FIXING THE BOOKS

The fellowship from which this book resulted was made possible with the generous support of Christopher Smeall.

School for Advanced Research
Resident Scholar Series

FIXING THE BOOKS

Secrecy, Literacy, and Perfectibility
in Indigenous New Mexico

Erin Debenport

School for Advanced Research Press
Santa Fe

School for Advanced Research Press
Post Office Box 2188
Santa Fe, New Mexico 87504-2188
www.sarpress.org

Managing Editor: Lisa Pacheco
Editorial Assistant: Ellen Goldberg
Designer and Production Manager: Cynthia Dyer
Manuscript Editor: Merryl Sloane
Proofreader: Kate Whelan
Indexer: Margaret Moore Booker

Library of Congress Cataloging-in-Publication Data
Debenport, Erin.
  Fixing the books : secrecy, literacy, and perfectibility in indigenous New Mexico / Erin Debenport. — First edition.
       pages cm. — (Resident scholar series)
  Includes bibliographical references and index.
  ISBN 978-1-938645-47-1 (alk. paper)
  1. Pueblo Indians—Languages—Social aspects. 2. Keres language—Orthography and spelling. 3. Tanoan languages—Orthography and spelling. 4. Literacy—Social aspects—New Mexico. 5. Sociolinguistics—New Mexico. 6. Anthropological linguistics—New Mexico. I. Title.
  E99.P9D326 2015
  306.44—dc23
                              2014031204

Library of Congress Catalog Card Number 2014031204
International Standard Book Number 978-1-938645-47-1
First edition 2015

Cover illustration: *Path of Life*, acrylic on canvas by Marla Allison, 2010. Courtesy of the School for Advanced Research. Catalog number SAR.2010-4-1A-D. Photograph by Addison Doty.

The School for Advanced Research (SAR) promotes the furthering of scholarship on—and public understanding of—human culture, behavior, and evolution. SAR Press publishes cutting-edge scholarly and general-interest books that encourage critical thinking and present new perspectives on topics of interest to all humans. Contributions by authors reflect their own opinions and viewpoints and do not necessarily express the opinions of SAR Press.

For Cabin,
My Family,
Ki'i Moonlight,
and Jacob

Contents

Acknowledgments

Many people have supported me while I worked on this book and continue to help me in countless ways. While I cannot thank specific individuals at "San Ramón Pueblo," I am forever grateful to my friends, colleagues, and Keiwa teachers there. I have also been fortunate to work as part of other Pueblo language projects with Evelyn Anaya Hatch, Melissa Axelrod, Geraldine Coriz, Shelece Easterday, Chris and Rocio Gomez, Richard Hernandez and Liliana Granillo-Hernandez, Jordan Lachler, Cora and Brenda McKenna, and Logan Sutton. Special thanks to Melissa who made it possible for me to work at San Ramón and continues to be a treasured colleague and friend at the University of New Mexico.

My committee was consistently patient and flexible, helping see me through a project that required continual fieldwork and a non-canonical defense, funding, and writing schedule. Thank you for having faith in me and in this project. My Chair, Michael Silverstein, was especially helpful in guiding me through the structure of the dissertation, and making sure I did a thorough job with the comparative lexicography section of the piece. Since my defense, he has continued to help me navigate the choppy waters of job searches and faculty life, for which I am very grateful. Amy Dahlstrom was my central source of encouragement and support at the University of Chicago, starting with serving as my thesis advisor for my Master's project, and continuing throughout my doctoral work. In addition to demystifying things like lexical-functional grammar, she knows all there is to know about food in Chicago, making this a very delicious journey. Jessica Cattelino, both during my time in graduate school and later during my post-doc, has proven to be an invaluable mentor. I am especially thankful for her suggestions regarding how to expand the project, especially evident in chapter 5, and for helping me situate my research within larger literatures on Native North America and the settler state. I remain deeply appreciative of all the hard work my committee members have done for me.

My work continues to benefit from discussions with other Chicago colleagues including: Mary Andronis, Chris Ball, Deanna Barenboim, Brian Brazeal, Megan Clark, Mike Cepek, Chris Corcoran, Cassie Fennel, Amy Franklin, Suzanne Gaskins, Lenore Grenoble, Kate Graber, Andy Graan, Katie Gruber, Courtney Handman, Joe Hankins, Nick Harkness, Elina Hartikainen, Laura Zoe Humphreys, John Lucy, Sean Mitchell, Sylvain Neuvel, Shunsuke Nozawa, Mike Reay, Jerry Sadock, Steven Scott, James Slotta, Henry Sybrandy, Jeremy Walton, Rihan Yeh, and Alan Yu. Gretchen Pfeil has provided incisive comments at critical junctures and I am grateful for her insights. This book has also been much improved from conversations with Richard Bauman, Tony Buccini, Andrea Berez, Nick Copeland, Alex Dent, Nancy Dorian, Mary Good, Bill Hanks, Pamela Innes, Graham Jones, Matt Liebmann, Barbra Meek, Robert Moore, Leighton Peterson, Sarah Trainer, and Tony Webster.

While at the University of California, Los Angeles's Center for Language, Interaction, and Culture, I was able to work closely with Paul Kroskrity and Jessica Cattelino, who both helped me envision how I could expand my doctoral work into a book. Paul continues to be very helpful concerning the politics of conducting linguistic anthropological fieldwork in Pueblo communities. Big thanks to Tracy and Ben Austin, Christian Havins, Sandy and Nick Luca, and Amanda Shaffer for putting me up while I was in Los Angeles. In addition, I have presented this material for audiences at UCLA, Sarah Lawrence College, SMU-Taos, First Presbyterian Church in Albuquerque, Southwest Seminars in Santa Fe, and at the SALSA, AAA, and SSILA conferences. Students in the Newberry Consortium for American Indian Studies Summer Institute, and especially my co-instructor, Scott Stevens, have become valued interlocutors who continue to help shape my thinking in important ways. Also, special thanks to Rusty Barrett, my fellow Arkansas ex-pat, and Albert Zapata, for hosting me at the University of Kentucky. This Red Tornado loves you.

Christopher Smeall generously funded a summer 2010 fellowship at the School for Advanced Research, where I greatly benefitted from conversations with Siva Arumugam, Cecilia Ballí, James F. Brooks, Minette Church, Suzanne Morrissey, Jason Ordaz, Nima Paidipaty, Jason Pribilsky, Cory Silverberg, Dan Usner, and Zoe Wool.

Throughout the project I have had excellent editorial help. Lisa Pacheco has seen me through this process from the very beginning, and offered a crucial initial edit. Justin Richland provided extensive feedback on the manuscript and remains an important source of information and support. Thanks also to Lynn Thomson Baca and Jessica Carr for editing assistance. Previous versions of chapters 4 and 6 appeared in *Journal of Linguistic Anthropology* 22, no. 3 (2012), and *American Indian Culture and Research Journal* 35, no. 2 (2011), respectively. Material from Chapter Two appeared in articles in *Language and Communication* and *International Journal of Sociolinguistics.*

Many thanks to all of my colleagues at UNM, in the Anthropology Department and beyond, especially David Bashwiner, Ann Braswell, Cathleen Cahill, John Carr, Patty Crown, Jennifer Denetdale, Les Field, Erika Gerety, Jennifer George, Alyosha Goldstein, Frances Hayashida, Amanda Heggan, Bruce Huckell, Lauren Hund, Kristina Jacobsen-Bia, Miria Kano, Louise Lamphere, Jeff Long, Tema Milstein, Keith Prufer, Rebecca Schreiber, Beverly Singer, Lindsay Smith, Sam Truett, Cristobal Valencia, JoNella Vasquez, Catie Wilging, and all of the graduate students I have been able to work with. Extra special thanks to Melinda Benson, Amy Brandzel, and Ronda Brulotte, who immediately jumped me into their informal junior faculty club, and to Michael Graves for being such a fantastic Chair. I cannot imagine getting to work with a more generous and insightful group of people.

Friends from all over have helped in many ways. Many thanks to Sarah and Brigham Bell; Stephanie and Marc Blumer; Joanna Bolme and Gary Jarman, Julia Bowsher, and Sean Burt; Emily Brigham; Benjamin and Lucy Caulfield; Ann and Brian Chenecka; Clint Coonfield; Emily Easton and Joseph Buszek; David and Linda Evans; Ryan Garcia; Rebecca Gates; Tracy and L. T. Goodluck; Carol Herzog; The Jicks; Sally Kane and Gregor Kretchmann; Jason Mitchell; Cathy and Keith Pettus, Jason Kaplan, Chris Kaufmann; Arif Khan; Moniqua Lane and Monte Workman; James Lawrence; John Moen and Sarah Dykes; Zach Moran and Ninah Hoffman; Erin Hansbrough; Marya Jones; Stephanie Kroack; Cindy Elliott and Dennis Fesenmyer; Michelle Marks; Sarah Mason; Shawn Miller; Claire McLane and Jonathan Zucchi; Judd and Colleen McRoberts; Kevin Moser; Bill and Betty Ann Poe; Joel, Amy, Sadie, and Zoe Ross; Brandon Ross and Maria Sanchez; Melinda Ritter and Steven Ramshur; Julie and Shipherd Reed; Scott Safford; The Tannex; Heather Trost and Jeremy Barnes; Kristi Trujillo; Bettie and Harry Wallingford; Lucy Wallingford; Mykl Wells and Mary-Lynn Greenhow; San and Jan Williams; and Jason Ward.

Finally, I could not have done any part of this project without my parents, Nona and Paul Debenport. They helped me get settled in Albuquerque (twice), fed me and housed me during fieldwork trips, and were waiting at the end of every day (with a beer) to talk about it. My sister, Rebecca Safford, has been right by my side through it all, and even gave me Tucson, which has become a second home. In the final, extremely difficult stages of the project, Jacob Ross was able to see me through with unfailing grace and strength. I love y'all very much.

FIXING THE BOOKS

o n e
Introduction

I press repeat on my iPod as I approach the stoplight, hoping to fit in some more Keiwa practice. It is early morning on a bright March day in 2008, and I am up early, winding through Albuquerque traffic on my way to San Ramón Pueblo. My Keiwa teacher, John (a pseudonym), and I have been preparing materials for the upcoming summer language program, writing and recording texts in this Pueblo language for the ten young-adult students who have signed up. During the long drive to San Ramón, through increasingly rural New Mexico towns, I continue to listen to the dialogues John and I have prepared, trying to understand the pronoun system, which has been eluding me for years.

I greet the few people sitting at the library computers checking their e-mail and make my way to the office that houses the pueblo's language program. John, the program's director, peers out the door into the library and hurriedly ushers me inside. "I want to show you something," he says, moving over to a file cabinet next to the locked storage closet that houses the tribe's archives. Checking again to make sure that I am the only one listening, he pulls out a copy of Elsie Clews Parsons's 1962 book, *Isleta Paintings*. "You won't believe what this lady did," he whispers, showing me the collection of paintings from one of the Rio Grande pueblos that Parsons commissioned while she was conducting ethnographic research in New Mexico in the early twentieth century. Depicting dozens of ceremonial practices inside the central Pueblo ritual space, the kiva, the paintings also contain written examples of Pueblo languages. John explains that the volume was produced under duress, with Parsons apparently purchasing the paintings from a recent Pueblo parolee who had few resources. As we look through the book, he continues to remark on the inappropriateness of these words and images being published, adding, "The artist's family still catches hell for this." Although it might appear that John himself was making these scenes inappropriately available by choosing to keep a copy of the book and by showing it to a non–community member, John was modeling the importance of indirectness, propriety, and the close management of cultural knowledge, stances that I saw enacted again and again during the ten-year period when the tribe introduced indigenous language literacy and I worked as part of the language program.

Parsons, although she published prolifically, had little to say about what it was like to work with Pueblos, especially regarding attitudes about controlling cultural knowledge. In Desley Deacon's biography, Parsons is quoted in a letter to her son: "High winds, sand laden, are bad for the throat particularly after nights of sleep broken by crying babies and by adults ceremonially wailing for a dead daughter. Besides, I had to play scientific detective unusually vigilantly to get meager facts, so suspicious are the Acomas of any White" (Deacon 1997:178). In *Pueblo Mothers and Children* (1991[1919]), however, Parsons presents a contrasting view to such conservatism, remarking, "The Pueblo Indian is unsurpassable as a pourer of wine into new bottles!" (Deacon 1997:226). Mirroring John's seemingly paradoxical attitudes toward controlling access to cultural information, Parsons presents apparently oppositional descriptions of the Pueblo people she worked with: conservative and uncooperative, but also resourceful and innovative.

Linguists, anthropologists, and other researchers interested in working in the Southwest are no longer warned of the uncomfortable conditions that Parsons described. At present, the majority of the nineteen New Mexican Pueblo communities (and one each in Texas and Arizona) have prosperous casinos and other economic ventures, as well as political, social, and geographic ties to the Hispanic and Anglo populations in Albuquerque, Santa Fe, and other New Mexico towns. Especially at pueblos like San Ramón, which are near large population centers, tribal members often go off-reservation to work, attend meetings, go out to eat, and engage in leisure activities, even at times residing in towns or suburbs near their home pueblos if housing is not available. Similarly, many tribes now employ a large number of nontribal members as part of their gaming and resort operations, potentially blurring the lines between Pueblo and non-Pueblo further and dimming the reputation Parsons advances of Pueblos' "suspicion" of outsiders. At the same time, despite these intersections of indigenous and non-indigenous populations in New Mexico, the pueblos are still perceived as distinct spaces, and prospective researchers are still likely to be cautioned regarding the difficulty of working productively in Pueblo communities. Pueblo people have a reputation for being friendly and welcoming but are also seen as secretive and cautious in ceremonial or research contexts. As I began to conduct research in New Mexico during graduate school, colleagues thoughtfully advised me regarding how difficult it would be to look at Pueblo languages. Even today, after more than ten years of participating in several Pueblo language programs, my ability to work in such settings continues to change. This book tells part of that story.

The idea of Pueblos' rigidity and conservatism coexists with Parsons's second remark, which highlights the flexibility and creativity she encountered when studying the intersection of Christianity and Native religions and child socialization throughout the region. The depiction of Pueblo people as innovators who are able to effectively respond to change would seem to contradict their reputation for secrecy, rigidity, and immutability. But current evidence of this proclivity is abundant, from the success of Pueblo gaming operations, to the ability of tribes to respond to and shape state policies, to tribal participation in pan–American Indian events. The decision to write down the San Ramón Keiwa language for the first time is another example of such innovation. At the same time, the potential for indigenous language literacy to compromise Pueblo secrecy presents a real threat to these communities. The focus of my project is to examine the paradox exemplified by John's copy of the Parsons book and by academic and popular depictions of Pueblo communities through the lens of Pueblos' literacy in indigenous languages.

In this book, I trace the short history of tribally directed indigenous language literacy at San Ramón Pueblo, beginning with the creation of a Keiwa orthography in early 2003, through the creation of a Keiwa-English dictionary and other pedagogical materials, up to the ongoing debate regarding writing in the pueblo, the eventual decision to return to oral-only language instruction, and the digital repatriation of language materials. First, I problematize the idea that the decision to produce written materials in this historically oral language is seemingly at odds with the linguistically and culturally "conservative" reputation shared by many tribes in the Southwest (Dozier 1983[1970]; Hinton and Hale 2001; Kroskrity 1993, 1998, 2000; Mithun 2001a) and potentially disrupts the control of both the intra- and intercommunity circulation of cultural knowledge at San Ramón Pueblo. This paradox is evident not only in the way Pueblo cultures are described by non–community members like Parsons but also in the fact that at San Ramón, some community members identify writing Keiwa as a controversial act. Tribal members are at once eager to innovate, producing written materials to aid language learning, yet wary of the possible risks involved with writing Keiwa. Potential hazards include the inappropriate circulation of cultural knowledge, language standardization, and damage to the religious system. It is precisely this tension that John illustrated when taking the book out of its special hiding place to show examples of the Keiwa language that had been inappropriately produced and circulated. Therefore, examining the paradox of San Ramón Keiwa literacy involves questioning the efficacy of such binary distinctions (for example, innovative-conservative and modern-traditional) in Indian Country and elsewhere while describing the implications of this tension for San Ramón people.

Second, by looking at San Ramón literacy ethnographically, I augment approaches in anthropology that aim to understand writing practices (Ahearn 2001; Bender 2002a, 2002b; Besnier 1995; Collins 1995), adapting these authors' arguments for the presence of numerous, situated, contingent literacies. Unlike Collins (1995), I do not engage in critiquing the "universalist" assumptions regarding the cognitive or psychological consequences of this example of emergent indigenous language literacy. Instead, I concentrate on looking at the role of literacy in the formation of groups and the ways that such groups have been connected to political participation in the social science literature, using the San Ramón case as a counterexample to some of the prototypical cases of textual circulation. At San Ramón Pueblo, literacy is a technology capable not only of spreading information but also of controlling it, in two ways: first, through regulating the circulation of cultural materials and, second, by shaping their formation during processes of editing and negotiation. At San Ramón, writing works both as a fixative for transforming language and culture into heritable objects and as a tool for revising forms of cultural property that can continue to be curated, managed, and perfected, two ways of "fixing the books" for current and future community members. My project also adds to the literature that foregrounds the importance of examining language in material forms and the status of written texts as valued and contested cultural objects (Blommaert 2008; Hull 2003, 2012; Keane 2003, 2007; Silverstein and Urban 1996).

Third, as part of looking at San Ramón literacy, I also look closely at the texts themselves. Throughout this book, I ask how the choices that authors make when crafting indigenous language texts index the larger goals and visions of a community. I describe the formal properties of various types of text, including dictionary example sentences, personal narratives, and pedagogical language dialogues, and the ways these pieces are intertextually linked with other written and oral texts. I show that the apparent contradiction surrounding San Ramón literacy actually reflects the often unexpected uses of texts that occur in contexts of revitalization and emergent literacy (Moore 2006) and the multiple language ideologies that are being indexed and utilized by community members. What are often thought of as "neutral" types of written work—dictionaries, curricula, and pedagogical dialogues—are used to teach community members vital cultural knowledge and ways of speaking, but they include fragments of local information in decontextualized illustrative materials, which in the current political climate at the pueblo is seen as risky. The overarching goal of communicating San Ramón cultural knowledge, rather than simply teaching grammatical structures or phonological rules, is revealed through the elements of established registers and genres in the dictionary example sentences and written dialogues. Current and future audiences are imagined as being able to correctly recontextualize San Ramón speech forms and the values they index.

In addition to looking at indigenous language literacy and the content of San Ramón texts, my ethnolinguistic study of San Ramón Pueblo contributes to theories explaining secrecy in two ways: by broadening understandings of concealment, avoidance, and information control among the Rio Grande Pueblos and by contributing to theorizations of secrecy in non-Pueblo contexts. In addition to transmitting salient cultural knowledge and information about the Keiwa language, community members reinforce language ideologies that privilege secrecy and indirectness. Conveying salient cultural information in pedagogical materials depends on triggering specific indexical associations, which are apparent in the creative manipulations of authority, audience, and temporality by Keiwa authors. Such linguistic and stylistic devices are used as resources to index collective local identities, an appropriate indirect stance, and other values. The simultaneous suppression and dissemination of information found in these examples of textual creation and circulation at San Ramón Pueblo mirrors the logic of secrecy itself, which depends on a certain measure of shared knowledge to communicate the significance of limited information. For me to fully understand the importance of the "secret" information contained in the Parsons book, for example, John had to give me access to the forbidden words and images contained in it.

Connected to this focus and my other research questions, I ask how secrecy is related to indigenous language literacy and whether approaches to information control and emergent writing practices mirror aspects of other social phenomena at San Ramón centering on perfectibility. In Pueblo and non-Pueblo contexts, processes of continual refinement, editing, and perfecting highlight the importance of the social work being done, assert the right of authors and participants to control the shape and circulation of cultural forms, and index idealized—in this case, indirect and collective—forms of sociality. Perfectibility thus resembles Pueblo secrecy and other proprietary practices in that it allows for the owners of cultural objects—in this case, written indigenous language texts—to exert greater control over their value and circulation. The dictionary, as an endlessly perfectible work worth painstaking editing and re-editing, accrues value just as the hidden copy of *Isleta Paintings* gains value through limited circulation and careful revelation.

By our considering the San Ramón example and looking at the connections between writing and secrecy, perfectibility, and various other practices, a critique of the formation of publics arises. What I show in this analysis is that theorists of the public sphere miss a large part of what literacy is all about: the ability to revise. Scholars, including Jürgen Habermas (1989), Michael Warner (1995, 2002a, 2002b), and Benedict Anderson (1991), have described the technology of literacy as one capable of disseminating information, contributing to the formation of publics and counterpublics, and creating particular forms of liberal democracy and conceptions of nationhood and community. By studying the proprietary practices in Pueblo writing, I show that literacy also has the potential to regulate and control the circulation of cultural knowledge and, in turn, both reflects and reinforces local models of interaction and personhood that privilege indirectness. I look at the public-private distinction in order to argue that the consequences of literacy do not always derive from the unbridled circulation of texts. As the example of Parsons's book illustrates, the lives of texts and the consequences for their authors also hinge on limiting viewership.

Community Background

As readers familiar with the Rio Grande valley or Native North American tribes have likely surmised, "San Ramón" is a pseudonym I created for the community that is the focus of this book. San Ramón is the Catholic patron saint of secrecy. Because many of the Rio Grande pueblos are named for their patron saints, this choice seemed to be in keeping with those naming practices. Linguists will notice that I also created a pseudonym for the language, a portmanteau of some indigenous Pueblo languages in the region: Keres, Tiwa, Tewa, and Towa. Additionally, I use aliases for all community residents and have given them no surnames, and I have obscured facts that point too directly to the specific location of the pueblo or the identities of the individuals who participated in this research. Although the widespread availability of electronic information and the limited number of Rio Grande pueblos mean that these efforts to disguise both people and place could be circumvented, I made this choice (independently and without the insistence of my Pueblo colleagues) in order to reflect the importance that is placed on the careful circulation of cultural knowledge and the centrality of inference and avoidance in this community. Similarly, I have omitted tokens of the Keiwa language in this book or in any other of my publicly available materials, a decision made in collaboration with tribal members. This signals a methodological departure from many works in linguistics and linguistic anthropology, and I hope that this decision makes a methodological contribution to these fields since I analyze the data in translation. In combination, these aesthetic, methodological, and ethical choices help to illustrate aspects of San Ramón language ideologies, writing practices, and emphasis on avoidance, issues I will discuss at length.

San Ramón Pueblo is located in central New Mexico, on the east side of the Rio Grande valley. Consisting of approximately 25,000 acres, San Ramón is one of the nineteen federally recognized tribes in New Mexico,[1] often referred to collectively as the "Rio Grande Pueblos" due to shared aspects of history, religion, culture, and—with the exception of Zuni Pueblo—proximity to the major water source in the region. A twentieth pueblo, Ysleta del Sur, is located in El Paso, Texas. The Hopi reservation, located within the Navajo reservation in northeastern Arizona, contains within it a Tewa-speaking pueblo, and both have many cultural and social connections with the other pueblos. The tribal website lists San Ramón's population as approximately five hundred people. Some tribal members live off-reservation in Santa Fe, Albuquerque, or their suburbs, and still others reside in other parts of New Mexico or out of state. In addition, there are nontribal members living at San Ramón Pueblo, resulting from intermarriage, disenrollment, and a long-standing tradition of adopting children from other Native American communities in New Mexico.

Community members at San Ramón divide the pueblo geographically into two parts: the "old village" and, by process of elimination, everything else. At the center is the old village, consisting of the plaza, which is a ceremonial and community space, and the oldest homes, which are closest to the plaza. Aside from an occasional, temporary jacal (thatched hut) made of vigas (wooden beams or logs) used for ceremonial purposes, the plaza contains no structures, serving as a site for religious functions that can attract hundreds of dancers, drummers, singers, and spectators. During the day, kids play in front of relatives' houses, and people cross the plaza on foot to run errands or visit neighbors. The homes that surround the rectangular space are made of adobe, and most are a single level. These residences are in high demand. What they lack in square footage is made up for by the status that comes from living in centrally located buildings that serve as multifamily feasting places during community and religious observances, close to the plaza and other ceremonial sites. Currently, the tribe is rebuilding all the original houses surrounding the plaza, in some cases, razing structures and erecting entirely new homes. The large, adobe community center is also located in the old village and is used for daily senior lunches and for special events, such as wedding receptions and baptism celebrations. The tribal offices and the meeting room for the tribal council are housed in this same complex, which includes the offices of many nontribal employees, such as the administrative staff and the census director, who maintains the membership rolls.

Just outside the plaza area are additional houses, some built in the 1950s and 1960s as part of a Housing and Urban Development program. Many HUD houses and historic buildings have hive-shaped, adobe *hornos* (ovens) in their yards, for baking bread and pies for feasts and weddings. The "old day school" building now houses the tribal library and computer lab and is adjacent to the Head Start building, the gym, and the community health clinic. The new church, financed by gaming revenues, sits above the center of town; a view of San Ramón Mountain is framed by its large windows. There are three other main residential areas in the pueblo, two of which contain houses built in the 1980s, and there is one street of single-family homes that were recently completed. Tribal programs helped members to purchase these homes, which quickly filled, and plans for increased construction at the pueblo are under way.

Although more people at San Ramón are purchasing dwellings billed as single-family homes, the reality of household structures is more fluid. Most community members live in multigenerational households with grandparents, grandchildren, or godchildren sharing the space. Also, friends and family members frequently stop by to have meals or talk, and young children often sleep over at one another's homes, especially if they live in Albuquerque or Santa Fe and are visiting the pueblo. The houses of particular families, as well as the institutional spaces of the library, the gym, and the community center, are the places at the pueblo that people frequently pass through or where they gather to visit. Jewelry and food vendors from neighboring pueblos and the Navajo reservation, also, stop at these locations to sell their products and to catch up with people they know at San Ramón.

As at the other Rio Grande pueblos, the economy at San Ramón was, until recently, based on agriculture, hunting, cattle management, and day labor. Mirroring the experiences of numerous other North American tribes, the decision to focus on gaming for economic development has brought a rapid increase in salary and standard of living for community members in the twenty-first century. In 2001, San Ramón completed construction on a new casino to replace the existing bingo hall. Like the previous building, the new casino is located along a major highway near Santa Fe, the state's most popular tourist destination. It is one of the largest casinos in the Southwest, employing more than two thousand people. Tribal members are now guaranteed employment, and many people work at all levels of the operation and at tribal offices and other economic ventures supported by gaming money.

Expenditures from gaming revenues have built a new church and athletic center and financed other construction projects, provided private school, collegiate, and continuing education tuition for all children and adults at the pueblo, and established an after-school tutoring program. The tribe is in the process of designing a new cultural center and swimming pool, as well as remodeling the existing athletic facilities. Like many other tribes that have been successful in the gaming industry, San Ramón Pueblo has been diversifying its economic development projects, such as investing in sustainable land management projects and Native American art and opening a luxury resort, concert hall, and golf course adjacent to the casino. The pueblo has also used its funds for political contributions and charitable giving, including a donation of $1 million to Hurricane Katrina relief in September 2005.

Cultural anthropologist Jessica Cattelino's (2008) analysis of the effects of Seminole gaming on indigenous communities in South Florida shows that Native-owned casinos often accomplish a range of social functions, an observation that holds true in the San Ramón example. Many San Ramón couples now choose to hold their wedding receptions at the casino resort, and the large ballrooms are also the sites of birthday parties and other special events. The banquet facilities can accommodate large numbers of guests, an important feature since it is customary at San Ramón Pueblo to invite the entire community along with friends from Hispanic, Anglo, and other Indian communities. Tribal members regularly visit with friends and family members they encounter when having lunch at the buffet or listening to the casino house band during happy hour. Although gathering places in the village, such as the library, the gym, and the senior center, remain the principal locations for San Ramón social life, the casino is a shared space for tribal members, friends from Albuquerque and Santa Fe, and casino patrons.

The San Ramón casino also serves as a showplace for cultural and historical objects associated with the community and with Pueblo traditions more generally. Large color photographs of past and present tribal councilmen greet patrons as they enter the main rotunda at the casino. Framed black-and-white pictures of community members and photographs of the pueblo from the turn of the twentieth century adorn the grand main gaming space, which houses the slot machines and table games, and the walls of the buffet restaurant. Each time I visit the casino with tribal members, they pause to discuss the old photographs, trying to determine the identity of everyone in the pictures, recounting old stories, and remembering buildings that no longer exist.

The accomplishments and traditions of other pueblos are also on display at San Ramón casino. Successful Pueblo artists from other parts of New Mexico have works prominently exhibited throughout the complex, including sculptures, black-and-white pottery, and inlaid silver and stone jewelry. Many of these Pueblo people are celebrated participants in the Santa Fe Indian Market, an annual international art fair that is one of the most influential institutions worldwide for the sale and evaluation of indigenous art.[2] Simultaneously, the dominant artistic and architectural motifs in the casino's design index a regional style that many scholars have identified as part of the Southwest's emergence as a tourist destination (Mullin 2001; Wilson 1997).

One aspect of life at San Ramón Pueblo that has changed dramatically as a result of gaming revenues is education. Approximately one-half of the children at San Ramón Pueblo attend public schools five miles away in the county seat of Coronado, a school district that also serves four other neighboring pueblos and the primarily Hispanic community where it is located. The remaining children attend private, parochial, or federal Indian schools in Albuquerque or Santa Fe, including a charter school whose mission is to serve Native students in the region. The tribe has instituted a policy requiring that all enrolled tribal members receive high school diplomas in order to maintain their health benefits and receive other economic incentives. GED certification classes and college courses sponsored by the University of New Mexico are regularly offered in Coronado, and San Ramón's Head Start teachers and other staff are given time off for continuing education. Presently, most adults at San Ramón Pueblo earn associate's degrees or higher, mostly at New Mexico institutions. Many high schoolers study filmmaking at the Institute of American Indian Arts in Santa Fe, responding to the growth of the film and television industries in the state. Although tribal members talk about the pressure to stay close to home in order to help with family and community responsibilities, an increasing number of young adults from San Ramón Pueblo are attending four-year institutions out of state, traveling back during the summer and school breaks to participate in ceremonial feasts and dances.

It is outside the focus of this book (and would be highly inappropriate) to describe the religious and ceremonial practices at San Ramón Pueblo, but some basic information regarding the intertwining of the political and religious systems is necessary in order to contextualize beliefs regarding secrecy and cultural knowledge and to understand the current political climate at the pueblo.[3] The political/religious posts of governor, lieutenant governor, war chief, and lieutenant war chief are filled by appointment yearly, although in the twenty-first century, the same cabinet members have held these positions for several consecutive years. All governors and lieutenant governors become tribal council members for life. The lieutenant governor serves as the tribal judge in tribal court, and the war chief and the lieutenant war chief oversee the religious activities at the pueblo. Some pueblos have switched to a constitutional model with elected tribal officials, but San Ramón continues to use an appointment system. Similarly, many pueblos allow women to serve on tribal councils, but San

Ramón's council remains an all-male body. Tribal officials also take part in state and national political activities, as exemplified by a former San Ramón governor's speech at a Democratic National Convention and community participation in a joint House and Senate hearing on language revitalization in Native North American communities. The chairperson for the group charged with getting out the New Mexico Native American vote for Barack Obama's 2008 presidential campaign was a San Ramón tribal member, reflecting the widespread community support for Democratic Party politics at the national and state levels.

When asked about religious affiliation, people at San Ramón typically respond "Indian Catholic" or "Catholic, but I also practice the traditional faith." Describing the role played by the Catholic priest at the pueblo, a member of the education staff remarked, "The priest also does his thing for all in the white man's way," indicating that Catholic practices coexist with Pueblo religion but take somewhat of a backseat to the "Indian religion." Some community members participate in religious observances at other pueblos, because of their family connections or knowledge of a specific dance or ritual. Many elders were also active in the movement to canonize Kateri Tekakwitha, a seventeenth-century Anishinaabe/Haudenosaunee woman who many at the pueblo and elsewhere describe as "the first Native American saint."[4] Even though Kateri was successfully canonized in 2012 and many community members made the trip to Rome for the canonization, the annual conferences where members of Kateri prayer circles would meet and petition the Vatican continue. Many Pueblo ceremonial dances and feasts are open to friends and to members of the public, but details regarding religious practice are kept secret. For the purposes of this book, two dimensions of San Ramón's religious practice should be stressed: the interrelated nature of religion and politics at the pueblo and the belief that the careful treatment of secret knowledge (including the ability to speak the Keiwa language) ensures the health of the religious/political system.

Although active in international Catholic organizations and national political parties, when San Ramón people talk politics and religion, the focus is usually local. Decisions made by tribal leaders control almost all aspects of life in the community. Land and housing can be granted or taken away on an individual or familial basis; tribal and ceremonial jobs are assigned or revoked. Most significant, decisions about tribal membership are made by the tribal council, specifically, by a few individuals who control the bulk of the political and religious power at the pueblo. Predictably, different factions support or challenge specific actions of the political and religious leaders, as well as the system of governance more generally and the ways that religious doctrine is interpreted by the current leadership. Community members also compare their political and religious climate with those of other pueblos, discussing how other tribes govern and allocate resources and offering opinions on the merit of various approaches.

The issue of membership has become an increasingly prominent concern at San Ramón Pueblo. Tribal membership, like indigenous language literacy, has numerous and sometimes competing definitions in Pueblo contexts, and it is currently the most fraught political and social issue at San Ramón. When policies change, the membership shifts, and the threat of further shifts is always present. Community members worry about getting their children and grandchildren "on the rolls," they worry about whose tribal affiliation might be threatened, and they talk about what can get someone kicked off the membership list.

Until the start of the twenty-first century, tribal membership was determined by a combination of genealogy, clan affiliation, and participation in cultural activities. In 2000, the tribe announced that it would be switching to a system that utilized "blood quantum"[5] to determine tribal membership, and many community members were disenfranchised as a result. The Census Department at the pueblo created a list of all enrolled members—organized according to the percentage of San Ramón parentage, ranging from "full" to 1/32—which circulated through the tribal offices, seen by employees and curious onlookers. In 2007, women who were married to non–San Ramón community members, as well as the children of such unions, were expunged from the tribal rolls, a decision that radically affected many families' access to health care, housing, and educational benefits. According to critics of the recent tribal administrations, both the assignment of blood quantum percentages and the 2007 ruling have been unevenly enforced, with the prevailing assumption that such measures are being used to disenfranchise critics and to maintain political and religious control. Some opponents of these policies fear the political, economic, and religious consequences of direct protest, but opposition groups have formed in response to these developments. Their efforts have resulted in a degree of success, with some tribal members regaining their previous membership status. Still, the issue remains extremely contentious on all sides. Community members often remark, "We never had these problems before we had money," which echoes critiques of "casino capitalism" that John and Jean Comaroff (2009) identify in other Native North American and global contexts.

Other pueblos are struggling with similar membership controversies, which are a common topic for gossip at San Ramón, with community members reporting on the political developments in neighboring reservations. Santa Clara Pueblo, famous for its role in a groundbreaking Supreme Court case, recently modified its membership policy. The decision in *Santa Clara Pueblo et al. v. Martinez et al.* (1978) had established the right of Native American tribes to make their own decisions regarding membership, similar to other sovereign nations' ability to make decisions regarding citizenship and immigration. The case involved a Santa Clara tribal member whose children had been denied membership because they had a Navajo father. The US Supreme Court ruled that this was not a case of sex discrimination (the offspring of male tribal members maintained their membership status) and that membership decisions were subject to tribes' sovereign right to constitute their communities.[6] The 2012 change at Santa Clara, still being adjudicated, calls for the potential reenrollment of children born of nontribal men and Santa Clara mothers. A Santa Clara member, quoted in an article in the *Santa Fe New Mexican* (2012), described the general attitude toward membership in her community, echoing the feelings at San Ramón. The reporter wrote: "The member, who favored the change but asked not to be identified, called membership 'a touchy issue' at Santa Clara. 'It's affected every family in the community with such animosity and all sorts of issues that come up in any family,' she said. 'So much is at stake that people feel uneasy talking about it.'" Perhaps even surpassing the discussion of religious practice as a touchy issue, tribal membership remains a central political and social issue at San Ramón Pueblo.

Part of the reason for the centrality of membership status is that so much is at stake. Individual and family housing, education, and health care are potentially threatened by disenrollment. For example, children attending private schools in Albuquerque or Santa Fe and those riding tribal buses to get to school are no longer able to take advantage of the tribal money or services that make these things possible. Houses and fields are distributed on an individual basis, with membership status often given as a reason for making housing and land decisions. Virtually all of these tribally funded benefits and programs have expanded during the twenty-first century as casino revenues have increased, making the gulf between enrolled and non-enrolled community members even starker. The effects of disenrollment and uncertain membership status, however, do not end at the tribal level. Many federal programs, including those run by the US Department of Housing and Urban Development and the Indian Health Service, require proof of enrollment in order for people to receive services. Tribal membership is thus a political classification rather than an ethnic designation, since exclusion from such services by virtue of being disenrolled does not violate the equal protection clause of the US Constitution (Justin Richland, personal communication 2013).

Although analytically distinct, the political, economic, and affective consequences of membership often overlap at San Ramón and figure into how families and individuals experience disenrollment. A friend whose children had been removed from the rolls and who feared that other family members might lose their tribal membership status asked, "Would that mean that we're still Indian?" Although there were economic consequences (both of her children were excluded from attending private schools), when talking about it, she stressed the ways that disenrollment intersected with indigenous subjectivities. This is one example of how discourses regarding affluence and membership are intertwined at San Ramón Pueblo. Many community members link discussions of the positively perceived aspects of greater wealth (greater casino revenues lead to greater political power and control over language and cultural policies) with the negative developments (the casino engenders more greed and therefore tighter membership standards).

In addition to being "on the rolls," there are concomitant and competing ways of discussing San Ramón subjectivities. Invoking or using the Keiwa language is certainly one of the most salient (and contentious) dimensions of embodying what is considered to be an authentic San Ramón identity, but looking at how historians, anthropologists, and linguists have theorized notions of identity and belonging helps to further explain this issue. In *Real Indians* (2003), the sociologist Eva Marie Garroutte considers four approaches used by Indians and non-Indians to decide who can appropriately claim to be Native American, tracing how assertions of indigeneity have been grounded at various points in US history by using legal means, racial and biological discourses, cultural foundations, and self-identification. This model is useful in outlining many of the ways San Ramón people identify themselves as community members and as indigenous people and how processes of identification are changing.

The legal definition of who is a San Ramón Pueblo member is determined by the tribal council. It is there that decisions affecting membership are discussed and voted on, such as the recent rulings removing certain groups from the rolls. At present, the census director is a non-Native employee whose responsibility is to maintain the current enrollment data as determined by the council and to confirm tribal status when individuals or families require proof of enrollment. As already stated, such legal definitions of San Ramón indigenous identity are potentially impermanent, depending on the decisions made by the tribal council and the patterns of enforcement. While it might seem that being on the rolls is only an economic issue rather than a true reflection of ethnic or cultural identity, for people at San Ramón Pueblo, it is also a powerful symbol of indigeneity and belonging. After having their tribal membership revoked or called into question, many community members, like my friend quoted above, express doubt about "really being Indian" and lament the loss of the economic advantages of being tribal members. More important, they see membership status as a central part of San Ramón identity. At the pueblo, being on the rolls is not a bureaucratic detail, but a powerful symbol of emplacement and authenticity.

Racial and biological definitions of indigeneity also increasingly have entered into discussions about Native identity at the pueblo. Unlike the anthropologist Circe Sturm's (2002, 2011) accounts of comparisons made among Cherokees that describe how physical characteristics are used to talk about indigenous identity, San Ramón community members do not usually discuss ethnic identity in terms of physical traits. At the pueblo, tribal and community members exhibit a wide range of skin tones, eye colors, body types, and other possible variations, but the greater context of New Mexico also contributes to this stance. In the 2010 US Census, 9.4 percent of the state's respondents identified as Native American, and 46.3 percent identified as Hispanic. Given these large Hispanic and Native populations, both as percentages of the total population and in comparison with other states, racial ideologies do not necessarily uphold whiteness as the unmarked racial category in New Mexico. The added complexity of the potential distinctions between Nuevomexicano, Chicano, Mexican, and Hispanic designations (among others), which are central to discussions of race and ethnicity in the region, further disassociates physical type from descriptions of ethnic or racial identities.[7] I have been present during numerous conversations at San Ramón in which certain traits were held up as ideals and others devalued, but it is not typical to align particular attributes with being Indian (although racial ideologies are often invoked when describing nonregional tribes). However, because blood quantum is being used as part of the tribal council's legal definition of San Ramón identity, "blood" is becoming a more central metaphor. Many people speculate about the "full-blooded" status of individuals, often asserting that this is a status impossible to prove or calling out individuals for claiming certain amounts of San Ramón blood. As Kauanui (2008), Sturm (2002), TallBear (2013), and others point out, linking racial ideologies to national identity can be a dangerous process. Whereas many people are hopeful that future administrations at San Ramón will reverse some of the decisions based on racial and biological definitions, some community members speak privately about the need for "a second Pueblo Revolt"[8] if such trends continue.

One way in which the community has been affected by these changes in the reckoning of indigenous identity is exemplified in Ellie's son, Michael. Ellie, who passed away in 2010, was a founding member of the San Ramón language program and a central contributor to the dictionary project. San Ramón Pueblo has a long history of adopting children from other indigenous communities in New Mexico. All the adoptees are given San Ramón names, have kiva ceremonies, and are raised in the same manner as other children in the village. Differing from this pattern slightly, Ellie and her husband adopted their son while they were stationed abroad fifty years ago. Michael's adoptive family on both sides is from San Ramón, he participates in ceremonial activities, and he is a Keiwa speaker. However, the tribal government made a decision to remove Michael and his children from the membership list because he is "white." Because he and his wife, who is from a neighboring pueblo, are tribal employees, they have been able to keep some benefits, but their children are no longer able to attend private schools at the expense of the tribe or participate in after-school programs. Community members largely reject this focus on race and associated repercussions such as these. However, directly protesting this or other membership decisions is risky, and critics fear that their families could be adversely affected and their own membership status reversed.

Most Pueblos adopt the third framework that Garroutte (2003) outlines for indexing Indian identity: establishing membership through cultural definitions. Often, this is framed in terms of lineage and descent, with speakers saying things like "My mom is from Taos, and my dad is from here" or "My dad was Spanish, but the rest of my family is from San Ramón." Although occasionally utilizing racial ideologies, such discursive moves establish cultural continuity and the place of the individual or family within it by describing a continuous Pueblo family history. In fact, San Ramón residents and members of other Pueblo communities pride themselves on being some of the only Native North American groups who were not forcibly relocated by the US government and who remain on their ancestral lands, making this link between land and culture an additional resource in the construction of indigenous identity.[9] The inverse of this discourse is that there remains tremendous anxiety about their forebears having to flee and then repopulate their pueblos following the

Spanish reconquest of New Spain in 1692. However, talking about what their ancestors must have struggled with in terms of Spanish retribution during this period and during other eras of colonial and federal rule serves as an additional way for San Ramón people to discursively link themselves with the history of the Rio Grande valley even as they work to save face as part of such interactions.

Another way that San Ramón people commonly utilize cultural foundations to establish Indian identity is their participation in specific practices. If an individual has had a kiva ceremony, was given an "Indian" name, or participates in dances and other ceremonial activities, then he or she is "Indian." This label also extends to members of other Pueblo communities, who share many of the same political and religious practices, and to Navajos, Apaches, and urban Indians from other parts of the country living in Albuquerque and Santa Fe. These pan-Pueblo and pan-indigenous regional identities are manifested in countless ways: dancing at events in other communities, selling traditional clothing to friends and at area feast days, listening to the Shiprock-based hip-hop group Robby Bee and the Boyz from the Rez, or putting a "This Truck Powered by Frybread" bumper sticker on your vehicle, among many other formal and informal practices. As the sociocultural linguists Mary Bucholtz and Kira Hall (2004) enumerate in their study of the various "tactics of intersubjectivity" used during processes of identity formation and the semiotic processes such approaches rely on, Pueblos utilize a variety of linguistic and visual resources to distinguish, authenticate, and authorize behaviors, discourses, and symbols associated with and constitutive of the embodiment of a San Ramón identity. Conversely, other processes of identification rely on "acts of alterity" (Hastings and Manning 2004), calling out certain behaviors, styles, or stances as decidedly non-Indian or non-Pueblo, themes I explore in chapter 6.

A central component of daily life at San Ramón Pueblo that also serves as a marker of indigenous identity is the importance placed on controlling access to cultural information. This book focuses on how control is embodied and ratified through linguistic practices, but this central feature of San Ramón life is evident even to the casual observer. At all entrances to the pueblo, signs are posted that state "No photos," "No sketching," and "No cell phones during religious events," along with prohibitions regarding alcohol and firearms. Another example of this emphasis occurs at the pueblo when a member of the community passes away. Tribal members are notified immediately of a death in the community, and the deceased's clan immediately makes preparations. Nontribal employees either are sent home from work to avoid witnessing certain ceremonial events or must remain in their offices and away from the old village. Non-clan affiliates who are tribal members must avoid "seeing anything," which is how one person vaguely described this process of active avoidance. These policies are not explicitly stated but are known to tribal members and eventually intuited by non-Indian employees and friends. Nontribal employees who are perceived as not respecting or understanding these prohibitions do not typically remain in their positions for long. All friends and family members are welcome to attend the memorial service at the Catholic Church and the wake at the community center, which normally occurs the following month. Although the people at San Ramón are happy to answer questions regarding the proper behavior for outsiders in this situation and others that require the appropriate recognition of distance,[10] local ideals of information control are largely communicated indirectly, which works to reinforce the local models of knowledge transmission. Such avoidance permeates language use and other practices at the pueblo, a central theme of this book.

Garroutte's (2003) fourth category of figuring indigenous identity, self-identification, is largely absent at San Ramón Pueblo. In Sturm's study of Cherokee processes of identification, *Becoming Indian* (2011), she shows how for some individuals, indigeneity is expressed at the individual level, with "racial shifting" becoming more common as people no longer identify as white. Community members at San Ramón, however, openly scoff at such definitions, deriding people who "decide to be Indian" as "wannabes," "not real Indians," or "fake New Agers who hang out in Santa Fe." At the same time, disenrollment practices are forcing community members to discuss indigenous identity at the individual level because families are increasingly made up of not only Pueblos and non-Pueblos but also enrolled, disenrolled, and unenrolled members.

Language Use

In this shifting and politically charged context, the San Ramón language program was created. At San Ramón Pueblo, English had been increasingly replacing Keiwa due to centuries of religious and cultural persecution, the forced assimilation at federal Indian schools, and the prevalence of English-language mass media—patterns of language shift that resemble those found in other indigenous North American communities. For years, tribal members worked to teach Keiwa orally to their families and groups of friends. Now, gaming and resort revenues have enabled the creation of a language director position and increased funding for institutionalized language-learning programs. In 2002, decisions about indigenous language policy began to be made at the tribal level, with the language director responsible for deciding how best to promote the increased use of Keiwa at the pueblo.

Community members refer to Keiwa, the Native language spoken at San Ramón Pueblo, by using the Keiwa words for "Indian speech," "Keiwa," or, most commonly, "Indian." The Keiwa language is spoken at two other pueblos, and a related dialect is spoken at two additional pueblos in the area. At San Ramón, there are approximately thirty fluent speakers of Keiwa, all of whom are over sixty-five years old. This mirrors the patterns of language shift at the other Rio Grande pueblos, whose populations comprise speakers of languages from the Kiowa-Tanoan and Keres families and Zuni, a language isolate. Across New Mexico, English is increasingly replacing Native languages and, to some extent, Spanish as the dominant code at home, work, and school.

Although data that reflect levels of fluency aid in illustrating the general patterns of language loss in Pueblo and other indigenous communities, they do not adequately describe language use at San Ramón Pueblo. Information about the number of fluent speakers depends on local political and ceremonial pressures, as well as the immediate context surrounding the inquiry. For example, tribal members who play significant religious or political roles are more likely to be counted as "speakers" than are the community members who use the language for everyday interactions, regardless of actual Keiwa ability or frequency of use. This hints at an ideology shaping ideas about speakerhood at San Ramón Pueblo. Far from a static definition based on an individual's facility for producing or understanding referential regularities in Keiwa, the idealized speaker is a ceremonially knowledgeable male, tasked with using the language for religious purposes.

Despite the sensitivity of the topic, there are situations in which community members openly discuss language shift. I observed a discussion at the San Ramón senior center regarding the importance of the language program, during which the names of individual speakers were listed one by one, called out while the group was finishing lunch. Some members have asked that information on levels of fluency be enhanced, especially in contexts that include community members from other tribes in the region. Finally, many people are able to comprehend but not produce utterances in the language, further complicating the ability to adequately capture levels of fluency. The number of San Ramón Keiwa speakers mentioned above is culled from the enrollment lists, which members of the dictionary committee divided into speakers and nonspeakers, but it should be considered only an approximation.

The limited contexts in which San Ramón Keiwa is spoken at the pueblo also restrict the use and transmission of the language. All tribal business is conducted in English, as are the continuing education and wellness classes for adults. The San Ramón Pueblo Head Start program has a predominantly English curriculum, although the school's directors have started to require employees who speak Keiwa to use the language in the classroom and have hired several teachers from a neighboring pueblo to better meet this requirement. After-school and summer programs are conducted in English, as are the majority of religious services, including Catholic masses and some portions of the ceremonies of the traditional faith. Moreover, the majority of non-institutional, casual interactions in the community take place in English, with only a few speakers supplementing their speech with Spanish greetings and terminology and fewer still employing San Ramón Keiwa greetings and expressions.

Geography has always played a role in patterns of language shift and transmission. The proximity of many Rio Grande pueblos to the colonial capital of Santa Fe during the period of early contact with the Spanish often subjected people to punishment for speaking Native languages (Simmons 1979). For most of the twentieth century, indigenous people in New Mexico were forced to attend Indian boarding schools in Albuquerque and Santa Fe, where students often roomed with children who spoke different languages. The students were brutally punished for speaking their Native language while on school property.[11] Many of the San Ramón Keiwa speakers I work with say that the decision to speak English with their own children is based on their experiences at Indian school but lament the fact that their children and grandchildren are not speakers of their Native language. During their lifetime, they have been castigated both for speaking Keiwa and for not speaking Keiwa, and many people express confusion and guilt regarding this shift.

Forced assimilation is the most frequent reason for language loss cited by community members at San Ramón. However, geography and size have also hastened the shift to English. The pueblo is close to some of Albuquerque and Santa Fe's fastest growing suburbs and several primarily Spanish-speaking communities. In addition, unlike some Rio Grande pueblos, San Ramón Pueblo cannot support schools, stores, and other institutions. As a result, the community has numerous institutional and economic connections to Albuquerque and Santa Fe, the political, economic, and educational centers of the region. These ties have increased with the surrounding population growth and the greater mobility engendered by economic prosperity at the pueblo.

Paralleling the trajectory of the other Rio Grande pueblos, San Ramón has only recently chosen to participate in language projects that involve nontribal members. This reflects a long-standing reluctance in Pueblo communities to host non-indigenous researchers and anger over the misuse of written materials that have detailed aspects of Pueblo religion and culture (Deacon 1997; Dozier 1951, 1983[1970]; Kroskrity 1993, 1998, 2000, 2012b; Norcini 2007; Spicer 1961). Scholars who have conducted linguistic or anthropological research in New Mexico pueblos have discussed this reluctance to share cultural knowledge or to write indigenous languages. Parsons, for instance, sees the difficulty she had in gaining access to several New Mexico pueblos as simply a methodological hurdle (Deacon 1997). Elizabeth Brandt, an anthropologist who worked at several pueblos under the direction of the linguist George Trager in 1970, links the avoidance of writing and the reluctance to participate in language programs to the religious and ceremonial structure: "I believe it could be demonstrated that secrets would not be given away unless the traditional religious organization had begun to disintegrate. After this process got underway, we would expect that the political system would show serious changes and realignments, and that a village would accept writing and other forms of data storage" (1980:143).

It is interesting to note that writing has been adopted at San Ramón Pueblo during a period characterized by increased political and religious organization, when tribal leaders have gained even more influence over secular and nonsecular aspects of life at the pueblo. Brandt's analysis ignores secrecy's continuous productivity. As I detail in the following chapter, discretionary practices are iterative, with new information to be kept hidden always being put into play, making the full-scale religious disintegration Brandt predicts always out of reach. Despite the persistence and transformation of avoidance practices, there is a growing anxiety regarding indigenous identity and language use, and the decisions to write the language and to partner with outside researchers came at a time of great uncertainty and upheaval. It is in this context that I began to work as a documentary linguist, curriculum designer, teacher, and ethnographer at San Ramón Pueblo.

Project History

While visiting family members in New Mexico during summers and holidays over the years, I noticed and eventually began following several stories in the popular press about Pueblo communities. Such articles emphasized the rapid increases in revenues for tribes that had opened casinos. These pieces often expressed concerns about the loss of indigenous culture that are similar to those Cattelino (2008, 2010) describes in her analyses of attitudes toward Indian wealth in South Florida, with indigenous and non-indigenous New Mexicans talking about the corrupting influence of gaming on Native ways of life. At the same time, stories appeared discussing the increased interest in Native language learning among indigenous people, the greater degree of community control over language policy that indigenous people now enjoyed, and the sometimes conflicting views that Pueblo communities had about using writing as part of language revitalization programs both in their communities and in the New Mexico public schools. What both discourses emphasized was that this was a critical time for indigenous communities in New Mexico, a time when "Native culture" was at its strongest and at its most vulnerable. These discourses are embedded in a larger framework of ideas about multiculturalism in New Mexico, including the idea of tripartite cultural harmony that scholars have shown to be a strategic simplification (Guthrie 2010; Mullin 2001; Trujillo 2009; Wilson 1997).

In 2002, I moved to New Mexico with the goal of studying language ideologies in a Pueblo community during this particular historical moment. Melissa Axelrod, a linguist at the University of New Mexico, invited me to meet with tribal employees in the Education Department at San Ramón Pueblo who had recently contacted her about starting a dictionary project. They had obtained from a neighboring pueblo a document written in the late 1970s by missionaries working for the Summer Institute of Linguistics (SIL) and wanted to create a version of the lexicon that would reflect the form of the language spoken at San Ramón. Axelrod, graduate student Jordan Lachler, and a group of three Keiwa speakers, John, Ellie, and Betty, had just finished developing a preliminary orthography and generously invited me to join the project. Later that year, I began working as a tutor for the tribe's after-school program, which is housed in the library. In between helping students to design science fair projects and trying in vain to remember algebra, I started to work more closely with John, the language director, and Domingo, another Education Department employee and tribal member, whose offices were nearby. Before long, I was going to San Ramón every weekday, helping to refine the orthography and making headway on the dictionary project.

During the initial meetings, the community members participating in the language program emphasized the importance of making written materials easy to use.

For example, they chose not to represent contrastive tone as part of the orthography for fear that diacritics would intimidate potential language learners. For the same reason, tribal members also made the decision that the first edition of the dictionary would not include "too much grammatical information" as part of the individual entries; later versions could possibly include "some rules" of their language at the end of the document. For each entry in the existing SIL dictionary, committee members began by deciding whether the word was used at San Ramón and, if the word was Spanish, whether it should be included at all. Following this, the group would agree on a spelling for each lexical item and determine whether they liked the extant example sentence. As the project continued, most of the committee's work went into the evaluation and creation of illustrative material, since the majority of the SIL dictionary's example sentences were judged to be inadequate. Most of the SIL sentences were excerpts from a New Testament translation and were judged to be either ungrammatical or culturally irrelevant. "We can do better than that," members of the committee remarked. They then took turns authoring sentences while I served as scribe, and new lexical items and accompanying examples were continually added.

After hours of entering example sentences into the database following the completion of the first draft, I noticed that the majority of the illustrative material was instructive in tone; most of it seemed like parts of a conversation rather than what I thought of as "reference" material (by this I mean atomized, contextually neutral sentences designed for the general reader); and, most important, the example sentences included information that I intuitively felt or was explicitly told was secret—and also culturally important. This apparent paradox was reaffirmed by the way community members discussed the dictionary and other written texts in the language, stressing the importance of controlling access to cultural information but emphasizing that texts created by the language program could "teach people how to be San Ramón." Statements such as this made clear the competing goals reflected in the dictionary example sentences and in more general discussions about language and identity.

With the permission of the language committee, I began to conduct ethnographic research while volunteering as a linguist and curriculum designer at the same time. For a year and a half, beginning in January 2003, I lived in New Mexico and spent my weekdays at the pueblo, working with members of the language program on the dictionary and on the creation of pedagogical materials. From 2004 to 2010, I made regular visits to the pueblo, ranging from one-week stays to accomplish a particular project with the language committee or attend a community event, to longer visits over holidays. For three summers (2007–2009), I helped to design and implement a summer language program for young adults and served as a co-instructor during the eight-week programs. While working in these capacities, I continued to conduct ethnographic and linguistic research. When I was not in New Mexico, I communicated with colleagues at the pueblo by telephone and e-mail, working with Keiwa speakers to add entries to the dictionary database, discussing ongoing projects, and chatting about events at the pueblo. During this time, I invested in a telephone landline that I answered only in Keiwa, which also turned out to be an effective way of avoiding solicitors. Since joining the Anthropology Department at the University of New Mexico in 2010, I have continued to do ethnographic research at San Ramón while also working at two other pueblos as part of their language programs.

As the project developed, I began to devote more time to analyzing particular institutional sites at San Ramón where decisions about language revitalization and the creation of written materials occurred. An example of one such context was the series of dictionary committee meetings to edit the first draft of the lexicon. As mentioned above, a group of fluent Keiwa speakers made decisions about the inclusion or exclusion of particular lexical items, about spelling, and about whether to approve the existing example sentences or create replacements. Observing these sessions (while also working as a scribe) enabled me to ascertain the favored example sentences, the reasons given by community members for the superiority of these, and the variables privileged during processes of reaching consensus among the dictionary authors.

In addition to institutional environments directly related to creating language materials, I continue to have access to numerous other contexts at San Ramón and in the region generally where language use and language policy are explicitly discussed. These include discussions at the senior citizen meal site regarding the language program, meetings with Head Start parents focusing on second language acquisition and preschool language curricula, and monthly meetings of the educational staff, the division at the pueblo responsible for establishing and implementing language policy. Working as a tutor enabled me to get to know many younger community members not directly involved with the language program, as well as their parents and grandparents. These and other instances gave me an understanding of how community members characterize the utility of the dictionary and written materials more broadly, who has access to written materials and how this is negotiated and controlled, and why community members participate in (or avoid) the language program.

The fieldwork I continue to conduct in non-institutional, social contexts also informs this book. Keiwa speakers' and nonspeakers' opinions regarding what the language revitalization program should encompass, how language has changed at the pueblo, and why being able to speak or read Keiwa is important continue to be frequent topics of conversation at parties, weddings, feast days, and other events. Since I started teaching at UNM, I also have discussed language and community events with community members and other Pueblo people who work on campus or go to the university. I am sure that talk about language occurs with more frequency in my interactions as a result of my professional identification as a linguist and my history of work with the tribe. However, my continued ethnographic research has shown that community members perceive this to be a critical time in their community for language preservation, and discussions of language policy and laments about the state of the Keiwa language are common. Additionally, I believe that my status as an outsider, but one who has knowledge of Keiwa and local affairs, has led to frank discussions about sensitive topics, such as membership, identity, and San Ramón culture. In order to honor the confidence that individuals place in me by sharing such information, I neither quote from such conversations nor include them directly as part of my analysis. Although such talks between friends have contributed to my understanding of both the San Ramón community and Pueblo culture as a whole, I do not consider them part of my research.

Project Methodologies

Conducting ethnographic and linguistic research that has been both lengthy and regular has given me a greater understanding of the Keiwa language and social life at San Ramón and how these things have changed over time. And, it is the key to my ability to work in this community. Such a project would not have been tenable without my spending a great deal of time at the pueblo establishing relationships with the language program staff and other tribal members. Concomitantly, the ability to accurately interpret and write about my findings depends on my understanding and observance of local attitudes regarding appropriateness and propriety, for example, using only English translations of Keiwa texts in this book. In this sense, the methodology both reflects the focus of this project and makes the project possible.

In addition to the ethnographic and linguistic fieldwork I conducted, I analyzed the syntactic and stylistic features of the San Ramón Keiwa dictionary's example sentences and lengthier texts in Keiwa. To better understand grammatical regularities in the language, I consulted the few available resources that describe the grammar of Pueblo languages (for example, Brandt 1970; Harrington 1909, 1910a, 1910b, 1912; Leap 1970a, 1970b; Speirs 1966, 1972; F. Trager 1968; G. Trager 1936, 1942, 1943, 1946, 1948, 1954, 1960, 1961; Watkins and McKenzie 1984). To augment my understanding of the Keiwa language, I also consulted with Logan Sutton, a graduate student in linguistics at the University of New Mexico whose research centers on the grammar and phonology of the Kiowa-Tanoan family, along with Keres, Uto-Aztecan, and Zuni materials held at UNM's library.

For each San Ramón dictionary example sentence, I created an interlinear gloss to compare the Keiwa texts according to various grammatical features. For instance, my analysis of pronoun choice, in chapter 3, relies on my assessment of preferred methods of person marking throughout the document, a task made possible by the initial step of creating glosses. Along with all the approved dictionary example sentences, I explored the structure of sentences that were not selected for inclusion in the final draft, which provided a means of characterizing which criteria were being used when choosing illustrative material and which information was deemed to be too sensitive to risk circulating. Like my treatment of all information at San Ramón Pueblo that is not intended for general circulation, I do not disclose the content of these sentences as part of this book or any other project I am involved with. Instead, I use this approach to enhance my understanding regarding the shifting nature of information control and the broadly preferred, grammatical and stylistic features of the example material.

Finally, as part of situating the creation of the San Ramón lexicon in a larger framework, I utilized a comparative approach to studying dictionary design. This involved the investigation of hundreds of lexicons in numerous traditions and resulted in the analysis in chapter 3. Furthermore, I conducted interviews with Steve Kleinedler, a lexicographer who currently works for a mainstream English reference dictionary, the *American Heritage Dictionary*. Utilizing comparative lexicography as a methodology accomplished several tasks. Primarily, it allowed for a systematic understanding of the ways that the San Ramón text differed from other lexicons by comparing its function, design, use of illustrative material, and other factors. Simultaneously, the dictionary's similarity to a few key texts provided me with a better insight into the imagined audiences that are being indexed as part of the creation and circulation of the lexicon. Comparing examples of extant dictionaries also allowed me to ascertain what my colleagues on the San Ramón dictionary committee valued in the project, ranging from aesthetic preferences to the identification with particular values and goals espoused by various lexicographers.

Particular individuals' approaches to language study have played large roles in my methodologies, my questions, and my understanding of language use at San Ramón Pueblo. In particular, John, the former language program director, was responsible for many of the texts I analyze in this book, as well as being my primary Keiwa teacher. Because of his family background and community position, he is highly knowledgeable about ceremonial language and local ideologies involving how and why to control cultural information. His influence guided my research in the direction I eventually took. Although I do not single out agency as a central theme, my book shares a methodological focus with Paul Kroskrity's study of "the types of agency exhibited by an elder and language activist" (2009a:191). Tying together analyses of language structure, individual action, and community transformation, he details the work of a Western Mono speaker and "emphasize[s] an especially robust agency that is something more than merely a 'capacity to act'; it is rather an awareness leading to the transformation of selves and systems" (192). John's work as a language activist and community leader mirrors this case, reflecting the changing ways that the San Ramón community and language are being figured as part of an emergent indigenous language literacy in the twenty-first century.

Plan of the Book

This book roughly follows the chronological development of Keiwa literacy over a ten-year period, 2003–2013. Throughout, I return to my original research focuses: the paradoxical nature of San Ramón literacy; the formal and intertextual dimensions of Keiwa texts; Pueblo and non-Pueblo secrecy; and the relationship between literacy and information control. In chapter 2, I theorize two concepts central to understanding the decision to write (and eventually to forbid writing) the Keiwa language: literacy and secrecy. I look at the dominant and emergent language ideologies at San Ramón Pueblo and how these beliefs about appropriate language use have been reflected in new practices with texts.

In chapter 3, I focus on lexicography, examining the significance of a dictionary being the first written work in this community and its properties as a text. I summarize a comparison of various dictionaries in order to highlight the ways that the San Ramón lexicon resembles and differs from other works. Following this, I survey the central syntactic and stylistic resources employed by the San Ramón dictionary authors when constructing example sentences. I pay close attention to person-marking strategies and tense/aspect use, highlighting the notions of audience, authority, and temporality in these short texts.

In chapter 4, I look at the ways that Keiwa literacy expanded after the initial dictionary project. I analyze a recorded (and, eventually, written) text that was produced as part of a language curriculum but ultimately had a very different purpose. I use this example to develop my critique of how literacy has been depicted in the West and to formulate an alternative reading of how texts can be used as part of the constitution of private, rather than public, spheres. Additionally, I connect this text to the generic features and content of the dictionary example sentences, showing how the dictionary's illustrative material draws on established San Ramón speech genres and associated goals.

Chapter 5 draws on ethnographic and textual examples from San Ramón to illustrate a new way of characterizing language revitalization projects: as social movements that draw on tropes of nostalgia, hope, and faith to accomplish various types of social work. I draw on works of religion scholars to support my argument regarding the focus on the past in language-learning materials and in discourses about language loss, planning, and revitalization.

In chapter 6, I return to the chronology of San Ramón indigenous language literacy by looking closely at another ostensibly neutral, pedagogical text: a soap opera written by members of the young-adult Keiwa language class. Describing the end of the era of tribally sanctioned, institutionalized Keiwa literacy, I devote the book's conclusion, chapter 7, to detailing the implications of San Ramón writing both for community members and for understandings of secrecy, publics, and circulatory practices, as well as the construction and presentation of anthropological knowledge.

This ethnographic study of emergent literacy provides a more complete picture of Pueblo secrecy and propriety by examining the relationships between prevailing linguistic ideologies, intertextual connections, and the contexts surrounding the production of Keiwa texts. San Ramón Keiwa literacy, rather than representing a break with linguistic ideologies privileging information control, is, as Parsons observed, an example of pouring the same wine into new vessels, of honoring existing local ideologies while utilizing additional, sometimes unexpected, discursive and ideological resources.

two
Ideology, Literacy, and Secrecy

In this chapter, I contextualize the shift to indigenous language literacy at San Ramón Pueblo by examining various understandings of writing and secrecy. I outline language ideologies at San Ramón, emphasizing how this body of work can help explain Pueblo attitudes toward writing and information control. I look at various ways scholars have typified literacy and circulatory practices, comparing these analyses with the San Ramón case. I then survey approaches to understanding secrecy, including social scientific definitions, work on politeness and information control, and the division between public and private. What emerges from this analysis is an understanding of the linguistic, ideological, and discursive resources informing Pueblo literacy and secrecy, showing that information control in these communities is an interactional phenomenon.

San Ramón Language Ideologies

A linguistic ideological framework is central to explaining literacy and secrecy at San Ramón Pueblo and the community's ways of creating and using texts, ways that initially seem to be contradictory. Judith Irvine defines language ideologies as "the cultural system of ideas about social and linguistic relationships, together with their loading of moral and political interests" (1989:255). Michael Silverstein's definition, "sets of beliefs about language articulated by users as a rationalization or justification of perceived language structure and use" (1979:193), highlights the reflexive aspect of these phenomena in speech communities. Susan Gal adds, "We can understand 'ideologies' as metadiscourses that comment on and regiment other communicative practices" (2002:79). Like these and other linguistic anthropologists working in this tradition, I see language ideologies as a means of simultaneously examining the micro- and macro-level processes of valuation and differentiation inherent in and created by local ways of speaking and envisioning appropriate uses of language. Rather than consider language ideologies as a theoretical concern apart from other social and linguistic practices, I take Francis Cody's approach and present them as a "presupposed backdrop" (2009:200) to work in linguistic anthropology. I highlight particular language ideologies in order to examine San Ramón attitudes toward writing, language purism, contextual appropriateness, indigenous identity, and information control.

Maintaining "pure" forms of San Ramón Keiwa and using the language only in particular contexts are prominent linguistic ideologies at San Ramón Pueblo. These proclivities are evident in the act of dictionary creation, in the production of other indigenous language texts, and in any discussions of language use and cultural knowledge. As scholars have observed, the emphasis on maintaining particular forms and registers and ways of using language to the exclusion of other codes and ways of speaking is often heightened in situations of rapid social change (see Eisenlohr 2004; Errington 2003; Hanks 1987; Hill 1985; Jaffe 1999; Liebmann 2008). Dictionary creation and other emergent uses of language at San Ramón Pueblo are examples of what the linguistic anthropologist Patrick Eisenlohr calls "new genres of entextualization" (2004:28) and typify the situations he describes: writing practices solidify specific registers and grammatical patterns, and there is a prevalence of purist ideologies. At San Ramón, these ideologies are displayed in the contrasts speakers draw between Keiwa and Spanish, Keiwa and English, and the form of Keiwa spoken at other pueblos and the dialect spoken at San Ramón, as well as in the idealized depictions of the San Ramón Keiwa language as it was spoken before contact and at other points in the past.

The linguistic anthropologist Paul Kroskrity has elaborated on the historically vague character of such distinctions drawn by Pueblo community members as embodying a "linguistically conservative" view. He describes the central "cultural preferences" held by the Arizona Tewas, an indigenous group that left its pueblo near Santa Fe after the reconquest following the Pueblo Revolt of 1680 and now resides on the Hopi reservation on First Mesa, near the villages of Sipaulovi and Walpi. Kroskrity traces the origins of these preferences to ceremonial speech, or "kiva talk," locating such linguistic practices in the central Pueblo ceremonial site, the kiva, and arguing that "the more explicit rules for language use in ritual performance provide local models for the generation and evaluation of more mundane speech forms and verbal practices" (1998:104). These preferences and their associated language ideologies also help to describe beliefs regarding the appropriate uses of language at San Ramón Pueblo, especially the premium placed on using forms felt to be specifically San Ramón in certain contexts.

Kroskrity defines the first of these preferences, indigenous purism: "During ritual performance, there is an explicit and enforced proscription against the use of foreign words and/or native vocabulary clearly identified with an equally alien social dialect" (1998:107). Community members at San Ramón Pueblo often lament the amount of English spoken in the kiva and the inability of certain religious officials to understand Keiwa, which undermines their efficacy in leadership positions. The consequences of not being able to "speak Indian" in this setting include, of course, the possibility of not being able to follow what is happening but also, invoking Kroskrity's observation, the possibility of referencing social values associated with speaking other languages. For older community members, Spanish carries negative connotations associated with conquest and discrimination. Although English does not index similar links, any language other than Keiwa represents an ideological step down from being able to perform and understand rituals in the Native language.

Like the mutable associations tribal members exhibit regarding the uses of writing as a technology, the negative social values assigned to Spanish and other dominant languages are varied. Irvine and Gal's (2000) analysis of semiotic processes of fractal recursivity is applicable in this case because meaningful oppositions between these languages and their associated significances serve as discursive resources in the construction of difference and solidarity, which are endlessly transferable to new contexts. While it would be easy to say that San Ramón Keiwa is generally the most valued of these codes, carrying associations of authority, indigenous authenticity, history, and difference from other tribes and groups in the region, fluent Keiwa speakers often defer to and speak English or Spanish. This is sometimes due to the presence of those who do not speak Keiwa but also concerns the appropriateness of specific languages in certain contexts. For instance, someone might choose to use San Ramón Keiwa in front of younger community members, knowing that they do not understand, in order to assert the importance of indigenous language learning. Speaking English or Spanish in most situations would be an unmarked activity, simply business as usual in multilingual New Mexico, but would be highly inappropriate when asserting one's indigenous identity in a regional or tribal setting is required. In such situations, Spanish is associated with past colonial repression and English with mass American culture and linguistic decline. However, the most salient ideological distinction in this case is the opposition between Keiwa and all other languages. English and Spanish carry their own indexical values, but in most situations, they are simply everyday languages, whereas speaking Keiwa is never a neutral act in this community. Its uses are specialized, its contexts of use are demarcated, and its presence heightens the saliency of the speech situations in which it is used.

One afternoon while I was in town to work on Keiwa pedagogical materials, Ethan, a young man who had recently been installed in a ceremonial position at San

Ramón, came to visit John at his office in the tribal library. John's knowledge of the language and religious ceremonies make him a popular resource for community members who need help with particular songs or speeches, and Ethan needed some advice. In the week leading up to the first ceremonial event where Ethan would be called upon to speak publicly, John worked with him to memorize the speech Ethan would need to present. Nervous about the presentation, Ethan asked John several times whether anyone else could make the speech or whether it could be done in English. Wanting Ethan to "do it right," John told him that he should be the one to do it, and they continued to practice together. Following the event, John told everyone how impressed he was with Ethan's speech: "He didn't forget anything, didn't use any English, and didn't even speak with an accent." The successful performance of this speech rested on Ethan's ability to adhere to local language ideologies by using the pronunciations considered to be strictly local and maintaining a uniform code, San Ramón Keiwa. The success of the speech event was not compromised by the fact that he had memorized the text.

This emphasis on linguistic purism is related to the second cultural preference rooted in Pueblo ceremonial practice, which Kroskrity labels "strict compartmentalization," or "the maintenance of a distinctive linguistic variety that is dedicated to a well-demarcated arena of use" (1998:107). This highlights the importance of certain words being used only in the kiva, since their use in other situations diminishes their overall ritual efficacy. At San Ramón Pueblo, community members who are active in ceremonial events frequently discuss such "preaching words," describing them as words or expressions that are to be used only in ritual contexts by those warranted because of their clan affiliation or political/religious position. People often describe instances when someone accidentally said such a word in a nonceremonial environment, and some speakers use circuitous ways of communicating in order to avoid contextually inappropriate utterances. Resembling situations in which strict adherence to linguistic purism is not observed, uttering certain words and expressions in nonritual contexts has the potential to reference social values associated with Spanish or English, values that are seen to be contrary to those promoted by local religious practices.

These two preferences are components of the language ideologies that are frequently indexed at San Ramón Pueblo in nonceremonial settings, cementing Kroskrity's observation that the cultural preferences inherent in kiva talk are also present in everyday language use. Such ideologies were especially apparent during meetings of the dictionary committee. Beginning at the inception of the dictionary project in January 2003 and continuing for three years, regular meetings were held to revise and create entries for the document. Four Keiwa speakers employed by the San Ramón Pueblo Education Department were regular participants in these meetings, which I, also, attended: Ellie, Frances, and Betty, who were in their mid- to late seventies, and John, who was in his early sixties. During the early meetings, Melissa Axelrod, the linguist from the University of New Mexico, was also present, and community members, tribal employees, and children participating in the after-school program regularly dropped by to say hello. Often, John stepped out to help people with specific language projects or to tend to his cattle; Ellie, Frances, and Betty periodically left to fulfill their duties as Head Start language teachers; and I made sure to keep the coffee cups refilled.

During these meetings, the group evaluated each entry individually, which involved converting the orthography used for the SIL document into the San Ramón alphabet, refining the English gloss, and agreeing on which example sentences to include. Although most of the meetings were spent creating and evaluating example sentences, effort was made to purge the document of any borrowed words, whether from Spanish, English, Apache, or Navajo, and of words or pronunciations used exclusively at neighboring pueblos. Words were then created to replace these deletions. It was decided, for example, to refrain from calling coffee *café* (which is Spanish) and instead craft a new Keiwa dictionary entry, which translates as "yellow brown stuff." This drive to purify and standardize the language as part of the dictionary project signals the importance of asserting the individuality of the San Ramón language, as opposed to following the Western lexicographic model and including all attested forms. One of the committee members said about this process, "It's hard because some of those Spanish words, like *manzana* for 'apple,' I have been using all my life. But now we have a better word for it, in Indian, so I have to learn to use it. I'm learning right along with the kids!" She went on to comment on the importance of switching certain words in the SIL dictionary to forms found at San Ramón: "It's like we're making their words into ours." As in many other language revitalization projects, such as the standardization and reintroduction of modern Hebrew following the establishment of the state of Israel,[1] the efforts of the San Ramón dictionary's authors to invent new words can be seen as one means of asserting cultural and political legitimacy and independence.

The creation of neologisms that are strictly local is related to a language ideology connected to the ideologies originating in kiva talk, one that envisions dictionaries as emblematic of group identity and nationhood, serving as a resource for the construction of difference. Scholars have detailed language ideologies that position modern nation-states as inextricably connected to a single, national language, thus reinforcing or creating political and economic boundaries based on perceived difference (Blommaert and Verschueren 1998; Errington 1998; Irvine and Gal 2000; Silverstein 2000). This is evident at San Ramón Pueblo, where the dictionary and orthography are often presented as necessary to make clear distinctions between San Ramón and another pueblo that speaks the same dialect of Keiwa. Increasingly, the New Mexico pueblos are economically competitive in relation to one another, and this is especially apparent in these two communities, both of which have a profitable casino. Creating a dictionary asserts the robustness of the San Ramón language compared with the form of Keiwa spoken at the neighboring pueblo, even though the other pueblo has many more speakers and is much larger. This ideology is also evident in the committee's desire to produce a "thicker" document than the SIL dictionary, with more entries. Here, it is clear that language in its written incarnation is being envisioned as a material object, whose merit is at least partially related to its size, as embodied in a larger text.

The Pueblo preference for strict compartmentalization that Kroskrity describes—ensuring that Native language use occurs only in ratified environments—was also evident during the meetings of the dictionary committee. Often, Keiwa speakers decided to omit a dictionary example sentence that contained too many "preaching words" or descriptions of religious practices that they felt were too detailed, indicating the importance of using certain expressions only in ceremonial contexts. An additional dimension of this focus on contextual appropriateness was the importance of maintaining indirectness when including culturally salient information. If preaching words were included in illustrative materials created for the dictionary, the authors talked about "sneaking them in" or included only partial descriptions of activities, leaving the burden on future language learners to correctly infer the intended indexical associations. At San Ramón Pueblo, indirectness and avoidance are as important as content, a belief that is modeled and reinforced along with the grammatical regularities that example sentences are ostensibly designed to illustrate.

Interestingly, the language ideologies stressing contextual appropriateness and purism that speakers made use of in the context of dictionary creation were, themselves, not pure. Many Spanish words were judged to be Indian and were included in the dictionary without any discussion of their etymologies. At times, members of the committee did point out the Spanish origin of a particular word, but, depending on the perception of the word's utility and the mood of the group, it was sometimes included in the Keiwa document anyway. Also, Keiwa speakers frequently made explicit efforts to include lexical items with close associations with ceremonial practices in dictionary example sentences and other learning materials in order to communicate this knowledge to other community members. In addition to the absence of total adherence to the various preferences, beliefs about how such preferences should be exhibited varied as well. Dictionary committee members spoke of a range of community opinions regarding the project and writing the language, from individuals who want written Keiwa to be taught in the public schools that serve the reservation, to those who believe that it should remain strictly oral and local. Thus, the ideologies of purism and contextual appropriateness held by people at San Ramón Pueblo are reflections of communally held beliefs regarding language—what it is and what it can do—and individual beliefs concerning how such ideologies are best upheld. Ideologies foregrounding "authentic" forms and uses of San Ramón Keiwa are resources available to speakers, enabling them to use Keiwa creatively by contrasting the uses of this code with other linguistic options. Also, the knowledge Keiwa is thought to contain and convey can be communicated in new contexts, including written works such as a dictionary. This makes clear that explaining Pueblo cultural attitudes as merely "traditional" or "conservative" ignores the fact that such values are not absolute. Jane Hill's analysis of purist tendencies in an indigenous community in Puebla, Mexico, describes how speakers exploit the different associations between Spanish and Nahuatl: "The peasant use of Mexicano, far from being conservative, is a dynamic and highly creative endeavor which draws widely on the symbolic resources of its environment" (1985:735). Similarly, those making decisions about how the Keiwa language will be written and how it is to be used in other contexts creatively assert their right to make such decisions through employing these stances.

It is also important to examine how the term "traditional" is employed at San Ramón and in other Pueblo contexts. Rather than refer to certain types of social structures, as it often does in the anthropological literature (so-called traditional societies), "traditional" at San Ramón is a positive label indicating an adherence to Pueblo religious (and therefore linguistic) practices. While working at San Ramón, I would often hear community members lament that the village as a whole was "becoming less traditional" or that relatives living out of state were "losing touch with their traditional side." Conversely, I never heard people describe themselves or their community as "conservative." When colleagues and friends referred to the Pueblo propensity for information control, avoidance, and indirectness, they would obliquely refer to "doing things [their] way" or "how Indian people are." In such situations, avoidance itself is used in talk about secrecy practices.

A third cultural preference among the Arizona Tewas that Kroskrity describes, the linguistic indexing of identity, is another prominent language ideology seen at San Ramón Pueblo and helps to further frame the topic of indigenous subjectivity. The linguistic indexing of identity refers to "the preference for locating the speaking self in a linguistically well-defined, possibly positional, sociocultural identity and the belief that speech behavior in general expresses important information about the speaker's identity" (Kroskrity 1998:117). For Pueblos, "identity" in this model is both individual and collective, with the ability to speak Keiwa presented both as an individual responsibility and as a means of defining the tribe as a whole. Like the other attitudes regarding appropriate language use at San Ramón Pueblo, this language ideology is revealed in different ways, to varying degrees, and in the service of accomplishing various kinds of social work, as the following story illustrates.

In 2005, a mandatory meeting was called for all education staff at the pueblo. The new director of education (a non-indigenous, nontribal member) wanted to introduce himself to the Head Start teachers, the cooks, and the language program staff. He had prepared a handout with his educational philosophy and his goals as director. In the document, he used the standard Keiwa greeting, using his own spelling system, having apparently heard other Native and non-Native staff members use this phrase in casual exchanges. It is accepted practice for community members and outsiders alike to ask Keiwa speakers how to say words and phrases in the language after having prolonged contact with the community, but his usage was highly inappropriate: he did not ask permission to write this greeting, and he was a recent addition to the staff. Although part of the resulting outcry from the education staff in response to this document was partly a result of his failure to consult with them regarding the policies he advocated, many of the heated, negative responses in the meeting and following the event centered on his use of Keiwa. After the meeting, tribal members used this gaffe as a way to talk about his shortcomings as a director, a discursive move that depicted him as an overbearing, disrespectful snob who was inappropriately claiming aspects of Native identity and therefore was a poor fit for the position.

Like the varied adherence to the ideologies of purism and contextual appropriateness, the close link between Native language use and identity is observed to various degrees by different individuals, serving as a resource in the construction of difference or in the performance of shared ethnic identitification or social solidarity. One afternoon while I was working with the dictionary committee, we stopped for a break. Before I went to the kitchen to pilfer a snack from the Head Start cooks, I had a short conversation in Keiwa with the other members, asking whether they wanted some coffee and letting them know I would be right back. Several community members were using the computers in the library and heard this exchange. When I returned, John told me that Chris, one of the bystanders, had exclaimed, "Who was that?" after I left the room. Later, we all laughed at his apparent confusion about an Anglo speaking Keiwa. Since this incident occurred, John has told the story countless times, and it has become increasingly elaborate. It is still a funny story, and he has embellished Chris's reaction, quoting him as saying, "Who the hell was *that?*" which always produces a big laugh. He has also augmented our short exchange in Keiwa, re-creating the conversation in the language (and translating it if necessary, according to the audience). In the new and improved version, I am a Keiwa Shakespeare, using complex constructions and very descriptive language. In some retellings, I am not even asking about coffee but discussing something infinitely more interesting. This story illustrates that the linguistic indexing of identity is a strategy used by people at San Ramón not only to create a boundary between indigenous and non-indigenous people but also in much more nuanced, flexible ways. John uses this story to several ends. He communicates that it is unusual for an outsider to speak Keiwa, which, in its default or "natural" incarnation is spoken only by community members, hence Chris's surprise. At times, this irony is accentuated when John is trying to encourage his interlocutor to learn more Keiwa, and he will add, "Jeez, she knows more than you!" (not a pedagogical approach I necessarily support). In addition, in each retelling, through humor, he is simultaneously conveying that it is appropriate that I have knowledge of this language and that community members should support the decision for me to work with the language committee. Thus, the link between the ability to speak Keiwa and indigenous identity is a highly adaptable discursive resource, available to use in multiple situations when the line between indigenous and non-indigenous can be exploited to accomplish communicative goals.

Understanding Pueblo Literacy

The decision made by community members at San Ramón Pueblo to begin writing the Keiwa language is, initially, a surprising one. At all the nineteen New Mexico pueblos, at the single Texas pueblo, at Hopi, and at the Tewa pueblo near there, literacy in any of the indigenous languages spoken in these communities has historically been viewed negatively and continues to be a controversial issue. Linguists and anthropologists have highlighted the Pueblo emphasis on secrecy, the importance of controlling the circulation of local information (with knowledge of the language itself seen as the prototypical form of local knowledge), and the fear of local languages being commodified (Anthes 2006; Dozier 1951; Ortiz 1969; Parsons, 1929, 1991[1919]; Peshkin 1997; Sando 1992).

However, as James Collins (1995) has pointed out, multiple literacies exist. In San Ramón and Pueblo communities more broadly, writing practices with indigenous languages have varied historically and contextually. What can be thought of as academic literacy—linguists using writing to circulate examples of Pueblo languages in extratribal contexts—is extremely rare and has most often occurred without the consent of Pueblo interlocutors. Similarly, indigenous language texts produced by religious organizations working in Pueblo communities are scarce, and missionaries have been expelled from pueblos for creating and disseminating written materials. But several pueblos other than San Ramón have instituted tribally based language programs that employ limited writing as a documentary or pedagogical tool. Since the mid-1990s, school-based indigenous language literacy has been part of the Tewa language program in Pojoaque Valley Public Schools, a district that serves five pueblos. At San Ramón (and likely at all the other pueblos), there is also a rich history of individual indigenous language literacy, with community members developing orthographies and sharing them with family and friends. In each of these instances, indigenous language literacy is constantly changing and conditioned contextually: contributors to tribal or school language programs later might withdraw support for writing indigenous languages, and former opponents of literacy-based classes might become writing advocates. Thus, these multiple views of writing and the assessment of potential benefits and risks overlap and intermingle, problematizing designations such as "tribal language program" and "community permission."

Issues involving literacy have dominated discussions about how best to institute language revitalization programs at the Rio Grande pueblos. While this is certainly a component of discussions involving approaches to language revitalization in indigenous communities throughout the world, in Pueblo contexts, it is not usually framed as a methodological or pedagogical issue, but as an ideological one. Regis Pecos and Rebecca Blum-Martinez, linguists and community members writing about their involvement in designing a language program that centers on language immersion for Cochiti Pueblo, discuss this choice:

> Cochiti Keres remains an unwritten language, in keeping with the oral tradition of the community. There is widespread support for keeping it in its oral form, from the religious and secular leaders as well as from the general tribal membership. The oral tradition in this community has been an important element in maintaining its values and traditional way of life. The leaders know that writing the language could bring about unwanted changes in secular and religious traditions. (Pecos and Blum-Martinez 2001:76)

Here, the authors outline a zero-sum analysis of the potential for literacy in their community, implying that oral traditions or "traditional way[s] of life" cannot coexist with the production of written materials. Indicative of Pueblo opinion on how to best teach indigenous languages, this reasoning identifies the decision not to write Pueblo languages as an ideological one, tied to the political/religious system. Also representative of Pueblo depictions of literacy is the authors' assertion that the consequences for choosing to write Native languages are serious, representing a potential affront to Pueblo culture as a whole.

Analyzing the foundations of language rights rhetoric in a Hopi context, the anthropologist Peter Whiteley (2003) explores the implications of literacy in Pueblo communities that are confronting language shift. As with the other language rights discourses he analyzes, he shows that how language is depicted, archived, and circulated leads to sometimes unforeseen outcomes for indigenous communities, especially those producing written materials in indigenous languages for the first time. He summarizes the Hopi experience: "Writing and other technologizations of language, such as its use on radio, television, and the Internet, devalue language's performative powers and largely demystify the 'magical power of words,' reducing language to symbols with referential, rhetorical, and aesthetic capacity but without instrumental force. The sociolinguistic effects may be profound" (Whiteley 2003:717). At Hopi, the sociolinguistic effects of adopting writing practices and producing a literary tradition include anxiety over the ability to control sensitive cultural information in the midst of developing written materials, concerns shared by community members at San Ramón Pueblo. Whiteley's description of the controversy surrounding the publication of the Hopi dictionary (Hill et al. 1998) adds to the literature on the differences between oral and written languages and the local or national consequences of each mode (Anderson 1991; Bauman and Briggs 2003; Chafe 1994; Goody and Watt 1968); the consequences of writing, like other technologies, are specific to individual speech communities or even individual people.

By examining the new literacy at San Ramón Pueblo ethnographically, this book adds to the literature that examines such attitudes toward writing, by studying language use, writing systems, and means of circulating written materials in specific communities (Ahearn 2001; Bender 2002a, 2002b; Besnier 1995; Collins 1995, 1997; Schieffelin 2000; Schieffelin and Doucet 1998; Schieffelin and Gilmore 1986; Whiteley 2003). This contrasts with approaches asserting that literacy and technologies of writing follow comparable trajectories across interactions, eras, and speech communities and with approaches claiming that literacy reflects comparable values, such as modernity and progress, within broad eras or across multiple contexts (Anderson 1991; Goody 1978; Habermas 1989; Warner 2002a, 2002b).[2] San Ramón literacy is much more nuanced, with the presence of several dominant discourses involving writing and associated linguistic ideologies. As Gal (2002) has shown, speech communities display multiple, often competing, language ideologies. This helps to reconcile the attitudes about writing embodied in the quote from Pecos and Blum-Martínez and the emergent belief at San Ramón Pueblo that the technology of writing is uniquely suited to reversing patterns of language shift.

To some extent, community members at San Ramón Pueblo share the attitude of the architects of the Cochiti language program. People fear that writing will diminish the ceremonial efficacy of the Keiwa language since the knowledge of certain phrases and prayers is, ideally, limited to specific clans and certainly should not be available to non-Indians. This is an especially salient concern, given that the central reason offered by San Ramón community members for the importance of speaking Keiwa is to be able to use the language appropriately in ceremonial contexts. In many senses, the fear that the ritual utility of the language will be compromised by writing the Keiwa language is similar to the relationship described by the linguistic anthropologist Niloofar Haeri (2003) between classical Arabic, the written form of the language used in the Qur'an, and secular Arabic, such as the spoken form she studies in present-day Egypt. Like San Ramón Keiwa, the written form of Arabic that appears in sacred texts differs from other "classical" languages, such as Sanskrit and Latin, in that vernacular forms of Arabic continue to be spoken. Haeri describes the complicated situation that this produces: "Classical Arabic...as the language of the Qur'an, continues to separate the sacred from the profane, writing from speaking, and prescribed religious rituals from personal communication with God" (2003:1). In the case of San Ramón Keiwa, the ceremonial uses of the language and its everyday functions are not comfortably separated for most Pueblo people, and the shift toward writing further complicates the ability to isolate the secular from the nonsecular.

As in the discourses of nostalgia Hill (1992) describes in indigenous Mexican communities, community members at San Ramón Pueblo compare the need to use writing in order to teach the Keiwa language to what they see as larger processes of cultural deterioration. Community members remember that children were previously raised by all of their relatives and that the Keiwa language, in this context, was learned at home and integrated into activities structured by family and clan, discourses I analyze in detail in chapters 3, 4, and 5. The current situation, they assert, is characterized by divorce, migration away from the pueblo, and language loss. Community members emphasize that "Indian should be taught at home, not at school," and lament that this pattern was interrupted by forced assimilation at federal Indian schools and changes in family structure over the past fifty years. Although the tribe initially chose to make writing a central component of the language program, literacy is typically described as a last resort. Expressing concern regarding the difficulty finding sufficient numbers of Keiwa speakers to participate in master-apprentice programs and other immersion-based activities, a member of the San Ramón dictionary committee said, "I want a dictionary for somebody to go to when they have nowhere else to go." Thus, literacy in the San Ramón context not only has the potential to compromise Pueblo religion and systems of knowledge but is also a potent symbol of new systems of bureaucratization, in which language learning occurs outside the institutions of family and clan.

One example of this fundamental concern regarding writing occurred at a Head Start parents' meeting I attended during the winter of 2006. A community member and fluent Keiwa speaker, who has a granddaughter in the Head Start program, voiced concern about introducing bilingual materials into the classroom. He expressed doubt that producing a children's book for use in the classroom would encourage language learning: "People would just memorize words from the page and not really understand what they meant." He was not concerned about protecting cultural knowledge, since the title in question, *Brown Bear, Brown Bear, What Do You See?* (Martin and Carle 1996), does not contain any sensitive material, but rather he believed that writing as a technology does not capture language use. This same individual went on to say that he would prefer that video materials be produced to aid in language learning, rather than written materials, which he sees as inferior.

This depiction of writing and its potentially deleterious effects on San Ramón culture and society coexists with a view that positions writing as a useful and unique technology. In the essay "Speaking and Writing," linguist Wallace Chafe assesses these two modalities, highlighting differences in permanence, a speaker's ability to evaluate content, spontaneity, the relationship to context, and the possible consequences for speakers and authors. He also discusses some ideologies associated with speaking and writing found in Western academic and literary discourses: "As we have seen, it is particularly common in literate societies for writing to be viewed as superior to speaking" (Chafe 1994:50). Similar language ideologies that privilege this technology are present at San Ramón Pueblo and are often connected to discourses foregrounding the importance of education and ideas about permanence. Community members present writing as a way of preserving "what old-timers used to say" for future speakers of the language.

The linguistic anthropologist Robert E. Moore (2006) describes such positive views of indigenous language literacy in his discussion of the politics of access to "endangered" language materials and the ways texts are utilized in academic and indigenous contexts. He identifies two dominant modes of encounter with endangered language texts: memorialization and regenerativity. Moore defines the former as "the creation of a permanent record of the language for posterity" and "an orientation to the beauty of linguistic (grammatical) structures" (2006:298). He defines regenerativity as "writing for reading aloud" and "an orientation to the representation (however inadequate) in writing of instances of language use, relying on Saussure's definition of parole" (298). He asserts that these modes of encounter condition the way texts are discussed, utilized, and consumed.

At San Ramón Pueblo, community members possess a decidedly regenerative orientation toward the dictionary and other written materials. Authors shape the content of example sentences and the stylistic and generic conventions such sentences contain in order to communicate appropriate ways of speaking to future language learners. According to Moore, this way of consuming texts depicts documentary materials, including written works, as memory aids, tools that can engender future interactions in indigenous languages. Unlike the relationships between consumers of texts and indigenous language materials that are conditioned by memorializing discourses, regenerativity positions texts as self-contextualizing, "mediated by kinship, descent and ethnicity" as opposed to academics' relationship to archives, which is "mediated by forms of scientific expertise licensed by institutions" (Moore 2006:310). Regenerativity diverges from the stance of memorialization, in which texts are read retrospectively with an implicit assumption of the demise of contemporary indigenous communities. Instead, a regenerative orientation to written materials engages with texts prospectively, positioning indigenous language materials as being able to reflect both specific indigenous cultures and the appropriate contexts of use by giving language learners the ability to speak their language in future speech events.

Discussions about the value of written language at San Ramón Pueblo are not limited to the decision of whether to write the Keiwa language and the potential utility of written texts; they also concern the implications of choosing certain ways of writing. The first task for those working on the San Ramón Keiwa dictionary project was to formulate an orthography capable of capturing all the sounds of the language. Over the course of a year and a half, the dictionary committee members, Melissa Axelrod, and I produced several versions of an alphabet. Throughout this lengthy process, tribal members working on the project stressed the importance of designing an alphabet that would be easy for people to use and that would "correct" the problems they saw in the orthography used by the SIL missionaries in the Keiwa dictionary. Although the alphabet the missionaries utilized did contain some inconsistencies and difficulties—for instance, [y] was used both as a consonant and to mark vowel length or diphthongs—most of the corrections made by San Ramón Keiwa speakers were aesthetic or ideological, in order to "accommodate future language learners." For example, Keiwa exhibits vowel length and contrastive tone, but the community members who helped to design the orthography decided to "wait until later to mark those things." This echoes analyses of the symbolic dimensions of orthographic choice (Romaine 2002; Schieffelin and Doucet 1998), which highlight situations in which certain orthographic conventions come to be associated with particular social values. In the San Ramón case, the use of diacritics is associated with foreignness and difficulty (and possibly Spanish); a skill to be developed at a later stage of language learning. In analyses of Cherokee literacy, Margaret Bender

(2002a, 2002b) identifies similar attitudes toward language socialization in Eastern Band communities in North Carolina. She describes how teachers "delay" instruction in the syllabary (one of four standardized orthographic possibilities in Cherokee), believing it to be a specialized skill ideally used by few people in particular settings. In both the Cherokee and San Ramón cases, the possibility for close transcription must be sacrificed in the early stages of language learning in order not to discourage community members from language learning and also in order to set apart Cherokee or Keiwa literacy as more difficult (and, consequently, as specialized and important).

This survey of literacy practices at San Ramón Pueblo illuminates several important distinctions. First, the basic division between the spoken Keiwa language and the newly produced, written language materials, including the dictionary, is apparent, with the former seen as the natural form of the code, indexing values such as authenticity, indigeneity, locality, difference, and solidarity. Written language carries other associations, at various times signaling the right of the tribe to develop and implement its own learning materials, or the "selling out" of a commercially and financially successful people, or the ability to control the historical record. As we have seen, sometimes what is at stake is the right to *use* spoken San Ramón Keiwa—to produce utterances using the indigenous language in various settings—an ability that is potentially conditioned by the creation of written Keiwa materials. In other contexts, the ability to *write* the Keiwa language and to display written language tokens is the controversial aspect of new literacy in this community. Finally, the right to control cultural knowledge is at issue, with the production of written Keiwa texts changing the possibilities for the dissemination of such knowledge and creating new ways of limiting intra- and intercommunity access. When "Indian language" is discussed, community members are selecting from these various depictions and manifestations of San Ramón Keiwa.

The language ideologies that present literacy as a potentially corrupting influence at odds with local patterns of language transmission *and* the ideologies that position writing as a useful technology for language learning and identity expression coexist at San Ramón Pueblo. Although some individuals adhere to a single side of the issue, positioning written Keiwa solely as a threat or as the only salvation for language and community, most people utilize both ideologies according to the context. The same person who reacts positively to the number of Keiwa signs at the casino might bristle at the idea of a written adult curriculum; a fan of the soap opera *As the Rez Turns* might not support the dictionary project. Thus, the social value of literacy (and indigenous language) in this community is mutable and varying, with writing used as a topic in which opinions regarding identity, propriety, and the future of the San Ramón community can be organized and expressed. This was illustrated in a comment made by a member of the dictionary committee at the end of a long day creating example sentences. He was suffering from a cold and cough, and I suggested that we stop for the moment and then convene the following day to finish the entries we were working on. "No thanks," he said. "I really want to get this stuff down while I'm thinking about it so that we can get it in the dictionary." Then, after a particularly punishing bout of coughing, he said, pointing upward, "Who knows, maybe we're not supposed to write it." I first interpreted this comment as a sardonic remark meant to alleviate my worry, but the fear of reprisal aligns with larger Pueblo attitudes regarding misfortune. Similar to the Hopi practice of *maqastutavo*, or "fear teaching" (Justin Richland, personal communication 2013), at San Ramón, adversity—either at the individual or the community level—is usually explained as directly resulting from inappropriate action. Here, writing is presented as a potential way to fall from grace, bringing judgment and misfortune to those who have used this technology improperly.

Theorizing Pueblo Secrecy

Theorizing secrecy at San Ramón Pueblo requires both the examination of local ideologies governing information control and an understanding of how secrecy and concealment have been treated in the social science literature.[3] Some scholars of secrecy have studied the phenomenon from within, by becoming initiated into exclusive groups (for example, Tanya Luhrmann's study of English witchcraft, 1989a, 1989b, and Graham Jones's 2012 work with French performance magicians). Others have conducted ethnography in institutions that keep the researcher away from sensitive information (for example, Joseph Masco's work with the Los Alamos National Laboratory, 2002, 2006, 2010). Because I have been permitted to learn the Keiwa language and to access limited cultural knowledge, this book is somewhat of a combination of both types of projects. Rather than detail what constitutes secret information or the criteria that must be met to classify types of knowledge as necessarily controlled, I look at how people at San Ramón talk about the practice of information control: why it is important, who can make decisions about the circulation of knowledge, and how concealment practices intersect with emergent literacy. This is not an insider ethnography at the level of clan or community, but an ethnographic examination of the social work that secrecy accomplishes, especially as it relates to Native language literacy.

The benchmark publication on secrecy in the social sciences is the sociologist Georg Simmel's 1906 work on secret societies. In this essay, Simmel argues for the ubiquity of secrecy, concealment, and other discretionary practices controlling the amount of knowledge that individuals or groups share. Beginning with discussions of individual interactions, marriage, and friendship, he goes on to present historical examples, including information control as practiced by Freemasons, members of Parliament, and Gallic druids. Throughout, Simmel emphasizes that "every human relationship has, as one of its traits, [a] degree of secrecy within or around it" (1906:466), presenting concealment as an essential part of interaction and the creation of groups. Simmel describes the elemental features of secret societies and formulates a series of propositions regarding the constitution and continuation of such groups. In this essay, he is also concerned with connecting instances of information control with theories of functionalism and modernity, positing that secret societies become more prevalent as life becomes more public and that they help to maintain social cohesion during times of rupture and change.

This last point speaks to popular understandings of Pueblo secrecy and the reasons that outsiders are not permitted to learn Pueblo languages or observe certain ceremonies. When I explain that I do not publish any Keiwa examples in my work or that people at San Ramón do not want Keiwa taught in schools, most non-Pueblo interlocutors identify such practices as purely reactive. "That's understandable after all they went through," "They had to keep their language hidden from the Spanish because that's all they had left," and "They only need English to get ahead these days" are common explanations for the well-known Pueblo emphasis on information control and limiting the circulation of Native languages. Indeed, these theories align with Simmel's propositions. He claims that secrecy arises as a response to the dominant society, a "concession to outsiders" (Simmel 1906:487) that serves the group "until strength may be developed to defer interruptions" (471). In this view, many aspects of secrecy can be understood functionally, with less powerful groups employing information control in times of danger or change. Information control can construct "barriers" (466) that differentiate subordinate groups from the dominant majority, asserting their moral superiority and creating a "secondary structure" (483) that exists within the larger society. This productive ability of secrets to impart control and structure would be a more complete explanation of Pueblo secrecy if community members at San Ramón and other Pueblo people themselves pointed to concealment as a means of differentiating themselves from non-Indians or simply as a reaction to colonization and the pressure to assimilate. Instead, colleagues of mine at San Ramón and other pueblos assert that keeping cultural knowledge appropriately restricted is an integral part of their religious system and the ability to correctly use the Keiwa language is inextricably tied to secrecy practices.[4] The need to hide the Keiwa language or cultural knowledge is not simply reactive, nor an assertion of agency by the less powerful.

Another issue that complicates thinking of secrecy as being solely about constraint is that access to cultural knowledge, although widely discussed at San Ramón Pueblo, is not always tightly controlled. A few years ago, John was asked to testify before the House Committee on Education at a hearing in Albuquerque to gather information about indigenous language loss and revitalization programs. He wrote a draft of his testimony and submitted it to the tribal attorney and council for approval. His statement began with a greeting in Keiwa, followed by an English translation. He then detailed his experience with the language program, discussing language use at the pueblo and the reasons for language shift. John outlined the various efforts to promote the use of Keiwa, the benefits of learning the language, and suggestions for supporting these efforts, including more federal funding for language programs and voting against English-only legislation. He closed by thanking the committee in Keiwa.

When John received feedback regarding his draft, the tribal attorney and the council members took issue with only one part of his testimony: his description of language loss. They inserted a sentence that stated, "San Ramón Pueblo has approximately 500 tribal members, over a third of whom are fluent speakers of our language." When John told me about this change, he was frustrated, remarking that the number of speakers was far from accurate. When he delivered his testimony, he used his original draft, which was printed in the program for the event. Following his appearance before the committee, neither the tribal attorney nor the council members spoke to him about which version he had used.

In addition to exemplifying the unevenness of concealment practices, this incident illustrates several discourses deployed during the negotiation and performance of speaking publicly about language use. Both John and those who edited his testimony relied on established ways of speaking in the public negotiation of indigenous identity. John employed greetings and closings in Keiwa, an act that is analyzed by the linguistic anthropologist Jocelyn Ahlers (2006) as a means of foregrounding Indian identity through a nonreferential use of language. The editors, in their adjustment of the draft, relied on enumeration to make a claim about the relative health of the Keiwa language, one of the discursive strategies used to talk about "endangered" languages highlighted by Hill (2002).

An overarching pressure that shapes these different uses of language is the often opposing indexical associations inherent in the performance of Indian identity during public discussions of language policy. As expressed in John's original draft, the goal of participating in this hearing was to raise the profile of indigenous language programs and to advocate policies that support them. The concerns that the editors expressed with their revision indicate the potential for presenting a compromised indigenous identity to the audience at the hearing, which contained members of indigenous communities in New Mexico and Arizona. The anxiety regarding inhabiting an authentic Indian identity is most evident in pan-Pueblo settings as opposed to intratribal contexts, in which Keiwa language use and policies are not subject to the same types of comparison and, therefore, possible criticism.

This example of competing indexical associations between the utilization of dominant discourses to discuss language loss and the performance of indigenous identity mirrors Elizabeth Povinelli's (1999) study of performances of indigeneity in "contexts of recognition" and James Clifford's (1988) work on Mashpee land claims. Unlike the situations these authors describe, however, the conflict in John's testimony did not lie with the state, but with successfully referencing a regional indigenous identity while recounting an accurate picture of language loss. This tells us that Pueblo concerns about secrecy are focused more on the intracommunity control of information (in the pan-Pueblo sense) than on simply keeping local information secret from non-indigenous people. The aspect of this story that most informs analyses of secrecy, though, is the lack of enforcement on the part of the tribal authorities to ensure that John would use the revised testimony, as well as the absence of

KEIWA LANGUAGE LEARNING MATERIALS

THESE MATERIALS ARE THE PROPERTY OF SAN RAMÓN PUEBLO AND ARE NOT INTENDED FOR GENERAL DISTRIBUTION. THEY ARE NOT TO BE COPIED, SENT ELECTRONICALLY, OR OTHERWISE REPRODUCED OR MADE AVAILABLE TO NON-COMMUNITY MEMBERS. DISTRIBUTION OF THESE MATERIALS TO NON-TRIBAL MEMBERS OR NON-TRIBAL EMPLOYEES MAY RESULT IN DISCIPLINARY ACTION OR TERMINATION. IF YOU HAVE ANY QUESTIONS, PLEASE CONTACT THE SAN RAMÓN PUEBLO LANGUAGE PROGRAM AT (███) ███-████.

Figure 2.1. The cover of the San Ramón Keiwa adult curriculum. Image created by author.

consequences for his choosing to use his original draft. In the end, the critics of his speech concentrated their efforts on the negotiations surrounding the appropriate use of language and its potential circulation in printed form rather than on the direct control of information by regulating the eventual content of his testimony.

Lack of strict control when regulating the spread of secret information also appeared in the ways the adult language curriculum was distributed. This text was envisioned as a pedagogical tool to be used in future language classes or by tribal members who wanted to work independently on learning Keiwa. Each of the fifteen lessons contains a dialogue written by John, Ellie, Frances, and Betty; an explanation of a grammatical and phonological aspect of the language; and vocabulary and practice exercises. A compact disc with all of the dialogues and Keiwa vocabulary performed by these four speakers accompanies the text. Although this was the second text written in the language, it was the first to be circulated, due to the lengthy nature of the dictionary project and the editing it necessitated. The adult curriculum's cover appears in figure 2.1.

The title in Keiwa appears first, followed by its English translation. In block letters, a warning sternly asserts the right of the tribal language program to control the circulation of the curriculum and to limit the text's readership. The next line, which refers to "disciplinary action" and "termination," is intended for the San Ramón Head Start teachers who come from neighboring pueblos. Language committee members felt that these employees might show the language materials to people in their community, who might disapprove of the tribe's decision to write the language.

The account of the actual textual circulation, however, tells a slightly different story. Although members of the language committee decided to number all the volumes and create a sign-up sheet for community members to check out copies, the curriculum was freely given to people who showed interest in the language, some of whom were no longer on the tribal rolls. This shows that the right to control indigenous language materials and the right to learn the language are what is being modeled here rather than actively controlling the circulation of written materials and, by extension, the cultural knowledge contained in the volume. As Lilith Mahmud outlines in her study of Italian Freemasons, secrecy should be considered to be part of practices of "discretion," which she describes as "a set of embodied practices that conceal and reveal potentially significant information" (2012:429). At San Ramón, the lack of consistent enforcement of access to indigenous language materials and information on language use is an integral component of discretionary practice, showing that revelation works in concert with concealment and models ownership and other values while adapting the circulation of cultural knowledge to multiple contexts.

An additional aspect of Simmel's analysis that further explains Pueblo secrecy is the ability of concealment to confer value: "scarcity" (1906:491) and managing reciprocal knowledge increase the value of the information being controlled. Luhrmann outlines the relationship between secrecy and exchange more pointedly: "Concealment creates property, something that is possessed, and the existence of this special property distinguishes possessor from nonpossessor and alters the attitudes of both toward the thing possessed" (1989a:136). However, Jones points out that disclosure is also involved in producing value: "Because concealing knowledge produces value through the exclusion of outsiders and revealing knowledge produces value through the incorporation of insiders, centripetal and centrifugal forces pull and push on the secret" (2012:78). Both Simmel and Luhrmann also discuss the difficulty of acquiring secret knowledge, through either intense study or prolonged trust, and how this also creates value in that more time and effort have been invested in procuring concealed information, augmenting in many cases systems of expertise and bureaucratization. In a study of Simmel's influence on how best to understand new patterns of electronic circulation and concealment, the sociologists Gary T. Marx and Glenn Muschert describe information as moving in flows similar to money and commodities (2009:9), with knowledge increasing or decreasing in relative value as it is exchanged and controlled.[5] These studies recall some classic texts in anthropology regarding exchange (Malinowski 1922; Mauss 1967; Munn 1986; Weiner 1988), with secrecy engendering fame and influence through rumor, inference, and the awareness that people and groups do not possess equal knowledge.

Secrecy—specifically, limiting access to the Keiwa language—confers value in four fundamental ways at San Ramón Pueblo: by tightly controlling cultural objects (texts); by elevating textual content; by positively or negatively affecting the status of people associated with indigenous language use; and by contributing to the reputation of the entire community. Writing turns San Ramón Keiwa materials into valued cultural objects whose circulation is closely guarded. Community members are supposed to sign out any language materials, and copies of the adult curriculum, the alphabet, and other pedagogical materials are protected. Community members speak positively about the difficulty of "getting ahold of language stuff" for any of the Pueblo languages and take seriously their responsibility as caretakers of these objects. A few years ago, one member of the young adult summer class left language materials in the library of the high school. The tribe was contacted by the librarian about the missing items. Although the student never came forward to claim them, gossip continues to swirl about the student's culpability and carelessness, and there is concern about the slip-up: "Just anyone could see our language." Such examples of improper levels of control and concealment help to establish written Keiwa materials as valued pieces of material culture in need of careful stewardship.

The scarcity of language materials also serves to elevate the words, expressions, registers, and stories contained in the texts. Not only do community language learners depend on written materials more and more as the opportunities to hear and use Keiwa decline, but also the fact that access to the texts is controlled and that the texts themselves are the product of assiduous creation and editing raises the importance of the few that exist. Significance is also imparted to the small group of community members who have been responsible for creating these texts, at times, elevating their status and, at others, casting the language program participants as contributors to overall community decline.

Another way that secrecy potentially confers value at San Ramón involves non-community members. San Ramón people pride themselves on successfully keeping their language and written language materials within the confines of the pueblo. People talk disdainfully about pueblos that teach their language in schools where "anyone can take the classes" and emphasize, "We will never put our language on the internet, where anyone could see it." That outsiders are largely banned from learning or using Pueblo languages also increases these codes' cachet in the region and beyond. On several occasions, I have talked to tourists visiting New Mexico who speak as reverently about "getting to learn a few words" of a Pueblo language as about hiking the remotest canyons or sampling the hottest green chile. The exclusivity of Pueblo languages indexes the idea of an untouched, authentic New Mexico, available only to those in the know.

There are also affective dimensions to the withholding of knowledge at San Ramón, aspects of which are found in other works on secrecy. Simmel discusses the ways that concealment can engender feelings of trust and solidarity among the members of secret societies. Secrecy removes knowledge from potential (un)verifiability or ridicule, according to Luhrmann, who describes secrecy's emotional timbre in the following way: "It is therapeutic: the magician learns to handle his feelings and actions more effectively because of magic's secrecy" (1989b:132). She goes on to describe other "psychological" functions of concealment, including "elicit[ing] awe and deference toward its hidden contents" (137) and "alter[ing] the attitudes of both insider and outsider toward the thing concealed" (161). And "secrecy is exciting" (162). Clearly, the practice of keeping secrets and alluding to their existence has the potential to produce or reflect affective states in both insiders and outsiders, including pride, jealousy, and stimulation.

Examples of concealment's affective power are plentiful both in and around the New Mexico pueblos. Most obvious, limiting access to the Keiwa language engenders feelings of solidarity among those sanctioned to speak or learn the language. For example, I asked the participants in the young adult language class to fill out an evaluation at the end of the summer to see which activities the students found helpful and to gather ideas for the following year's class. Several respondents talked about liking the "group dynamics" and "being able to say things no one else understands with other people from the class." Controlled access to Keiwa is also awe inspiring, as evidenced by the tourist example mentioned above. Outsiders, including linguists and anthropologists, are especially prone to secrecy's affective power. Throughout the history of both disciplines, there has been a relative emphasis on analyzing examples of speech genres that are somehow limited in circulation, such as ritual chants or creation stories, and on studying previously undocumented languages. Mahmud comments on the close ties between anthropology and secrecy, pointing out that secrets are often characterized by ethnographers as automatically central and important and are often studied precisely because of their detachability compared with other forms of knowledge. In addition, she argues, "Secret societies...have often served a metonymical function in ethnographic writings: They have appeared as bounded communities within larger social groups, small parts that come to stand in for the whole" (Mahmud 2012:427). Thus, the affective power of concealment is not a phenomenon limited to anthropology's "subjects" but is part of the motivations and methodologies of its practitioners.[6]

Here is an example of secrecy producing excitement. One hot summer day, Michelle and I drove a group of second graders from the summer recreation program up to San Ramón Mountain, the focal point of the pueblo and purportedly the location of numerous hidden shrines and religious sites. In addition to serving as the tribal librarian for many years, Michelle works with the language committee and other education programs. After driving past abandoned sheep farms and unused roads, we pulled the Suburban over and settled under a tree to visit while the kids played. One of the children, Matt, was playing with his cousin Marissa nearby. Sotto voce, he said, "Listen, I can hear our ancestors singing in Indian!" He followed this up by saying, "Don't let *her* know [*nodding in my direction*]. She shouldn't hear it." Marissa squealed with excitement, visibly impressed. Of course, feelings of excitement and awe connected to language secrecy also have the potential to set up the kinds of barriers Simmel cautioned against, and some disenrolled tribal members felt the sting of being cut out of the San Ramón language program or not being allowed to view the language materials.

A final affective dimension of secrecy found in the San Ramón case is described by Simmel: "Secrecy involves a tension which, at the moment of revelation, finds its release. This constitutes the climax in the development of the secret; in it the whole charm of secrecy concentrates and rises to its highest pitch—just as the moment of the disappearance of an object brings out the feeling of its value in the most intense degree" (1906:465). Hence, the affective and value-producing qualities of secrecy are at their most potent during moments of revelation, and divulgence is again revealed to be an integral part of the logic of concealment. This proves that a measure of revelation is absolutely necessary in order for value to be conferred on controlled knowledge. In order for secret knowledge to accomplish social work, some degree of information sharing must occur. Revelation could potentially range from simply knowing that San Ramón Keiwa is to be spoken only by tribal members, to being initiated into how to utilize highly controlled ceremonial words or genres. Affect and value are produced only if the sense of scarcity that Simmel describes is made present through mention, inference, or direct initiation.

As Simmel and other theorists of secrecy make clear, concealment is an interactional process, with language being the central medium used to share information. Philosophers of language have long weighed in on the amount or quality of information necessary to successfully achieve reference (Donellan 1966; Frege 1952 [1892]; Kripke 1980; Putnam 1975; Russell 1905; Strawson 1950). Sociolinguists, sociologists, and philosophers have built on this tradition to describe the rules that lie behind the appropriate dissemination of information in interactions (Brown and Levinson 1987; Goffman 1955; Grice 1975). Like Simmel's approach to secrecy, many of these works rely heavily on theorizing an idealized, individuated speaker who acts rationally to achieve social and interactional cohesion, mirroring depictions of societies' structures found in functionalist theories in anthropology (Durkheim 1997 [1893]; Malinowski 1922).

Since these studies appeared, linguistic anthropologists and sociolinguists have expanded the narrow focus on Western rationality, allowing for analyses of interactional practices of indirectness and veiling across countless speech communities.[7] Andrew Cowell's work on Arapaho narratives expressly criticizes individualized notions of face, specifically as they apply to understanding interactions in Native North America: "As for many Native American communities, respect is fundamentally based on the principle of non-imposition of excess authority and its counterpart, non-derogation of legitimate authority. Central to this process is the use of indirectness, as students of Native America have noticed" (2007:55). At San Ramón, such patterns of avoidance occur across many types of interactions. As I detail in subsequent chapters, dictionary example sentences are used to indirectly convey sensitive cultural information, a language pedagogical dialogue becomes a political tract, and a fictional soap opera serves as a trenchant critique of tribal membership policy. As we consider approaches to understanding concealment, it is useful to view secrecy practices as essentially intense forms of indirectness and avoidance, and they should be analyzed accordingly.

A third means of explicating information control can be found in the extensive literature on the public and private spheres. Most crucial for the present study is that the division between public and private is where theories of literacy and secrecy meet. Central to the theorization of this divide is the place of texts and their ability to reflect or engender certain types of social action, behaviors that are then prototypically associated with either the public or private sphere. Thus, the distinction between the public and private spheres is one of the most important means to describe the implications of textual circulation and the creation of modern publics. In the San Ramón case, it beomes a means of discussing the various ways written language is used, imagined, and controlled.

The literature on the dichotomy between public and private is voluminous, from Habermas's (1989) foundational work positing the existence of the public sphere and its implications for liberal democracy, to critiques of this theory (Calhoun 1992), to Michael Warner's (2002a, 2002b) work on counterpublics. In terms of analyzing what theories of publics mean for understandings of secrecy, Gal's "A Semiotics of the Public/Private Distinction" (2002) is most efficacious. Overcoming the inability of some depictions of this divide to apply to non-Western contexts, Gal argues that "when the public/private distinction is analyzed as a communicative phenomenon—a product of semiotic processes—it shows a complex and systematic logic" (2002:77), one that can encapsulate cross-cultural and transhistorical iterations of this divide. She points out the "error in assuming stable boundaries between public and private" (78), echoing misguided attempts to depict ideas about appropriate language use or secrecy as stable phenomena. Gal shows that the public-private distinction, like attitudes regarding proper language use, is "ideological" (78), with these categories serving as "tools for arguments about and in" the social world (79). Throughout the essay, she provides examples of how definitions of private or public are constantly shifting according to context, and this distinction is used again and again, constituting an example of "fractal recursivity" (see also Irvine and Gal 2000).

Illustrating Gal's point, the use of the public-private semiotic at San Ramón Pueblo both differs from other examples of this divide and is conditioned by the immediate contexts of use. Her approach is especially useful in describing the various audiences that are allowed to view San Ramón Keiwa texts. In subsequent chapters, I detail many of the more controlled, or "private," uses of Keiwa writing. However, Pueblo writing, at San Ramón and elsewhere in the region, has been used in many ways that align with aspects of the Western folk views of "publics," since they have the potential to be viewed by disinterested, anonymous audiences, constituting another example of the necessity of divulgence in discretionary practices. One innovation has been the use of Keiwa in commercial settings, specifically in the casino complex located on the reservation. Increasingly, Keiwa names are used for many of the attractions in this tribal venture: the lounge is called Rain Water or Rain Drop; Ice is the martini bar; Sunrise is the buffet; and Blue Mountain is the fine dining restaurant. When I asked bartenders and servers at the casino about the Keiwa words, they helpfully supplied more or less accurate translations, although in some cases, they had to double-check with other employees. One server assured me, "Everything means something," while nodding earnestly and gesturing at the various casino attractions with Keiwa names. The fact that he did not single out English signs (which also "mean" something) points to the nonreferential functions that such signs embody and indicates the specificity of the San Ramón Keiwa language and the applicability of this code for use in commercial settings. In fact, most tribal members utilize English phrases when referring to places in the casino ("the lounge," "the buffet").

The San Ramón employee's helpful but cheerfully uninvested attitude was echoed by employees at the Hotel Santa Fe. Owned and operated by another Pueblo community, this tribal venture also uses indigenous language in signs throughout the hotel. The indigenous words for "Welcome, Welcome" are posted in large letters above the entry. When I asked one of the employees what the words mean, he told me, "Uh, 'Welcome,' I think.... Yeah, it means 'Welcome,'" but he was unfamiliar with any of the other terms.

The management at the San Ramón casino has begun to contact members of the tribal language program before naming new attractions. Community members, however, place little importance on the accuracy of the signs once these are posted, even though they acknowledge that the casino signs are sometimes misspelled and contain letters not found in the standardized San Ramón orthography. Much more effort is put into the negotiations between the marketing department and tribal members and among members of the committee itself regarding the choice of appropriate names. Language committee members consult for hours about spelling and the appropriateness of using particular words and expressions. Once the signs appear in print, however, their status as important sites for the discussion of public indigenous language use fades. At San Ramón, the right to make such decisions—both among tribal members and in partnership with nontribal casino employees—and to comment on what constitutes the "perfect" written forms is of greater consequence.

The use of Pueblo languages in civic settings is another emergent trend in the public, written, indigenous language materials in the region. On US 84 just north of Santa Fe, two overpasses display the Tewa words for the nearby pueblos: K'uuyemugeh (previously hispanicized to Cuyamungue) and Posuwaegeh (Pojoaque). In 2008, San Juan Pueblo officially changed its name to the Tewa word for the community, Ohkay Owingeh, and in 2010, Santo Domingo Pueblo changed its name to Kewa, the Keres designation. These decisions have resulted in sign changes on the reservation, as well as changes in all legal and commercial tribal documents. Although most people at San Ramón Pueblo view such changes positively, these do not necessarily connect to their own decisions about public language use. When I asked a colleague there whether she agreed with these decisions, she said that she did but that if similar changes were made at San Ramón, "it would be hard for emergency vehicles to find the right houses."

In 2007, a contractor from the city of Albuquerque contacted me to see whether community members at San Ramón Pueblo would be interested in including Keiwa in a public works project by the Rio Grande that was also to include English, Spanish, and binary code. The plan was for all the languages spoken in the area to be represented. Because there were Keiwa-speaking pueblos throughout the region, it was decided that this language should constitute the indigenous contribution. I put him in touch with the tribal member who handles such decisions, and after the exchange of several e-mails, it was decided that the two-word Keiwa phrase for "river of life" would be included. The tribal member who made the decision stipulated that the contractor "make sure to spell it right" and that everyone involved with the negotiation remain anonymous, in order to avoid any political fallout at the pueblo and elsewhere from those who might object to this public use of the language. Although the discussion of whether to participate in the project was lengthy, in the years since this decision was made, none of the tribal members who were involved have inquired about the status of the project. Again, time and energy were spent on discussing the imagined consequences, both positive and negative, of using written Keiwa, but after the negotiations were concluded, the issue did not require any attention.

In addition to commercial and civic settings, the circulation of new written texts occurs in public spaces in the San Ramón community. Several summers ago, the eight students in the young-adult Keiwa program began each day by visiting the kitchen at the tribal education complex and asking the cook what she was preparing for the Head Start lunch so that they could post the menu in Keiwa. This initially provided a way for the group to practice asking questions and writing (not to mention the added bonus of grabbing a cup of coffee or a snack). As the summer progressed, their use of language became more ritualistic than referential or pedagogical, a way to talk about Native language learning and to elicit approval from the Keiwa speakers and other adults who work in the building. The language students and the community members teaching the class took great care to spell each word correctly and to use Keiwa words whenever possible, collaborating on neologisms when Spanish loanwords were the norm. One of the cooks, a Keiwa speaker from another pueblo, devoted a folder in her recipe file to the menus, archiving the diligence of the students and their teachers in attaining the appropriate orthographic and visual representations of the local vocabulary.

Of course, public uses of Pueblo languages often overlap among commercial, civic, and community contexts, and nowhere is this more obvious than in electronic media. The website for the Indian Pueblo Cultural Center, a museum, gift shop, and conference center in Albuquerque serving all the pueblos, is one example. The site has information for potential visitors on the center's upcoming events, hours, and the like, but it also has a historical and cultural component, enumerating the various language families represented at the pueblos and providing recorded examples of five Pueblo languages. Most individual pueblos split the commercial, civic, and community uses of Native language online, maintaining separate sites for the tribe and for the casino or other ventures. For instance, one pueblo uses Keiwa on its hotel website but not on its tribal website, which has an extensive section on the culture and history of the community. Perhaps such commercial uses of Native languages, like the place names for the lounge and other locations at the San Ramón casino, are less controversial sites for the public display of written materials. However, other than listing the restaurant names mentioned above, San Ramón Pueblo uses no Native language on either its casino website or its tribal site.

These examples of language being used in multiple public settings show that the written form of the Keiwa language is a nonreferential resource used to highlight indigenous identity. Another part of embodying an ideal San Ramón identity, which is also revealed in such actions, is the respectful discussion of appropriate use, which asserts the right of community members to control access to indigenous language materials. Adherence to these local standards of negotiation also occurs in non-institutional and informal settings at San Ramón. In a trend that started during the weekly sewing club at the pueblo, community members make baby books and Christmas stockings using written language, embroidering the letters of the Keiwa alphabet next to words beginning with each sound or sewing the Indian names of family members. One year I received several phone calls the week before Christmas from seamstresses asking for help with spelling because they were completing last-minute presents. Whereas it could be argued that the baby books serve a pedagogical function, teaching children (and their caregivers) the sounds of San Ramón Keiwa and some basic vocabulary, the Indian names on the Christmas stockings serve a decidedly nonreferential function. Like the commercial, civic, and community uses of Native languages, these private, familial uses of indigenous language foreground an Indian identity through the use of written materials and assert a personal right to use the technology of writing, not an uncontroversial choice at San Ramón Pueblo.

Conclusion

Language ideologies, literacy, and concealment practices are not only central aspects of the ethnolinguistic context at San Ramón Pueblo but also interrelated concepts. New practices with texts are conditioned by extant and emergent language ideologies and practices of concealment. Writing becomes a new platform upon which community members perform acts of purism, veiling, avoidance, and indirectness. All of these are interactional phenomena, requiring a close look at how spoken and written texts are produced, what they contain, and where they are circulated.

One final aspect of information control is important to emphasize, especially as it relates to indigenous language literacy and Pueblo language ideologies: the deliberateness of secrecy. Simmel observes, "Secrecy does not grow, but is built by design" (1906:479). Similarly, San Ramón literacy continues to be an extremely thoughtful process, one that, like secrecy, requires constant vigilance and management in order to produce appropriate texts and interactions and their associated social effects.

three
Setting an Example

The San Ramón Keiwa Dictionary

> A dictionary of this sort is not just a collection of words and their meanings, but represents something of what the community it serves requires.
>
> —*Earle Waugh, foreword to* Alberta Elders' Cree Dictionary

One morning soon after I arrived at the pueblo to work on the first draft of the dictionary, I found John organizing his file cabinets. He showed me a document he had found while cleaning up, a word list from the 1930s that had ended up in the library cultural archive. A San Ramón community member had dictated a list of Keiwa nouns and greetings to an unidentified anthropologist from the Smithsonian Institution during a trip to Washington, DC. Together, John and I deciphered the script and the orthographic conventions, identifying the San Ramón Keiwa words for "dog," "arm," and "tree," among others, and a short list of greetings. John was surprised that this man had agreed to write down words to be kept in a museum. He remarked, "His name doesn't sound like he's from here, anyway," but the listed forms were accurate and clearly represented the Keiwa spoken at San Ramón (as opposed to the dialect documented in the SIL dictionary).

Although John was surprised to encounter such an early example of a lexicon of San Ramón Keiwa and although members of the dictionary committee frequently talked about being part of writing their language "for the first time," independent writing traditions and smaller lexicography projects have existed at the pueblo for many years. Individuals using self-designed orthographies have created word lists to aid in language learning or to record certain vocabularies. Over the years, Ellie, Frances, and Betty have made word lists for the children participating in the summer language program, concentrating on semantic categories such as animals, colors, food, and clothing. Although none of these efforts became actual dictionary projects, they shared several of the same goals and methodologies found in other indigenous and non-indigenous lexicons, including an emphasis on language learning, the use of elicitation, and a focus on concrete nouns.

In this chapter, I detail the creation and content of the San Ramón Keiwa dictionary, the first text created as part of the pueblo's tribally sanctioned, indigenous language literacy. I examine the connections between the material and historical aspects of the San Ramón project and other lexicographic projects, as well as some potential impacts of instituting a dictionary project. The bulk of the chapter is devoted to understanding the tools—both grammatical and poetic—that San Ramón Keiwa speakers used when constructing dictionary example sentences, which became the central focus of the dictionary project. I analyze the preferred person-marking patterns in the example sentences in order to examine issues of authority, audience, and stereotypic knowledge as reflected in the participant structures that the grammatical regularities reveal. After exploring the temporal dimensions of sentence construction by enumerating the prevalent tense/aspect markers used by dictionary authors, I concentrate on the grammatical methods used to express explicit or implicit desires or hopes as embodied in the use of the purposive modal enclitic, the subjunctive aspectual marker, and other common constructions in the dictionary example sentences. The chapter concludes with a discussion of register and genre in the text and the connection between preferred grammatical forms at the level of the sentence and larger ideas regarding San Ramón personhood and perfectibility.

The Genre of Lexicography

Commonplace to the point of being taken for granted, dictionaries are largely unexamined as a contemporary written genre, despite their ubiquity. Highlighting the features of this type of text helps to explain the significance of the San Ramón document by showing the ways that the dictionary adheres to and diverges from lexicographic traditions.[1] In prototypical incarnations, such as the *Oxford English Dictionary* or other well-known examples, dictionaries are envisioned as neutral reference works, designed to describe the grammatical and semantic regularities of individual lexical items. Definitions are crafted to help readers distinguish between various shades of referential meaning, and example sentences further illustrate the various senses of each entry.

Reference dictionaries are also used as pedagogical tools to teach new words and their meanings. Dictionaries figure prominently in second-language learning or in familiarizing learners with specialized vocabularies for birding, geology, and any number of specialized pursuits. Often, knowledge of such terms is part of an initiation into a particular group, as Rusty Barrett illustrates in his study of how lexicons circulated by party promoters serve to introduce men into specific parts of a gay subculture (Barrett, forthcoming). The San Ramón Keiwa dictionary, created expressly as a language-learning tool to be used by an extremely circumscribed group of people, relies on the often mundane, neutral associations with reference and pedagogical materials in order to include potentially sensitive information in the text.

For most dictionary projects, there is a considerable convergence in the methods authors use to craft lexicons. As illustrated by the Smithsonian Keiwa text, the first (or only) step in many encounters between linguists and linguistic consultants consists of making a word list, with the speaker translating words into the language being documented. The linguist Marianne Mithun outlines this methodology, identifying the elicitation of translated forms as a tactic that must be employed alongside other approaches, including the recording of longer stretches of speech and the production of grammatical judgments (2001b:48). Elicitation tends to yield easily isolatable forms, such as nouns, to the exclusion of more grammatically complex forms. Although some members of the Keiwa dictionary committee consulted notebooks with word lists they had independently produced, elicitation was never a central component of the project. At no time did I or any of the other participants elicit forms to complete verb paradigms, add to semantic fields, or fill in grammatical descriptions.

Using an existing corpus or employing data-mining techniques are two lexicographic methodologies that seek to remedy the focus on nouns. In a sense, this approach was utilized by the Keiwa authors, although in a circuitous way. The material in the 1970s SIL dictionary that the San Ramón authors used to begin their dictionary project was selected using a corpus: a translation of the New Testament. Every word that appeared in the Keiwa translation (which was guided by missionaries from the Summer Institute of Linguistics) was then made into a separate lemma, or entry. These are the same lemmata that eventually served as the word list used by Keiwa speakers at San Ramón Pueblo to aid in the construction of their volume. Although numerous texts have been written or recorded in the years since the dictionary project started, committee members did not look to those texts as source material, eliminating corpus lexicography as a direct methodological component of the project.

Corpora are also frequently the source of example material. With the advent of the internet, lexicographers can more easily search for sentences that help to illustrate the meaning of dictionary entries or disambiguate between meanings. However, example sentences are also created by lexicographers themselves. Steve Kleinedler, a senior editor for the *American Heritage Dictionary*, describes the process his organization uses: "We make them up. There are some dictionaries that only use corpora, but those can sound stilted or contextually bizarre. If we have citations from journals, we will use those. But when it comes to finding example sentences for complex words like 'take' and 'give,' it is better to use constructed examples. You can base the constructed example on corpora, especially if it is used in a particular collocation, but mainly, we use corpora as a guide" (personal communication May 2008).

The invention of exemplification material diverges from methodologies historically used in lexicography, which drew on existing literature to illustrate usage (Jackson 2002:26). Although the dictionary authors at San Ramón created their own example sentences for the majority of the volume, these sentences were not envisioned as a way to disambiguate the meanings of individual lexical items or to enhance definitions. Instead, the Keiwa dictionary sentences focus on imparting necessary cultural information, imploring readers, "Listen so [that] you can live life the way it's supposed to be lived," as one sentence explicitly instructs.

To summarize, the Keiwa authors eschewed elicitation and corpora analysis to isolate entries and provide illustrative material in favor of using the SIL text as a jumping-off point, focusing most of their attention on crafting example sentences. The central lexicographic methodology employed at San Ramón Pueblo can thus be thought of as perfecting words and sentences according to local ideological and aesthetic preferences. The team of dictionary authors looked to the SIL text as an example and began, as they described it, by "correcting" the spelling of each lexical item. Following this, they corrected the example sentences they felt were ungrammatical and replaced the ones that were culturally irrelevant by authoring their own sentences. They also omitted example sentences that were no longer felt to be appropriate to include in the dictionary. What emerged is essentially an endlessly perfectible work—a quality that many dictionaries share in that they are constantly being revised and augmented.

The overall formal aspects of the Keiwa text both align with and diverge from prototypical lexicons. One structural aspect shared by almost all the dictionaries I surveyed was the use of alphabetical entries. While this may seem obvious, its ubiquity is important to note since it emphasizes a central lexicographic ideology: dictionaries are collections of words. Their alphabetical arrangement renders them orderly and searchable, and the arrangement itself signals the totality of a language (from *A* to *Z*, so to speak). This view, which often works in concert with elicitation as a central method, depends on and creates a depiction of language as a collection of discrete words or characters rather than as a set of rules, patterns, sounds, morphemes, ways of speaking, ways of being in the world, or other possibilities. This Western linguistic ideology also has credence at San Ramón Pueblo, as evidenced by the push to collect "more words" for the dictionary and by the assumption that a San Ramón Keiwa lexicon would consist of a collection of alphabetically arranged "words." This is a difficult task, considering Keiwa's synthetic morphology, in which pronouns appear as prefixes on the verb and nouns are often incorporated into the verbal complex.

In addition, when surveying dictionaries for this project, I noticed that almost all of these texts have extensive introductions. The introductions contain orienting material for dictionary readers, elaborating on how best to "use" the volume and providing information on the text's authors and their authority to write such a work. Unlike authors of written texts whose utility or appeal is revealed during the process of reading, such as novels, plays, or even other types of reference works, dictionary authors emphasize the codified uses for their works by including lengthy introductory sections. Appeals are made to ideal audiences, explanations are given for scope and organization, and especially in the case of most published indigenous language dictionaries, lexicons are identified as intrinsic to language revitalization projects and assertions of linguistic and cultural uniqueness.

The introductory material in the San Ramón Keiwa lexicon contrasts with prototypical dictionary introductions in marked ways, most notably in its brevity. The sole introductory information that dictionary committee members planned on including in the final printed version is a warning (that the text is intended only for tribal members' use) and words of encouragement (for Keiwa learners). It does, however, perform one common function of dictionary introductions in that it states who is licensed to view and use the text, limiting this only to "community members at San Ramón Pueblo" rather than to undifferentiated, inclusive categories such as "English speakers." On the single introductory page, the dictionary authors do not include information about their identities or qualifications, although many committee members have college degrees, hold tribal positions of authority, and are locally recognized as language and cultural experts.[2] Instead, they credit authorship to the "San Ramón Pueblo Education Department." This is partially because everyone in the community knows the identity of the staff members involved with the language program. But it is also the case that the dictionary committee members do not want their names listed as authors, nor do they want to include information about their college degrees or language ability, for fear of negative political repercussions such as disenrollment and because of the cultural inappropriateness of claiming authority in such a direct, public way.[3] Although committee members were quick to emphasize my qualifications when I was introduced to new people, citing my school affiliation and Keiwa abilities, I am not listed as a co-author or consultant on this project. It would be inappropriate to claim association with the Keiwa language as a nontribal member, and it would be tasteless to foreground my own credentials.

Concomitantly, the tiny introduction to the San Ramón Keiwa dictionary contains no directions for future readers on how to use the text. In fact, language program members have devoted little discussion to how community members will learn the alphabet, either to use the dictionary or to read other written materials produced in Keiwa.[4] Although committee members discussed eventually including a copy of the alphabet in the front of the dictionary, as it stands now, the text begins with entries that start with the letter *A* on the page immediately following the introduction. The absence of extensive introductory material sets up an "if you have to ask" situation: if you do not already know who created this text, who can use it, and what it is to be used for, then you are automatically outside the group of appropriate viewers and users.

The final formal feature of dictionaries that helps to explain the significance of the San Ramón text is lemma design. After addressing particular audiences in introductions and arranging words alphabetically, what information do lexicographers choose to include in individual entries? Although varying in level of detail, all the lexicons I surveyed contain some amount of grammatical information, by listing parts of speech, crafting explicitly metasemantic statements about usage, or using example sentences illustrating specific grammatical processes. It is here that the San Ramón text differs most drastically from other lexicons, omitting any grammatical information and including only the headword, its English translation, and the carefully crafted example sentence(s). This serves to heighten the relative importance of the illustrative material.

The Keiwa dictionary's lemma design highlights the absence of referential ideologies of language in its authors. Dictionary creation in any community both depends on and foregrounds what Silverstein (1976) terms "the semantico-referential function of language," one facet of language, among others, that lets interlocutors achieve reference, allowing for predication and description. Indeed, elicitation as a methodology captures referential regularities to the exclusion of gathering information on language use, a legacy of linguistic methodology seen from Saussure to Chomsky.

The focus on referential speech events and the decision to create indigenous language lexicons as the central means of reversing language shift may result in part from North American tribes' increased participation in the US educational system and the influence of Western language ideologies. But perhaps another reason that many indigenous groups choose to create this type of text is practicality. Because of the rapidly declining use of indigenous languages in many Native North American communities, especially in everyday situations, speakers increasingly have less access to other functions of language, such as face-to-face interactions or ritual speech. As a result, in many communities that are using lexicography in an attempt to reverse language shift, the archiving, teaching, and emphasis on the referential regularities of indigenous languages has led to a lack of description of other language functions or, in many cases, their exclusion altogether from language revitalization programs. Like the community member at the San Ramón parents' meeting who worried that students would only memorize Keiwa words and sentences, individuals in participating communities recognize the potential absence of other functions of language in language revitalization programs using dictionaries. As I detail in the following sections, many of the San Ramón Keiwa example sentences attempt to convey non-referential information regarding face-to-face interaction and ritual speech to future readers of the dictionary. However, the close association between dictionaries and the semantico-referential function of language is precisely what allows the authors of the San Ramón lexicon to accomplish their goals in creating such a text by including potentially sensitive local knowledge in seemingly neutral example sentences.

Standardizing the languages chronicled in dictionaries is another potential effect shared by lexicographic projects. As numerous scholars have shown (Collins 1995; Jaffe 1996, 1999; Lippi-Green 1997; Milroy and Milroy 1998; Nevins 2004; Rosa 2010), movements to standardize language, whether at the level of lexicon, dialect, code, or another axis of difference, are inherently ideological, connecting positive or negative social values with particular ways of speaking. Because the social values indexed by standardized language(s) often have political or material consequences and because processes of standardization occur in institutional frameworks, the establishment of a standard language reflects and influences social life outside the immediate issues of language policy.

A dictionary that focuses on an "endangered" language has an even greater potential for standardization since it is often one of only a handful of written or recorded materials in that language. The centrality of these dictionaries to the language communities they represent and to students of indigenous languages grows as fewer community members become fluent in such languages. Also, dictionaries reflect and enforce "the culture of standard[ization]" (Silverstein 1996:221) by presenting single, sanctioned compendiums of "correct" words and their pronunciations. Collins connects the processes of standardization surrounding lexicography to nationalist projects, using the revolutionary period in the United States and the efforts of colonists to distance themselves politically and culturally from Great Britain as an example: "Efforts to fashion a standard American English during this period—most notably Noah Webster's dictionaries and reading programs—expressed the democratic impulses of a common language" (1999:217).

Determining whether the San Ramón dictionary has a standardizing effect on the Keiwa language and how it will contribute to future discussions of "correct" language usage will depend on future language use in the community and how the text is utilized over time. While I was conducting my fieldwork, community members would often reply, "The way we spelled it in the dictionary" when there was a question about orthography, although many people, including Keiwa speakers, had not learned to use the alphabet or expressed little interest in writing Keiwa, making the adoption of a standardized spelling system uneven. Similarly, dialectal variation may be erased. The words and example sentences included in the dictionary were overwhelmingly created by only four speakers, all of whom come from families at San Ramón that display only minor dialectal differences. However, these same authors did not object to including examples of other dialects, including the occasional Keiwa word from another pueblo, provided that they did not "have a better word for it."

There is great potential for the dictionary to play a role in standardizing particular grammatical constructions, registers, and genres in San Ramón Keiwa by virtue of the authors' personal tastes and their goals in creating the text. John was the only tribal member who worked on the text as a full-time language program employee; being the youngest and healthiest member of the group also enabled him to complete more work on the volume. The speech forms appropriate for males in this community may thus become standard forms as a result of the privileging of certain registers. Of course, this type of institutional imbalance can also work in the opposite way. When creating example sentences that referred to clan, group, or familial affiliation, John consistently avoided referring to groups of which he was a member, feeling that dictionary readers might find this self-centered or conceited. Also, a concerted effort to standardize on the part of all the Keiwa dictionary committee members took place at the level of the register, what the lexicographers Rice and Saxon (2002:127) describe as privileging "conservative usages" or the language of elders. This is yet another example of the way that supposedly neutral reference works are ideologically laden, intensely political projects.

Such ideological aspects of lexicography are connected to the institutional history of the genre and to the characteristics of its material forms. In the Euro American tradition, dictionaries are "serious" books, to be consumed as part of research or pedagogical projects. People do not typically keep dictionaries by the bed for a casual read, but dictionaries are often housed in libraries; they do not have colorful paper jackets but are instead solid-color, hardcover books. The associations of dictionaries with difficulty and seriousness are apparent in the reactions I have had from nonlinguists when they hear that I am working on a lexicography project: "Ugh. I'm sorry"; "God, that must be *so* boring"; and my personal favorite, "You don't *seem* like a person who would be writing a dictionary" (meant as a compliment). Reading and writing dictionaries are not seen as activities to be savored, but as arcane, scholarly endeavors, activities enjoyed only by the nerdiest of word geeks.[5]

The seriousness that is associated with printed dictionaries is also related to ideologies concerning the archive and the museum in the Western tradition (Blommaert 2008; Silverstein 2003). Archives, museums, and dictionaries are associated with the institutional space of the library, which is a location that implies social values such as gravity, scholarship, and the shaping and preservation of the past. Dictionaries' association with teams of "experts" (lexicographers) also resembles the ways that archives and museums are created and governed. All rely on similar processes of assembling collections, whether they consist of documents, artifacts, or words, and are often created by groups of multiple authors or curators. Behind such ideologies lies the belief that museums, archives, and dictionaries—and in Blommaert's (2008) examination of colonial era documents describing African languages, grammars—house objects and texts (such as maps or grammars) that are convertible into geographic boundaries, spoken languages, or discrete national identities. As Blommaert points out, the production of grammars was part of colonial agendas throughout the world, depicting indigenous languages (and their associated speakers and cultures) as translatable, known quantities for the European or American colonizers, able to be understood and controlled by rendering such languages curiosities from a precolonial past.

Along with cartographers and grammarians, lexicographers have had a long relationship with indigenous languages and their speakers, from colonial word lists that were developed to send with clergy to New Spain, to Wycliffe Bible translators and SIL missionaries' efforts to disseminate religious materials throughout the world, to dictionaries written as part of descriptive projects. In Hanks's work chronicling the deliberate production of a new form of Yucatec Maya by Franciscan friars in the colonial period, *Converting Words* (2010), he shows how dictionaries, along with grammars and scriptures and other religious texts, were integral to the imposition of a new form of Yucatec and the corresponding transformation of Maya spaces and bodies. Currently, indigenous language lexicography is central to many language revitalization and documentation projects.

Finally, as the lexicographers and linguists William Frawley, Kenneth Hill, and Pamela Munro (2002:2) observe in the introduction to their edited volume, which includes works describing the challenges and goals specific to lexicographic projects in indigenous communities, dictionaries are increasingly being developed to directly reverse issues of language shift. The linguists Leanne Hinton and William Weigel assert, "A dictionary is a repository of tribal identity that can be used for a variety of purposes even after the language ceases to be spoken" (2001:156), referring to the ideology of regenerativity prevalent in discussions about language loss (see Moore 2006). In these and other works, texts—especially lexicons—are seen as integral to speakers' abilities to reanimate their languages and prevent them from being forgotten. They also connect being able to speak or read indigenous languages to ideals of indigenous identity and authenticity. Like fine art objects, dictionaries circulated through extant and new institutional channels are another example of "culture" embodied in material form. This is especially salient in contexts of cultural revitalization. As the archaeologist Matthew Liebmann (2008) indicates in his study of Pueblo material culture following the Pueblo Revolt, objects figure prominently in the articulation of cultural strength and difference. The functional and formal differences, as well as the ideological, historical, and material links or contrasts between the San Ramón Keiwa text and other dictionaries, become clear when we look closely at the lexicon's example sentences.

Preferred Grammatical Constructions in Dictionary Example Sentences

The San Ramón dictionary, like the Cree dictionary mentioned in this chapter's epigraph, reflects what the community members who wrote it "require," in order to accomplish particular goals, deviating from many prototypical ways of creating lexicons. As mentioned above, each entry contains the headword, its English translation, an example sentence, and its English gloss. Below are examples of several lemmata as they appear in the dictionary. (Throughout, the Keiwa words have been obscured.)

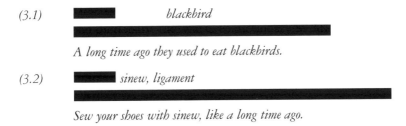

(3.1)　　　■■■■■■■　　　*blackbird*
　　　■■■■■■■■■■■■■■■■■■■■■■■■■■

A long time ago they used to eat blackbirds.

(3.2)　　　■■■■■■　*sinew, ligament*
　　　■■■■■■■■■■■■■■■■■■■■■■■■

Sew your shoes with sinew, like a long time ago.

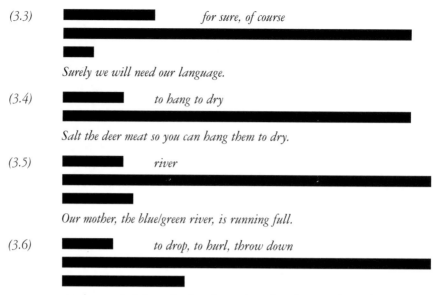

(3.3) [redacted] *for sure, of course*

[redacted]

Surely we will need our language.

(3.4) [redacted] *to hang to dry*

[redacted]

Salt the deer meat so you can hang them to dry.

(3.5) [redacted] *river*

[redacted]

Our mother, the blue/green river, is running full.

(3.6) [redacted] *to drop, to hurl, throw down*

[redacted]

At the sound of shots, the deer threw themselves down to the south.

These examples are representative of the majority of the illustrative sentences created for the San Ramón lexicon in that the sentences are utilized to describe the history of the pueblo (example 3.1); instruct community members about cultural practices and priorities (examples 3.2–3.4); or demonstrate components of local ceremonial speech genres or technologies (examples 3.5–3.6). This type of content is present in the majority of the sentences that the dictionary committee agrees are "good examples." However, it is precisely these particular uses of written language—instances that have the potential to communicate cultural practices specific to San Ramón Pueblo—that are continually presented by members of the community as potentially dangerous. Thus, the dictionary emerges as a paradoxical object: it is a tool necessary for preserving the ancestral language, but it is potentially at odds with locally held beliefs regarding secrecy. The lexicon is at once a neutral reference work and a potential place for creatively encoding salient cultural information.

In order to explore my initial thought about the dictionary—that the San Ramón Keiwa dictionary authors were using certain types of example sentences repeatedly—I analyzed all the illustrative sentences to determine the favored grammatical forms. The sentences that were deemed too sensitive for inclusion were also part of this sample, although they are not reproduced here, nor is their content discussed. As a result of this analysis, frequently used grammatical constructions became apparent, an unsurprising finding for a text constrained by generic and stylistic expectations, by pedagogical and cultural goals, and by the limited number of authors participating in the writing process. As in my comparative analysis of dictionaries above, this methodology revealed the differences between the preferred grammatical forms in the Western tradition and in the San Ramón text, making clear the additional resources employed by authors to accomplish their communicative and social goals.

First-Person Constructions

My analysis of the example sentences created for the San Ramón dictionary indicates the use of numerous first-person forms, with several recurrent constructions.[6] Plural imperatives are frequently used, as seen in example 3.7, which encourages participation in what was once a common practice at San Ramón Pueblo:

(3.7)   *Let's go pick grapes so we can make wine.*

This example illustrates of the prevalent use of first-person plural forms—to educate the reader about local technologies and to encourage their continuation, a theme favored by all the community members who worked on the dictionary project. Similarly, the following sentences use first-person plural imperatives that describe activities the authors lament are not practiced as much as they once were at San Ramón Pueblo:

(3.8)   *Let's go dig wild celery.*

(3.9)   *The neighbors are plastering their walls with mud. Let's go help.*

(3.10)   *Let's go pick wild spinach so we can put it in the beans.*

These examples also represent conscious attempts by the dictionary authors to, as they remarked during the editing process, "describe how things used to be," and they include words and expressions that "old-timers used to use." However, the first-person plural imperative is also found in example sentences describing more recent cultural practices, including alternative methods of acquiring food:

(3.11)   *Let's go to Church's to eat chicken.*

The contents of first-person plural imperative constructions provide a snapshot of the overall focus for all the example sentences. The ones that describe commonplace twenty-first-century activities are interspersed in illustrative material that mostly concerns specifically local practices closely associated with San Ramón Pueblo. The majority of the content chronicles practices that are largely obsolete but that are still salient to San Ramón identity. Thus, the authors' use of first-person plural imperatives not only advocates community participation in particular activities but also advances an alignment with the social values that such activities indicate.

These themes are echoed in the many non-imperative first-person plural constructions created for the document. In such sentences, the dictionary authors exhibit their direct knowledge of cultural practices and the history of the pueblo by placing themselves in the discourse as representatives of a body of collective knowledge. Also, those sentences often reference past activities, as in example 3.12, which uses the perfective aspectual marker to describe a method of food preparation that has fallen out of practice:

(3.12)   *We ate tomatoes with sugar.*

However, the use of first-person plural forms is not limited to descriptions of activities that took place in the past. They are also used in constructions utilizing imperfective and future forms, as in the following descriptions of the appropriate observances for various local events:

(3.13)   *For the dead we will be making food for All Souls Day.*

(3.14)   *Tomorrow evening we will sing songs at the kiva.*

Such sentences reflect the ways that community members at San Ramón Pueblo typically describe communal work and the preparations they engage in as part of following local ceremonial protocols. These are everyday conversations that take place in both Keiwa and English. The written first-person plural constructions and in spoken exchanges show inherently local practices—bringing food to the cemetery for the Day of the Dead or singing songs in the kiva—that also index San Ramón subjectivities. They are not being presented as lost technologies or as important activities that need to be reintroduced, but as descriptions of ongoing practices.

Displaying collective knowledge of the local geography, plants, and animals is another common use for first-person plural forms in the San Ramón dictionary:

(3.15)   *We go rabbit hunting to the east.*

(3.16)   *We're going to get evergreen for the dance.*

Example 3.15 was singled out as an effective sentence by members of the dictionary committee because it utilized the word that means "to the east," one of the many detailed terms for cardinal directions in San Ramón Keiwa, words that can also serve as place names, in this case, referring to the focal geographic and ceremonial feature of the pueblo, San Ramón Mountain. The command of this directional system also figures prominently in certain types of ritual speech, and this sentence constitutes another example of what the dictionary authors described as "sneaking in preaching words." These two sentences also represent a concerted effort on the part of the authors to create examples that capture both men's and women's knowledge, foregrounding the expertise of certain groups in the community by using specialized vocabularies and by modeling appropriate language use. Knowledge of favored hunting locations is effectively limited to groups of men at San Ramón, whereas women and children typically are part of the group that collects evergreen branches for dances.

The use of first-person plural constructions tying San Ramón people to the local geography is not restricted to the boundaries of the pueblo. It also describes activities that take place throughout the region:

(3.17)   *We're going to go buy food in Albuquerque.*

Again, dictionary sentences such as these, which use first-person plural forms when describing features of the local landscape, mirror the collection of sentences in their entirety. The authors display a preference for content that indexes their community, which perhaps counterintuitively includes references to regional place names that are not immediately identifiable as local.

Finally, first-person plural forms often appear in the San Ramón dictionary in illustrative sentences whose content explicitly references language shift and the importance of being able to speak Keiwa:

(3.18)   *Surely we will need our language.*

Here, language is presented as collectively possessed, something that everyone—referred to as "we," the entire village—will require in the future. This sentence and others like it underscore two central features of talking about language at San Ramón Pueblo: the presence of expressions of regret and anxiety surrounding the current state of language use and a preference for collective representations of the Keiwa language. Its survival is described as depending on the same type of cooperative mobilization that the dictionary authors describe as part of the preparations for ceremonial and community events.

The prevalence of first-person plural forms in the San Ramón dictionary example sentences serves several functions. The usage positions the author of an individual sentence as a member of a group, which achieves what Benveniste (1971), in his study of pronouns, calls the "amplified speaker." By amplifying the imagined speaker of such sentences, individual authors at San Ramón Pueblo are stressing statements designed to promote certain behaviors and activities. Thus, the use of first-person plural forms establishes the authority of the sentence's author by presenting first-hand knowledge of cultural practices and accentuating the importance of the actions being described by casting the author as a member of a collectivity. In addition, the pervasiveness of first-person plural forms in descriptions of history, place, and local technologies and in the presentation of specialized gendered or linguistic knowledge points to San Ramón ideologies that position these entities as being collectively marshaled or controlled. In San Ramón, the responsibility for correctly observing community practices—ceremonial, secular, and linguistic—is prototypically presented as belonging to particular groups or to the pueblo as a whole, as opposed to specific individuals.

Consequently, singular first-person pronouns are not as common in the San Ramón dictionary, although sentences using singular forms often exhibit characteristics that are similar to the examples containing plural prefixes. Such constructions include sentences that draw attention to obsolete local technologies (3.19); collective depictions of the community and anxieties regarding assimilation (3.20); and implicit moral instruction achieved by describing direct participation in locally valued activities (3.21):

(3.19)   *I was pounding deer jerky for dry meat stew.*

(3.20)   *I hope our people don't disappear; may they live a long time.*

(3.21)   *I brought wood in for grandma.*

Paralleling the subject matter of the plural first-person constructions, the dictionary authors occasionally deviated from their emphasis on valued practices associated with indigenous identity and wrote example sentences describing the individual life histories of specific dictionary authors. The following sentences were produced by two members of the committee in close succession after the creation of example 3.22 led to a general discussion about marriage:

(3.22)   My *daughter is getting married.*

(3.23)   I *got married right here at the church.*

Similar discussions among the authors regarding attending Indian school in Santa Fe, genealogy, and employment history resulted in the creation of other clusters of example sentences using first-person singular pronouns. Such constructions were also utilized when discussing hobbies, habits, and personal preferences (example 3.24) or when commenting on a specific interlocutor's state of mind at the time the sentence was written (example 3.25).

(3.24)   I *like fried chile hearts with eggs.*

(3.25)   I *need a happy hour.*

In this sense, the dictionary emerges as a place for recording individual life histories and adumbrated portraits of the people involved in its creation. Although the authors are not identified as individuals or in conjunction with the specific sentences they contributed to the text, family members and close friends could easily use the finished document as a site for accessing scattered biographical information rather than as an undifferentiated reference work.

Diverging from the San Ramón authors' preference for first-person forms, lexicographers working in the Western tradition do not frequently employ first-person forms in example material. Most example sentences in monolingual English reference dictionaries contain referents that are indicated by full noun phrases or proper names and, as a result, do not require the use of pronouns (unless, of course, they are entries *for* pronouns). In entries for common verb forms, however, dictionary authors occasionally include example sentences that utilize pronouns as part of presenting contrastive inflections, especially in reference dictionaries that describe a particular dialect. This tactic is used by the editors of the *Cambridge Dictionary of American English* (Landau et al. 2000), which contains example sentences utilizing personal pronouns, such as "We were woken early by the sound of the birds singing," one of several examples for "sing." Readers of this reference work are not expected to identify the referent "we" in this example by associating the pronoun with a particular group of which the "speaker" or sentence author is a member. Instead, readers are meant to notice that the form of the verb in question remains the same when used in this type of subordinate construction, despite changes in the subject of the sentence. There is nothing "personal" in this use of personal pronouns.

Unlike the usage in such reference works, the presence of first-person forms in the San Ramón text is not limited to the entries for verbs, nor do the authors display any interest in illustrating multiple verbal inflections. Instead, the use of first-person pronouns in the San Ramón document displays the collective focus of the dictionary authors and an assumption that those reading the dictionary will not view such constructions as confusing due to potential failures of reference. Instead, authorized readers will be able to correctly identify the speakers as San Ramón community members and will likely recognize the authors of individual sentences by virtue of knowing who was involved in the project, along with their life histories, tastes, and pet subjects. The architects of the San Ramón Keiwa dictionary implicitly identify themselves as authors of this text by utilizing first-person forms to exhibit knowledge, to extol the importance of particular cultural values, and, as we shall see, to position themselves as interlocutors in constructions that also contain second-person pronouns.

Second-Person Forms

The use of second-person pronouns is even more prevalent in San Ramón Keiwa dictionary example sentences than the use of first-person forms. The most common second-person construction is a directive. In the following examples, the San Ramón authors again exhibit a preference for sentences about practices that are felt to be lost and that should be reintroduced by imploring the addressee(s) to engage in such activities:

(3.26)   *Salt the deer meat so you can hang it to dry.*

(3.27)   *Straighten the sticks so we can make arrows.*

In addition to informing the addressee of the motivation behind such practices, a feature of many San Ramón example sentences that is discussed later in the chapter, the speaker/author often locates the utility of the directed action by explicitly invoking the past:

(3.28)   *Sew your moccasins with sinew, like a long time ago.*

Directives are also found in proverbs and adages, some of which were repackaged as dictionary example sentences, for instance, in this one created for the word "face":

(3.29)   *When you meet people, never turn your face to the side (be friendly to everyone).*

This is a revealing example, although by no means unique among the illustrative sentences, in that it includes parenthetical information in the English translation that does not appear in the Keiwa sentence. Frequently, there are noticeable discrepancies between the English and Keiwa versions of the dictionary example sentences. Extraordinarily descriptive Keiwa phrases are often reduced to straightforward English forms since the authors chose not to carry over metaphors or poetic language into the accompanying translations. The converse occurs in the preceding example: by including "be friendly to everyone" in parentheses following the English gloss, the author of this sentence is not leaving the point of her directive implicit. Instead, the English unambiguously states the behavior that should follow from the observance of this adage. Other commands are even more candid, eliminating the associated proverb and including only the moral segment of the directive:

(3.30)   *Don't you ever be jealous. All it takes is work.*[7]

In both instances, the dictionary example sentences adapt local sayings that employ second-person pronouns.

In addition to instructing future undifferentiated readers to participate in local activities, speak Keiwa, and behave appropriately, second-person constructions are used to admonish particular (although unnamed) community members. During breaks and in the meetings held for writing and editing example sentences, the dictionary authors would chat and joke, discuss the day's events, and make evening plans. They would also take advantage of the relative privacy and exclusivity of the library, as well as the shared views of the group, to voice their feelings about the current political and social climate at the pueblo. Often, such conversations would turn to specific political/religious leaders and what was presented as their lack of support for the language program, their arbitrary and destructive decisions about membership, or their general shamelessness and disregard for proper behavior. Frequently, a member of the dictionary committee would halt the (usually English) conversation and say, "Here's a sentence" or "Do we have an entry for _____?" using the interaction both as a prompt for particular words and expressions and as a source of inspiration for the creation of example material. If an entry already existed or a sentence had previously been created to illustrate each of the words in the new example sentence, it was simply added to an existing entry or, if the committee preferred, replaced the earlier example sentence.

(3.31)   *If you can't speak Indian, at least try.*

(3.32)   *You're nothing but an eavesdropper.*

Examples 3.31 and 3.32 are the result of such processes of entextualization. Both sentences were created with specific addressees in mind, and everyone at the table was aware of their identities even though second-person pronouns were used exclusively in the construction of both sentences. This recalls Kroskrity's (2009a) analysis of the ways that Western Mono speaker Rosalie Bethel simultaneously managed the face-to-face relationships and events in immediate recording contexts and the relationships with the imagined audiences she anticipated would be watching the video. Interestingly, after all the San Ramón dictionary entries were entered into the database, the immediate context and the individuals implicated in these sentences and others like them were effectively erased from the written, if not spoken, record.

Another way that second-person forms were utilized by the San Ramón dictionary authors is the construction of what can be thought of as mini-dialogues. Two sentences, written consecutively, were created for this single entry:

(3.33)   *Always speak in Indian. I will try.*

A similar exchange, also explicitly stating the importance of indigenous language use, is below:

> (3.34)   *I understand Indian. Do you understand Indian?*

These sentences were written as examples for the entries "always" and "to understand," respectively, and the authors chose to utilize both first- and second-person forms to create pair-part exchanges. The authors also decided that these pairs of sentences should be entered into a single field in the dictionary database, rather than each sentence appearing as a separate example, to preserve the "conversation" in its full form.

As discussed in my analysis of preferred first-person forms, the San Ramón dictionary authors display a preference for sentences that refer to ceremonial content, indigenous language, and local technologies but also include examples of quotidian subjects:

> (3.35)   *I won some money. Really? How much? Five hundred.*

These two complete exchanges between Person A and Person B were packed into a single HTML field in the dictionary database and emerge in the final printed version as they are displayed above.

In addition to mini-conversations in individual entries, the dictionary authors frequently constructed exchanges across several headwords. For instance, a sentence using first-person forms that was constructed as a response to a question similar to the one presented in example 3.35 might appear in a completely different part of the dictionary. Although these constructed exchanges are separated in an alphabetized print version, they demonstrate that the example sentences are to be used as tools in the construction of future conversations. They are not viewed by their authors as mere illustrations of isolated words but are examples of established ways of speaking at San Ramón Pueblo, including speech forms that necessarily include more than one speaker.

In Western dictionaries, example sentences that utilize second-person forms, like those using first-person constructions, are rare. First- and second-person forms do appear in the *Oxford English Dictionary*, but those sentences are not constructed. They are extracted from previously published sources. Like first-person forms, second-person pronouns are generally found only in texts focusing on discrete dialects of English or in lexicons for travelers that invent the illustrative material. By creating the sentence "Are you running against each other or against the clock?" the authors of the Cambridge lexicon are not trying to model future conversations or affect addressee behavior but are preserving an American English idiom.

The Uniqueness of First- and Second-Person Forms

In addition to signaling the interactional nature of the written text and the complex ways that pronominal forms index participant frameworks, first- and second-person forms exhibit unique characteristics across languages and speech events, individually and as a specific class. In an investigation of pronouns, Benveniste (1971) addresses these specifics, presenting the forms "I" and "you" as what he considers to be the only manifestations of the category of person in the English pronominal system and presenting third-person forms as substitutes for objects and entities that do not possess true deictic properties. As part of his analysis, Benveniste observes that, unlike formal texts, where first- and second-person forms are rarely found, "it would be difficult to conceive of a short spoken text where they were not employed" (1971:218). This observation highlights the presence of such forms in the San Ramón dictionary. A scientific text such as a dictionary can easily be imagined without "I" and "you," but the association of these forms with interactional texts helps to explain the sense, for the Western observer, that a very different sort of document has been written.

Additionally, Benveniste identifies individual properties associated with the first-person English form, making clear that such characteristics exist cross-linguistically. He establishes the inextricable bond between this deictic and its context by stating, "*I* can only be identified by the instance of discourse that contains it and by that alone" (Benveniste 1971:218), which shows that examining theories of reference (and failures to refer) can lead to observations regarding actual discourse (Kripke 1980; Putnam 1975). Additionally, the stances encoded by "I" can, as Benveniste points out, extend throughout a discourse, furthering the speaker's point of view through the use of spatial and temporal deictics anchored to a first-person form. By explaining the first-person form's centrality in the establishment of subjectivity, Benveniste alludes to its place in expressing authority and in avoiding implication in speech events. He explains that because such forms, like their second-person counterparts, do not "assert anything, they are not subject to the condition of truth and escape all denial" (Benveniste 1971:220).

Linguists and anthropologists have also weighed in on the special characteristics of second-person forms. The sociolinguist Susan Ervin-Tripp's inquiry into the nature of American English directives helps to frame some of these features as they pertain to second-person marking in San Ramón dictionary example sentences. She begins by describing common requests, analyzing the kinds of directives in English according to the relative power of the speaker and addressee and the obviousness of the directive, asserting that directives are "likely sensitive to addressee features" (Ervin-Tripp 1976:26). Breaking with previous sociolinguistic studies that attempted to describe and predict the presence of second-person forms of address as purely a function of politeness, Ervin-Tripp sees directives as varying according to the ongoing activity occurring between speakers and asserts that such forms "differ in the amounts of inference or knowledge they require" (51). Thus, looking at forms of address requires information about the context in which such utterances are being produced and not simply preordained social categories such as age and rank, categories that are meant to indicate relative economic or social power.

As seen in Ervin-Tripp's work, the prevalence of second-person forms, especially directives, points to an emphasis on the addressee(s) or audiences for the San Ramón dictionary. The audience is necessarily imagined and anticipated as part of this written text, and the actions advocated by its authors will necessarily be postponed. The central addressee feature indicated by the directives constructed for the dictionary is the requirement that addressees be San Ramón community members. Characteristics such as age and rank, factors that Ervin-Tripp examines, are muted but not entirely erased. For example, a future addressee will necessarily be from San Ramón Pueblo and will know the group of individuals involved and their positions. This prototypical addressee will also be able to infer that any speaker of San Ramón Keiwa would be older than any nonspeaker in the community, positioning the text's authors as knowledgeable and in positions of authority by virtue of age, authoring language materials, and speaking Keiwa fluently. Similarly, the content of the example sentences, which focus on imparting local information, positions the creators of the directives as experts who possess large amounts of knowledge about San Ramón culture. Thus, the future addressee would be appropriately directed by the dictionary's authors, whose authority is not automatic but is predicated on possessing linguistic and cultural knowledge and using such knowledge in a particular context.

The linguistic anthropologist Michelle Rosaldo's critique of speech act theory, "The Things We Do with Words" (1982), examines directives among the Ilongots, an indigenous group in the Philippines. Her work informs my analysis of the San Ramón dictionary authors' preference for second-person forms. She shows that speech acts, such as commands, need to be observed ethnographically in order to determine the types of social work they accomplish in speech communities and describes certain features of directives themselves. She argues that an examination of commands should acknowledge that the use of these forms in a particular community reflects specific "views of human action and of human social order" (Rosaldo 1982:209) and that the use of directives is "constrained by everyday concerns for orderly cooperation and expectations that decide what different persons ought to know and do" (206).

Rather than articulate inequality through the use of directives, as among the Ilongots, San Ramón community members negotiate and strengthen their group identity by directing the future behavior of imagined addressees. As Goffman observes regarding commands, "audiences hear in a way special to them" (1979:14). In keeping with Rosaldo's observation that Ilongots learn to speak by learning commands, it is hoped that by learning to speak Keiwa, community members will learn how to conduct themselves appropriately and exhibit behavior and engage in activities that connect them to the pueblo and identify them as Indians, both within and outside the reservation. Moreover, in exhibiting their command of cultural knowledge by grounding it through the use of first-person forms, the dictionary authors establish their authority to issue commands. Thus, the predominance of first- and second-person pronouns in San Ramón example sentences illustrates numerous "microlevel strategies of indexicality" (SturtzSreetharan 2006:173) that indicate the social positions of interlocutors and the responsibilities of the text's intended audience, simultaneously establishing the dictionary as an interactional text.

The Absence of Authority and Audience: Third-Person Constructions

The prevalence of first- and second-person forms in the San Ramón dictionary example sentences indicates that certain types of social work are accomplished or imagined by the participants in the text's creation, circulation, and use. I now consider some example sentences in which authority and audience are not directly referenced through pronoun choice. The dictionary authors instead employed full noun phrases or third-person pronouns in the construction of the sentences. Although the semiotic mechanisms and discursive strategies used by authors to construct an interactional text differ in such cases, the goals are similar: foregrounding a collective San Ramón identity and commenting on the immediate political and social situation in increasingly more veiled ways.

Of the example sentences that do not use first- and second-person pronouns, sentences that employ full noun phrases are most common. The following examples are representative of the dictionary sentences that utilize noun phrases as referents:

(3.36)   *Cow poop is good for fields.*

(3.37)   *Ground owls live in the ground.*

Like dictionary definitions in the Western tradition, these sentences are presented as conveying universal, enduring truths. However, they describe local agricultural practices and animal species indigenous to the area, (re)iterating these regularities for the dictionary's audience. When the dictionary authors at San Ramón Pueblo use third-person forms, it is most often in constructions that convey local patterns or practices:

(3.38)   *On Sundays, those that are holy go to church.*

(3.39)   *They used to thrash wheat at the hera.*

(3.40)   *They make bracelets out of turquoise.*

In the process of crafting sentences that convey cultural regularities, the authors often use undefined words, proper names, or expressions that are exclusive to San Ramón Pueblo, illustrated in example 3.39 by the word "hera,"[8] which is the word for a pueblo clearing where agricultural tasks used to take place. Additionally, almost all the sentences that use third-person marking use pronominal forms that are plural, again amplifying the statements.

Proper names are regularly used as referents in sentences utilizing third-person constructions. At San Ramón Pueblo, every community member has an "Indian name," a Keiwa first name given at birth,[9] and these are used frequently in the dictionary example sentences:

(3.41)   *Blue Mountain was saying there's snow on the mountain.*

(3.42)   ▬▬▬▬▬ *is older than everyone else.*

At times, the authors gloss the name using its literal translation in English (example 3.41); at other times, they retain the Keiwa form in the gloss (example 3.42). Nouns denoting local places are also used frequently:

(3.43)   *At the casino bar, drinks are expensive.*

(3.44)   *Our mother, the blue/green river, is running full.*

In example 3.43, it is assumed that the reader will be able to correctly infer that in this case, "casino" refers solely to the San Ramón casino and that the bar in question is the newly built martini lounge, as opposed to the other bars in the casino complex. The San Ramón Keiwa word for "Rio Grande" can be left undefined in example 3.44 because all community members would be able to identify this place name and would not confuse it with other rivers. Although sentences using full noun phrases, third-person forms, and proper names do not contain identifiable points of view, they still index stances that are in accordance with those more easily identifiable through the use of first- and second-person forms. The authority necessary to indicate what is felt to be an authentic San Ramón identity is displayed by referring to local places, names, and practices.

One way that third-person forms employed by the authors of the dictionary closely resemble definitional glossing in the Western lexicographic tradition is the use of metapragmatic and metasemantic statements. In the illustrative sentences, the authors model appropriate language use according to gender, as seen in example 3.45, which states the respective ways for men and women to say "thank you" in Keiwa:

(3.45)   *Women say* ███████████, *men say* ███████████

As in the majority of the other dictionary example sentences, the effectiveness of such statements depends on possessing knowledge specific to San Ramón Pueblo. In this instance, readers would be required to know basic Keiwa exchanges in order to understand the meaning, since "thank you" is not part of the English gloss. Example sentences that closely resemble dictionary definitions do not require resident knowledge to understand:

(3.46)   *Spanish people call bread* pan.

Using the Spanish word for "bread," the author constructs a statement of semantic equivalence, one of only a few sentences of this type in the entire document.

Dictionary example sentences that employ third-person constructions are not directly establishing or reinforcing participant structures, nor reflecting past or potential conversations, but instead are attempts to build "stereotypic" expertise at San Ramón Pueblo (Silverstein 2006). Stereotypes, Silverstein asserts, are characterized by a "relational conceptual distinction in knowledge structures; as sense conveyed in the process of using language, such concepts are indexed or cued by certain terms (words of consistent and recurrent denotational applicability)" (2006:487). By creating cultural "definitions" when authoring example sentences and by concentrating almost exclusively on local technologies, geographies, expressions, and the like, the San Ramón dictionary authors try to fill in what they perceive to be the gaps in the local conceptual structure, or, to borrow philosopher Hilary Putnam's (1975) phrase, what things are "like around here." In this view, it is not simply a matter of reintroducing the grammar of the Keiwa language. It also involves emphasizing the inherently local systems of knowledge that were previously conveyed through using Keiwa as the predominant language in the community.

Silverstein's analysis of stereotypic knowledge also delineates the connection between such "cultural concepts" and authority, power, and personhood: "The terms, in short, cue specific areas of cultural knowledge, the manifesting of possession or control over which is frequently critical to identifiability of someone's group membership or one's status within a group or position in a network" (2006:488).

Here, the authority of the dictionary authors, in addition to being revealed and ratified through the use of first-person forms and the issuing of directives, is conveyed through their command of -onomic knowledge specific to and appropriate for San Ramón Pueblo. Like the stereotypic knowledge brought to bear when using "wine registers," to use Silverstein's phrase, the Keiwa dictionary's authors are teaching cultural concepts associated with the past and creating new structures of coherence when writing example sentences. The types of regularities that the San Ramón dictionary authors convey are not solely grammatical but can be productively studied, in part, by examining the authors' grammatical choices.

Finally, third-person forms in San Ramón dictionary example sentences are used to communicate a different kind of local information. Unlike stereotypical concepts, which are represented as timeless truths that apply equally to all members of the pueblo, third-person forms are also used to construct veiled comments about particular individuals. The contents of such sentences resemble gossip and critiques of community members and their behavior. The following sentences are examples of this type of construction:

(3.47)   *He told a lie about me.*

(3.48)   *He doesn't have the strength to stay away from liquor.*

(3.49)   *He's done that a lot of times.*

Like the second-person constructions discussed above that address an unnamed speaker in order to comment on political and social issues at the pueblo, these sentences express indirect criticism concerning unnamed individuals. However, such sentences did not arise from the same processes of entextualization as their second-person counterparts.

Each of these sentences was produced by authors apart from discussions about current events, in isolation, and was not discussed further by the dictionary committee after I finished transcribing. The only way that such a sentence can be identified as being a veiled critique is by virtue of how it is presented and received, combined with knowledge of the immediate social context at the pueblo. The sentence's author would say, "I've got one," after the group members had been sitting quietly, ruminating over the creation of a sentence for a particular entry. He or she would then state the sentence and look at each of the other committee members pointedly. They would then nod, indicating that they knew exactly to whom the sentence was referring, and would perhaps offer "Yes" or "That's right," but otherwise, there was no further discussion. In some cases, not only was the person in the sentence left unspecified, but the cause for criticism was obscured as well, as seen in example 3.49. Thus, the dictionary authors creatively used third-person constructions to craft exceedingly indirect, exclusively local critiques. For these inferences to be successful, however, it was necessary for at least some of the participants to engage in more overt gossiping before convening to work on the dictionary, interactions I was sometimes a part of but more often was not. This presented another opportunity for us all to model appropriate discretion: I knew that it was not my place to ask and left it up to my colleagues, the arbiters of community knowledge, to decide whether to ask me if I knew whom they were talking about and, if I did not, whether to dispense hints that would reveal the identity of those in question. It remains to be seen whether the identity of the people referred to using third-person pronouns in such cases will be transparent to dictionary readers. Perhaps the sentences were written only with an eye toward establishing solidarity and performing discretion on the occasion of their creation and will henceforth be used solely to communicate grammatico-semantic regularities in Keiwa.

Tense, Aspect, and Mode

An additional focus of mine when examining the grammatical constructions used by the San Ramón dictionary authors is the preferred tense and aspect markers in the example sentences. I connect the prevalence of certain aspectual and modal particles to the overall focuses of the dictionary project, including the emphasis on communicating salient cultural knowledge.

Like the patterns that emerged from my analysis of preferred person-marking strategies in the San Ramón dictionary's example material, this analysis shows that the text's authors have relied on several favored tense/aspect markers. Often, tense/aspect markers are absent in the construction of directives (examples 3.2, 3.4, 3.27), making uninflected forms one of the most prevalent structures. The use of stative markers (examples 3.36, 3.37, 3.41–3.43) and habitual markers (examples 3.15, 3.31, 3.40, 3.45) is also common throughout the document to convey enduring truths or states of affairs. This signals that the dictionary authors depend on tense/aspect markers that illustrate semantic and pragmatic (if not grammatical) regularities over time, which is common among lexicons that, across all traditions, aim to establish rules governing language structure and use.

The habitual past aspect marker appears frequently in the San Ramón dictionary. Often, this form occurs in sentences that describe past technologies and practices closely associated with embodying what is felt to be an authentic San Ramón identity. I provide a complete analysis of the habitual past aspect marker and its relationship to established speech genres in San Ramón Keiwa in chapter 3, but it is important to note its prevalence as a grammatical form.

Another significant pattern in the San Ramón dictionary is the presence of the subjunctive aspectual marker. It is used in several different kinds of construction and carries multiple meanings. In sentences 3.7–3.11, this form appears in first-person plural imperative constructions, glossed by Keiwa speakers as "Let's go." The subjunctive marker is also used in sentences employing second-person forms where speakers translate the particle as "should" or "ought to" when constructing more elaborate directives than the single-clause constructions that omit tense or aspect suffixes. A third use of the subjunctive aspectual marker appears in sentences where the author expresses hope or desire (example 3.20). In this sense, the Keiwa subjunctive form can be productively compared to the use of the subjunctive in Romance languages (Zagona 2002): it is used to soften requests and to express wishes for the future, in addition to describing the utility behind certain actions.

This focus on utility, which is apparent in the reliance on the subjunctive marker, is also expressed in other common grammatical constructions used by the San Ramón dictionary authors. The modal enclitic ("in order to," "so that"), which I have glossed as the purposive marker, is a favored form throughout the document. Prototypically, the purposive is used as part of explanations of local technologies and cultural practices, as seen in examples 3.4, 3.10, and 3.50.

(3.50)   *Go get some yucca root so we can wash our hair.*

Often, this modal marker appears in constructions where the matrix clause contains the subjunctive aspectual marker and the verb in the subordinate clause describes the purpose of engaging in the recommended action. Although yucca plants abound throughout the Rio Grande valley, the fact that the roots of the plant can be used to make a frothy, soap-like substance when mixed with water and that this mixture is good for washing hair is not well known locally. The dictionary authors are communicating the utility of engaging in this past practice to current and future pueblo residents.

The focus on emphasizing the utility of certain actions is also expressed using grammatical means that lie outside Keiwa verbal morphology. Keiwa possesses a set of suffixes that attach to nouns to conjoin clauses, act as prepositions, and indicate sources, among other functions. When used as a nominal suffix, the particle prototypically encodes instrumentality (i.e., "with a knife"), but it is also used in constructions where speakers gloss it as "because." It is in this capacity that this nominal suffix appears frequently in the San Ramón dictionary, expressing the consequences for actors performing actions either correctly or, as seen in example 3.51, poorly:

(3.51)   *Because she didn't push hard on the rolling pin, her tortillas are thick.*

Being able to make tortillas, red and green chile sauces, Indian bread, dried meat, and other foods that community members consider to be "traditional" is closely associated by them with personifying an authentic Indian identity. The ability to adequately prepare for and to observe ceremonial feasts is especially important. Again, the need to perform such tasks correctly, even at the level of the tortilla, is emphasized by the dictionary authors' grammatical conventions.

Another way that San Ramón speakers describe the motivation behind the actions in the dictionary example sentences is by using the relativizer ("that's why"):

(3.52)   *There's a hole in the roof. That's why we need to fix it.*

The content of such examples usually calls attention to valued community activities. While the statement in example 3.52 may seem like an obvious conclusion, it is representative of common discourses at San Ramón that emphasize the importance of collective work and helping other community members, a topic explored in depth in chapter 4. This emphasis on motivation and consequence is revealed during the process of detailing the preferred grammatical patterns. In such instances, authors are not describing actions in order to present grammatical regularities but are highlighting the importance of particular actions.

Register and Style

The resources that the authors of the San Ramón Keiwa dictionary use to create example material extend beyond a preference for first- and second-person pronominal forms, beyond a reliance on habitual past aspectual marking, and beyond the level of the sentence itself. The authors draw on existing ways of speaking—local registers and speaking styles—when constructing the example sentences. They index, and simultaneously ossify, particular ways of speaking in Keiwa, favoring speaking styles associated with ceremonial speech and also including examples of less formal registers in order to aid future speakers in the construction of everyday conversations.

In an attempt to expand on the folk view that one should use certain ways of speaking in particular situations or to accomplish various things, scholars have refined the concepts of style and register. Eckert and Rickford chronicle efforts in sociolinguistics to describe variation, adopting a "view of variation as social practice" and describing style as a "resource for constructing categories and identities" (2001:6). Eckert and Rickford sum up Irvine's definition of style as "distinctiveness within a system of possibilities" (2001:6). Thus, a survey of the ways of speaking that the dictionary authors employ at San Ramón Pueblo involves enumerating the various possibilities available to speakers: the styles associated with particular codes (Keiwa, Spanish, and English) and the salient categories, subjectivities, and values associated with the social categories that speakers reference (including male, female, indigenous, non-indigenous, traditional, urban, good, bad, and countless others in numerous dynamic combinations).

However, studying variation is not simply a question of describing registers as social facts and connecting them to a priori groups of speakers and situations of use. It also involves delineating how ways of speaking come to stand for particular types of situations or social positions. As Agha states, "registers are not static facts about a language but *reflexive models of language use* that are disseminated along identifiable trajectories in social space through communicative practices" (2005:38). To understand such linguistic and social resources, he emphasizes the importance of describing how certain ways of speaking come to be associated with particular values, looking at processes of "enregisterment" (38). Because the dictionary is the first written text in San Ramón Keiwa and because patterns of enregisterment rooted in literacy practices are in the process of being codified, it is imperative to describe such processes when analyzing the authors' stated goals in writing the document.

As already mentioned, the authors of the San Ramón Keiwa dictionary display a preference for constructing sentences that include information about ceremonial life at the pueblo, often sampling ways of speaking that are appropriate in ceremonial contexts. As Kroskrity (1993, 1998, 2000) has described in his work with the Arizona Tewa, Pueblo linguistic ideologies that identify the kiva as the prototypical site for language use generate models for other forms of speech and often project the rules for appropriate language use into other contexts. Although it is difficult to ascertain whether authors are utilizing ceremonial registers at the level of the individual sentence, discrete lexical items recognizable as examples of ceremonial speech are apparent in the dictionary example sentences, such as the use of directional words. In certain sentences, it is clear from the definition or the context of production that a particular word or expression is associated with ceremonial practice. The following entries contain material openly associated with ceremonial registers, by virtue of using words or expressions not seen in less formal registers:

(3.53)   ▮▮▮▮▮▮ *is the lead dancer.*

(3.54)   *Tomorrow we're going to practice at the kiva.*

(3.55)   *The cacique is asking for good health for his people.*

Other sentences make no explicit mention of how a word is supposed to be used in a ceremonial context but include metapragmatic statements by the dictionary authors that highlight the ceremonial efficacy of the lexical item:

(3.56)   ▮▮▮▮▮▮ *is a preaching word for all wild game.*

(3.57)   *During these times* ▮▮▮▮▮▮ *is hard to find. (One of the clans uses* ▮▮▮▮▮▮ *in their doings.)*[10]

The fact that the dictionary authors felt the need to include such metapragmatic information points to the possibility that a central goal of the example material, and of the document itself, is to impart knowledge of the registers appropriate in ceremonial contexts.

Other sentences constructed for the San Ramón Keiwa dictionary rely wholly on the reader's ability to infer the ceremonial association with the activity being described or the word in question. Many of these sentences are the ones discussed in chapter 2, which moved in and out of versions of the dictionary, based on their perceived level of sensitivity and the immediate political climate. Because the dictionary's authors do not provide metapragmatic material for such sentences, their controversial nature would not be apparent to someone unfamiliar with local practices. This emphasizes that the text is not intended to be used outside the community and the only relevant opinions regarding the comparative appropriateness or effectiveness of the illustrative material are those of community members.

Numerous sentences embody such textual constraints. Example 3.58 is something that a dance leader might say to a dancer as part of the former's responsibility to assemble and correct the position of the participants:

(3.58)   *Stand at the front.*

Example 3.59 describes a small part of a curing ceremony:

(3.59)   *S/he was being massaged because s/he had bumps on the arm.*

For a non-indigenous person, or even for a local person unfamiliar with the potential use of a particular word or expression in a ceremonial context, these sentences would not be seen to contain sensitive information. However, the dictionary is only to be used locally, and community members potentially have access to such knowledge, making it necessary for the dictionary authors to treat such sentences carefully. Because the authors emphasize the need to include cultural information in the example material, such sentences are simultaneously effective and threatening, hence their status as impermanent examples, shifting in and out of subsequent editions. Keiwa speakers often explicitly referred to the need to obfuscate ceremonial information or to think of example sentences that would allow them to use particular words but in more mundane senses, not associated with ceremonial practice. After several tries, one dictionary author finally created an example sentence for the verb "to look out":

(3.60)   *S/he has acute eyesight.*

The group approved the sentence, and the author exclaimed excitedly, "I found a way to use it without giving anything away!" For me and for community members unfamiliar with the use of this verb in ceremonial registers, especially those whose clan membership might prohibit them from knowing certain aspects of Pueblo religion, the central meaning of the word remained successfully veiled. The goal of appropriately using this register in the context of dictionary creation was successfully accomplished by the author, who consciously produced several meanings simultaneously.

Although individual lexical items associated with kiva talk, ceremonial locations, or religious practices index the ceremonial registers they are associated with, there is little evidence that the dictionary authors adhere to the level of formality the use of such registers requires in actual ritual contexts, both at the sentence level and in longer stretches of text. In Irvine's (1979) analysis of formal and informal registers, she identifies four aspects of formality that are seen cross-culturally: increased code structuring; code consistency; invocation of positional identities; and the emergence of a central situational focus. In the San Ramón dictionary, there is scant indication of increased code structuring in the example sentences that utilize formal or ceremonial registers, but the limitations on length inherent in creating illustrative material makes it difficult to adequately evaluate this index of increased formality.

However, in the example material there does exist a greater avoidance of Spanish or English loanwords in sentences that include preaching words or that index aspects of ceremonial registers. When a potential sentence associated with this formal register was written but did contain loanwords, the dictionary authors invariably worked to find a word in Keiwa or to create a neologism for that particular sentence. This then led to the need to check the text to see whether the word or expression used to replace the more commonly used Spanish or English form was already in the dictionary, and if not, a new entry was created with its own example sentence. Thus, the growth of the entire document has been connected to the appropriately formal characteristic of this ceremonial register, again making it clear that the work as a whole is linked to the goal of ensuring the future of particular speaking styles and their associated values.

The third characteristic of formal registers that Irvine identifies, the invocation of positional identities, is also evident in the San Ramón Keiwa example sentences containing ceremonial content. This is manifested in the proclivity of the dictionary authors to include honorifics and other ceremonial forms of address that indicate respect, such as the form seen in example 3.61:

(3.61) *I saw my godmother.*

In example 3.62, the speaker utilizes the appropriate way of referring to the dead ("the one that used to be") when using a ceremonial register, another honorific construction in the language:

(3.62) *The one that used to be called* ██████████ *used to cut his beard with scissors.*

Again, the emphasis on formal contexts and ways of speaking appears in entries where the ceremonial associations are obvious (example 3.61), in those where the recognition of formal content depends on specialized knowledge, and in those where aspects of a ceremonial register are creatively included in an informal utterance (example 3.62).

It is more difficult to identify a central situational focus for sentences indexing ceremonial registers, the fourth facet of formality Irvine identifies, largely because of the nature of dictionaries themselves and the processes of enregisterment in this example of textual creation. In some sense, each example sentence can be simultaneously seen as a discrete text and as part of a larger work. The pressures faced by the dictionary authors, as well as the stylistic resources at their disposal, were calibrated at the level of the sentence. The social and political ramifications of the entire text, however, were considered at the level of the larger work, which will ostensibly be circulated within the community and evaluated as a whole. This duality is evident in the processes of enregisterment during meetings of the dictionary committee. During some sessions, the members wrote several sentences in succession, all utilizing aspects of ceremonial registers by including words associated with particular practices and sites, by avoiding the use of borrowed terms, and by using honorific expressions. Patterns were often triggered by encountering a particular word in the

SIL lexicon, with the authors utilizing formal stylistic resources throughout the next page or the next section or until it was time to break for lunch. In these cases, the situational focus might be identified as trying to create material that future speakers could use in ceremonial contexts. Nonetheless, when the dictionary authors discussed the eventual completion of the work and how it would be distributed and used, it was not presented as a collection of short texts that utilize ceremonial registers or traditional ways of speaking, but instead as a reference tool that would aid language learners, a depiction that reflects the Western view of this type of text.

The presence of example sentences in the San Ramón Keiwa dictionary with little or no evidence of the use of ceremonial registers indicates that the dictionary authors are utilizing numerous stylistic resources, making it necessary to consider the multiple situational focuses being indexed by such variation. For example, the authors employ what appear to be extremely informal exchanges, suitable for every-day conversation:

(3.63)   *The US is out in a battle in Afghanistan.*

(3.64)   *He lied about me, said I was pregnant.*

(3.65)   *How embarrassing, we didn't know he was sick.*

(3.66)   *Get up! The sun is shining on your butt!*

(3.67)   *Do you have any matches? (Once you start the match and it's flaming)*
          Light it!

These examples of informal registers are characterized by code inconsistency (example 3.63), content appropriate for gossip (examples 3.64 and 3.65), or off-color jokes and expressions (example 3.66). Many entries utilizing informal styles consist of tiny conversations, some including stage directions or background information (example 3.67). The situational focus of such statements and exchanges is to provide future language learners with phrases and portions of conversations to be used in informal settings, again establishing this as an interactional text. Augmenting my analysis above of pronoun usage in the San Ramón Keiwa dictionary, it is clear that the larger situational focus for the authors is to position the example sentences as records of the available ways of speaking in order for future language learners to have access to a wide variety of stylistic resources. In contrast with prototypical Western dictionaries, the San Ramón lexicon exhibits a wider variety of stylistic, rather than grammatical, variation in its example material.

A central question in examining register variation in San Ramón Keiwa example sentences is not only the extent to which the authors utilize specific ways of speaking and the social values associated with such styles but also the implications of such choices. As in other communities where language shift has led to fewer speakers and a paucity of texts in the respective heritage language, the texts currently being produced at San Ramón Pueblo may be one of the only ways future community members will have to access the Keiwa language. With this comes an ossification of the forms recorded in texts such as the dictionary, including the registers or styles favored by its authors. Of course, the authors are conscious of this development, hence their insistence on writing example sentences that are representative of what they feel should be communicated to their descendants. In the case of sentences containing the characteristics of formal, ceremonial registers, this may lead to the continued avoidance of borrowed words, not only in ceremonial contexts but in other contexts as well. Similarly, the archaic forms and neologisms created as part of respecting the conventions of formal registers are included in the dictionary alongside informal words and expressions in San Ramón Keiwa. Should the text be used in a "regenerative" capacity by future language learners (Moore 2006), it is this form of the language that will endure. Possibly, the nonformal registers in the San Ramón Keiwa dictionary could come to be associated with ceremonial contexts, changing the definition of what is appropriate in such environments. Conversely, aspects of speech styles that are currently considered to be formal could be utilized as resources in the construction of future everyday conversations if language learners do indeed use the dictionary as a resource for the production of everyday talk.

In any case, it is likely that, as Moore (2006) has described, "endangered" language texts may be used in ways their authors never anticipated. In keeping with his observation that in many indigenous North American communities, text artifacts themselves have often come to serve as ceremonial objects, the San Ramón Keiwa dictionary, because of content associated with ceremonial registers, could have a similar future and be held up as a material manifestation of indigenous authenticity and the vitality of San Ramón culture and language. There is also the possibility that the processes of enregisterment surrounding the use of formal speaking styles will also be communicated to future readers. Specifically, the emphasis on circumlocution and the need to obfuscate the ceremonial context of certain words and expressions may or may not be apparent if future readers are unable to correctly recontextualize these forms.

Genre and Intertextuality

Like the stylistic variation in the example sentences, the dictionary authors draw on different established speech genres when creating illustrative material, employing methods of structuring longer texts that mirror many functions of other types of speech events. Similarly, the authors also create adumbrated versions of existing speech genres when constructing example sentences, further circumscribing the intended uses for this text.

To describe the characteristics of longer speech forms in San Ramón Keiwa, how they are created, and how they circulate, I draw on work in linguistic anthropology on speech genres. Building on Bakhtin (1986), linguistic anthropologists have utilized this analytic to discuss how particular ways of speaking are isolated in various speech communities and how speech genres both refer back to previous occasions of use and shape future interactions. Bauman provides a synthesis of this work, defining genre as "one order of speech style, a constellation of systemically related, co-occur[r]ent formal features and structures that serves as a conventionalized orienting framework for the production and reception of discourse. More specifically, a genre is a speech style oriented to the production and reception of a particular kind of text" (2001:79). In "Discourse Genres in a Theory of Practice," Hanks emphasizes the importance of examining genre during periods of rapid social change, a characteristic of the current sociopolitical climate at San Ramón: "In this formulation, speech genres are seen as both the outcome of historically specific acts, and themselves among the constituting dimensions, interims of which action is possible. Genres then, as kinds of discourse, derive their thematic organization from the interplay between systems of social value, linguistic convention, and the world portrayed" (1987:671). The generic conventions in the San Ramón Keiwa dictionary are used to accomplish various goals in the current context, mirroring many functions of the dictionary itself.

Briggs and Bauman outline the history of using this analytic in anthropology and the implications of studying genre for the discipline more broadly. They expand the description of generic forms from simple classificatory types to a "conventionalized but flexible and open-ended set of expectations concerning the organization of formal means and structures in discursive practice" (1992:144). This allows for an understanding of forms that are emergent and those that are enduring in speech communities, in other words, how texts are connected through relationships of "intertextuality." In the San Ramón case, expectations regarding what written forms should look like and which types of texts should be created are negotiated and solidified in the project of indigenous language literacy.

Mirroring the use of multiple speaking styles in the construction of example material, the authors of the San Ramón Keiwa dictionary use conventions from several speech genres. Generic conventions associated with dictionary entry design in the Western tradition are rare but evident, including the use of example sentences to further elucidate definitions:

(3.68)  *sound of hitting your head; thud*

It sounded like ▮▮▮▮▮▮▮ *when he got hit on the head.*

Occasionally, the dictionary authors include two example sentences in order to show alternative word order (in the Keiwa version, in this instance), another function of illustrative sentences in the Western tradition:

(3.69) *inside*

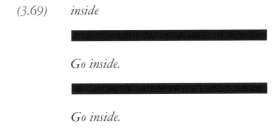

Go inside.

Go inside.

Explanations of multiple, alternative grammatical constructions, such as methods of clause conjunction, sporadically appear in the example sentences, resulting from the authors' efforts to "show how to speak good Indian":

(3.70)   or

I need to get up early or the cows won't eat.

At times, the authors include multiple verb conjugations in entries, showing variation in number or tense/aspect, among other processes:

(3.71)   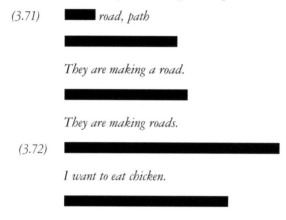 *road, path*

They are making a road.

They are making roads.

(3.72)

I want to eat chicken.

I ate the chicken.

Example sentences are also used to differentiate between homonyms, sometimes in the same entry:

(3.73)   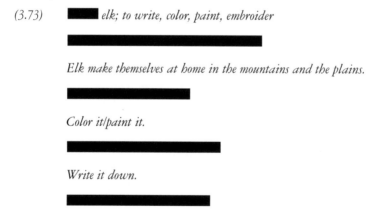 *elk; to write, color, paint, embroider*

Elk make themselves at home in the mountains and the plains.

Color it/paint it.

Write it down.

Paint the wall.

Examples that adhere to the generic conventions of Western dictionaries, as above, are exceptions, although most example sentences created for the San Ramón Keiwa dictionary emphasize content, style, and local speech genres. The lack of interest expressed by the dictionary authors in utilizing the preexisting fields in the dictionary database for singular and plural forms or for conjugations of past, present, and future verbs is an example of this focus. Although the complexity of the noun class system and the large amount of pronominal forms in San Ramón Keiwa would make it necessary to refine this part of the database in order to use the feature productively, dictionary committee members have not shown a desire to include such elicited forms in entries. In this local model, lexicographic methods, such as elicitation and the presentation of grammatical paradigms, as well as the written genres these approaches yield, such as contrastive example material or the grammatical sketches that appear at the front of many dictionaries, are not part of dictionary creation.

Conclusion

Comparing the methodologies, functions, resulting texts, and possible implications of lexicographic projects reveals the error in considering dictionaries to be a single type of work. Although there are historical, generic, and ideological similarities among works classified as lexicons and such similarities can be usefully manipulated to accomplish certain goals, detailing the differences between dictionaries helps to point to the specific conditions of their production. In indigenous communities, where lexicography projects are seldom ongoing, dictionaries accentuate the immediate linguistic, social, and political climates in which they are written to a greater degree than is seen in texts that are part of a continuing series. Clearly, in the San Ramón case, although the generic and ideological aspects of lexicography tend to position such texts as timeless, objective, and referentially neutral, in fact, they are more contextually bound than many other kinds of texts.

Also, as evidenced at San Ramón, local oral and literary traditions and language ideologies intermingle with approaches to textual creation, lexicography, and beliefs about linguistic practice from other speech communities, including textual traditions associated with former colonial powers and other Western traditions. For these reasons, there is a need to study dictionaries individually, utilizing ethnographic approaches and, as presented in this chapter, comparative methods that examine dictionary entries and these types of text in their entirety. A project of comparative lexicography embodies many theoretical and methodological characteristics of approaches to examining literacy in that it recognizes the myriad goals behind creating lexicons and the numerous ways of undertaking dictionary projects. Like multiple "literacies" (Collins 1995), there exist multiple lexicographies, as is apparent at San Ramón Pueblo. The differences between the Keiwa dictionary and other examples of this genre are revealed through ethnographic and comparative analysis, specifically, the emphasis on dictionary example material through the omission of other material and the intensely local focus of the sentences' content.

Another dimension of lexicography revealed by utilizing a comparative approach is the ability of such reference works to confer authority. In any community, this often results in the creation of new "experts." At San Ramón, this is evident in the way that the dictionary project has been institutionalized and, at an individual level, in the way that community members are recognized for their expertise in choosing which words and expressions will be included and in "correcting" dictionary material. This reconfiguration positions indigenous community members, not colonial educators or religious leaders, as those who control dictionary projects and who are increasingly involved in the processes of standardization and valorization associated with such texts. Although local systems of power and authority control who can participate in the dictionary project, the Keiwa text and other indigenous language lexicons reflect a change from previous patterns of establishing textual authority in the United States. Describing one example of such limitations, in a discussion of the ethnologist Henry Rowe Schoolcraft's collections of indigenous North American stories, Bauman and Briggs say, "Native Americans' rights to shape textual representations of themselves were thus limited in both theory and practice" (2003:282). Unlike several of the dictionaries I examined as part of this survey, such authority is not emphasized in the introduction to the San Ramón Keiwa dictionary, nor is it explicitly mentioned in other parts of the text. Instead, these qualities and variables are communicated in the content of the example sentences.

In the case of emergent genres—here, dictionary example sentences—authors use forms with indexical associations that evoke the properties of speech and the social norms that seem culturally appropriate for the ultimate goal of the document itself, which is, as one community member describes it, to help future speakers of the language to "be Indian." Hence, example sentences are included that refer to both ceremonial and everyday speaking styles, and shortened forms of established speech genres are created, which I analyze in the next chapter. The ability to successfully produce spoken Keiwa (which the dictionary authors make clear by including multiple speaking styles) is a local value indexed by much of the illustrative material, and the importance of qualities such as generosity and collective action, which are associated with embodying an authentic Pueblo identity, is emphasized as well.

In order to "be Indian," future language learners must glean local knowledge from the indirect ways that such norms are communicated in the example sentences, in part, by using features of established registers and speech genres. This, in turn, imparts another lesson to future community members: the value paced on circumlocution and the privileging of local knowledge. Concomitantly, the patterns of entextualization and circulation surrounding the creation of the dictionary and other new texts at San Ramón Pueblo reflect the local importance of observing indirectness when circulating cultural information, especially indigenous language materials. In chapter 4, I consider a Keiwa text that conveys moral lessons surreptitiously.

four
Perfecting Texts, Perfecting Community

The Bowl Story

For both New Mexico locals and tourists in Santa Fe and Albuquerque, the annual feast days held at area pueblos are the primary time that non-indigenous people are introduced to these communities, which have a reputation for being conservative and closed. From early summer through fall and again around Christmas, each pueblo recognizes its patron saint's day or king's day with ceremonial dances and songs. Friends and strangers go inside private homes and load their plates with green and red chile, enchilada casserole, and Jello salad between watching dances on the plaza and perusing the vendor stalls. Pueblo residents prepare for feast days for months, shopping for supplies, practicing dances, and making and freezing food to feed hundreds of people. Attending a feast day is popularly presented as a way of glimpsing what are imagined to be unchanging or "authentic" examples of Pueblo culture, as opposed to visible yet popularly contested examples of Pueblo culture and commerce such as the casinos and attached concert venues that line the interstate highways.

In many ways, the perception of these events as unchanging is accurate, based on the numerous feast days I have attended at San Ramón Pueblo. San Ramón residents and members of other pueblos point to their respective feast days as "traditional times" when you "need to do everything a certain way." As scholars who have examined Pueblo ceremonies have observed (Colwell-Chanthaphonh 2011; Fowles 2013;

Rodríguez 1996; Royce 2004; Sweet 2004[1985]) and as Kroskrity (1993, 1998, 2000, 2009b, 2012a) details in his studies of ceremonial Pueblo speech and related language ideologies, innovation is discouraged in ritual contexts. San Ramón community members consider songs and dances to be "successful" when the preferred forms are replicated exactly.

However, a new ceremonial position has recently been created at San Ramón within the "traditional" context of Pueblo feast days. A young adult male has been appointed by members of the tribal council as a supplementary "dance boss," in addition to an existing position with the same title. It is the responsibility of the original dance boss to walk up and down the lines of dancers, ensuring that steps are not missed and that clothing and regalia are perfectly worn. The dancers keep their eyes appropriately averted and their movements minimal, all qualities patrolled by the dance boss. It is the responsibility of the new dance boss to gaze outward from the plaza, looking for audience members who have visible cameras or cell phones and confiscating any devices for taking pictures or recordings. Outsiders attending Pueblo dances are restricted from any "image making practices" (Colwell-Chanthaphonh 2011). The new dance boss's vigilance is shared by the other dance boss, by religious leaders, and, it could be argued, by the community members watching the ceremony. This new development, like the continual refinement of the dancers' clothing and comportment, is an iterative process; the new dance boss does not make a sweep of the crowd at the beginning of the event but instead constantly patrols throughout the day.

The ritual efficacy of Pueblo feast days in both their traditional and more recent manifestations depends on this aesthetic ideal of "continuous perfectibility," a facet of a larger constellation of preferred forms of sociality shaping interactions, technologies, and exchanges, which I describe as Pueblo "propriety." This stance is "characterized by highly mediated forms of address and veiled authorship, a focus on the continuous perfectibility of texts and interactions, and controlling the circulation of cultural objects in order to highlight their importance" (Debenport 2011:89). As in the cultural anthropologist Hirokazu Miyazaki's (2000, 2006) description of the "aesthetics of completion" that shapes Fijian gift exchanges, Pueblo dancers follow what can be thought of as an aesthetics of continual refinement. The iterative quality of such practices closely aligns with Whorf's (2012 [1956]) analysis of the Hopi phenomenological distinction between events that are "manifesting" and those that are "manifested," with dances and other rituals serving as primary sites for the enactment of ongoing perfectibility.

Pueblo propriety and its associated aesthetic practices are found in prototypically traditional cultural forms, such as child rearing and food distribution practices, but are also present in new forms, making this a contemporary concern. Just as the new dance boss displays tenets of this ideology by dealing with the cell phones and digital cameras at San Ramón Pueblo, indigenous language literacy has opened up new opportunities for enacting proprietary practices. As I have shown in the preceding chapters, Keiwa language literacy has proved to be adaptable to Pueblo settings, where it is used for refinement, perfectibility, and control. In this chapter, I look closely at the creation, content, and circulation of an indigenous language pedagogical text and how writing was used in prototypically Pueblo ways. I also compare this text, as a prototypical example of a prominent Pueblo speech genre, with the dictionary example sentences, which exhibit similar features.

I outline the context in which this text was created, paying special attention to how discourses regarding indigenous language, tribal membership, gaming, and the future of the community are intertwined at San Ramón Pueblo. I analyze the original recording of the text in its English translation, identifying its salient stylistic and grammatical features, and compare these with generic features of language pedagogical dialogues in US classrooms and extant Pueblo speech genres. I then show how the generic conventions shaping this text mirror those found in many dictionary example sentences. I trace the lengthy editing processes surrounding the subsequent written versions of the text, highlighting the changes that were made and the indexical values of the embedded stories that were inserted into the final version. My examination of the creation and eventual use of this text shows that indigenous language literacy practices at San Ramón reflect different understandings of citizenship and political participation, relying on known but indirectly addressed individuals rather than on anonymous publics for their realization.

The Bowl Story *and Pedagogical Dialogues*

The text that came to be known as *The Bowl Story* emerged from a recording session in the San Ramón tribal library during the spring of 2008. During a visit at the pueblo to plan the summer language program, I sat down with John to record pedagogical dialogues to be used in the community language classes. Our goal was to create language materials that the eight young adult students could use to practice pronunciation and transcription both in class and at home. Like the dictionary and other Keiwa materials produced as part of the San Ramón language program, the recordings and resulting transcriptions were to be used only by tribal members.

In addition to collaborating on the San Ramón dictionary, John, Ellie, Betty, Frances, and I had worked together on creating pedagogical language dialogues as part of a written adult curriculum, whose circulation I discussed in chapter 2. For these initial dialogues, the authors began in English, constructing exchanges between Person A and Person B, trying to balance the conversations so that each student practicing the dialogues would benefit equally and also to adhere to the theme of the particular lesson, such as numbers, colors, and animals. Following this, the group would translate the sentences into Keiwa. To a great extent, these texts adhered to the style of pedagogical dialogues prevalent in US foreign language classes and popular language-learning materials, such as Rosetta Stone. The following example is taken from the lesson focusing on adjectives:

(4.1) *Dialogue: "People Watching"*

A: Let's go to Cottonwood Mall so we can watch people.

B: Let's go!

A: Look at that tall man. Maybe he plays basketball for the Lobos.

B: Look how big his feet are. Maybe he wears an 18-D.

A: Look at that stocky woman going in the Big and Tall Store.

B: Yeah. She needs big pants!
And her friend is tall and skinny.
I think she needs suspenders so she won't lose her pants.

A: How cute—look at that fat little infant!

B: Pinch her cheeks!

A: No! The baby's mother might slap me.

The content of all fifteen dialogues displays an overwhelmingly local focus, seen here in the use of nearby place names (Cottonwood Mall) and the reference to the University of New Mexico's basketball team. However, the author also uses the pair-part construction and attends to the chapter topic, reflecting Western pedagogical conventions. Almost any person who has taken a language class at the secondary level in the United States would recognize this as an example of the genre of the pedagogical foreign language dialogue. Most of the dialogues are dyadic, designed to give each speaker equal amounts of practice, and each dialogue is designed to convey a selection of grammatical or semantic phenomena. Although it was understood that no one outside San Ramón Pueblo would have access to the adult Keiwa curriculum, its content was designed for a general audience and covered topics such as greetings and commands. In contrast, the recording session on that spring afternoon in the library represented a methodological departure from previous curricula creation by starting with an unscripted Keiwa recording and then generating pedagogical dialogues from the audio texts.

Like other indigenous language texts produced at San Ramón Pueblo, including the dictionary and the "first Native soap opera," *As the Rez Turns*, which I describe in chapter 6, in the original recording of *The Bowl Story*, John used several features of local speech genres, but one most prominently. This generic framework is characterized by descriptions of the history of the area and of cultural practices at the pueblo that are no longer observed, correlating the loss of such practices with moral decline. It is used in both formal and informal contexts, by adults speaking to their peers or to children, in Keiwa, English, and, in a few cases I have observed, Spanish. The themes of this speech genre include the importance of working hard, respecting elders, being generous, and working together. These texts exhibit goals and strategies similar to the Arizona Tewa speech genre that Kroskrity (1993) calls "speaking the past."

Kroskrity describes this speech genre when discussing the use of the evidential marker -*ba* in Arizona Tewa "traditional stories" (1993:143). This particle is a formal characteristic of this genre and is used to connect the discourse with an "imaginary ideal native speaker of Tewa" (146) in order to imbue the story with the appropriate authority while distancing the author or animator from the account. Kroskrity details the utility of this speech form:

> These stories, in the traditional Arizona Tewa view, are regarded as necessary for such seemingly unrelated things as the moral and educational development of young listeners and the maintenance and progression of the agricultural cycle. They are fable-like narratives…which often contain instructive episodes depicting traditional technologies…. Tewa stories depict a moral universe that rewards "good" characteristics and punishes the "bad." (Kroskrity 1993:143)

Although the performance of the related speech genre in San Ramón Keiwa does not exhibit the same grammatical features as the Arizona Tewa stories, speakers use other means to displace authority to idealized Native speakers, and they emphasize local technologies and practices in an effort to construct a local "moral universe." Thus, instead of producing a prototypical language pedagogical dialogue, John employs aspects of "speaking the past," producing a monologue designed for a specific audience and without regard for imparting particular grammatical lessons.

(4.2)   The Bowl Story (*original transcription of English translation*)

1 The old timers, a long time ago, used to say
2 when we ate we used to sit on the floor to eat
3 they used to eat out of one bowl
4 just by dipping the bread in the bowl
5 that's the way they used to eat
6 Once an old man said
7 If we all have our own little bowls and we are eating like that
8 older brothers, younger brothers, older sisters, younger sisters
9 will not care for each other as much
10 all of the pueblo
11 male children, girl children, groups
12 male children, female children, groups, clans
13 they will also not care for each other as much
14 In the future there will be more jealousy
15 I still remember we all used to help each other
16 If somebody was plastering their walls
17 fixing their house
18 the neighbors would come over to help
19 the person that owned the house
20 would then get ready and fix lunch for the helpers
21 and also we used to get alfalfa
22 Also if the neighbor saw he came to help
23 Also, when they were working cows
24 if they were branding them or if they were cutting their horns
25 Everyone also used to help each other
26 And now, just as he was saying

27 If we're not eating together
28 if we're not eating, sitting together
29 out of one bowl
30 we will not care for each other
31 And that's the way it's getting to be
32 Now our people
33 our people are more greedy and stingy
34 they are getting more jealous
35 we don't help each other anymore
36 we don't help each other like we did a long time ago
37 we used to take care of each other
38 when children were playing
39 anybody could advise them
40 they used to correct them
41 and now if the children are talked to

42 their mothers and fathers don't like it
43 and that's the way we're going now
44 maybe we need to be careful
45 so that once again we can be together
46 so everybody in the community
47 is of use and is a contributor, of one mind, heart, and effort
48 Now we're seeing divisions among ourselves
49 It is not necessary for us to be so stingy
50 there's plenty for everybody
51 and it will even be better
52 if we help each other
53 if there is not jealousy
54 That's the way it needs to be.

When we examine the formal characteristics and content in this example of speaking the past, the goals of this genre and its connection to other texts, practices of perfectibility, and local characterizations of community become clear. In the recording, John shows a preference for the Keiwa habitual past aspectual marker (most often glossed as "used to"), a central formal characteristic of this San Ramón speech genre (lines 1–3, 5, 15, 18, 21, 25, 37, 40). It serves to describe previous ways that food was served in the community, along with other practices he feels have been abandoned. An additional way that he positions the action of the narrative in the past is by using the modal ("a long time ago") as seen in line 1 and as an adverb in the expression "like we did a long time ago" (line 36). Perfective markers, which also place the action in the past, are utilized throughout to provide background for situations in which community members acted generously.

The use of perfective aspectual markers and expressions, which enable John to describe local practices that are presently obsolete, is coupled with the use of imperfective aspectual markers (lines 33–36, 43, 45, 50). These allow him to contrast with current habits the routines he feels have been wrongly abandoned. This rhetorical move allows John to align the positive qualities of generosity and helpfulness with the past and the negative qualities of jealousy and greed with the current social and political climate at San Ramón Pueblo. He makes these associations unambiguous by using future tense/aspect marking to outline what he sees as the implications of such changes (lines 9, 14, 30), as well as the good things that will result from returning to values he associates with the past (lines 44–47, 51–53). This strategy recalls Kroskrity's analysis of one component of Tewa storytelling: "carrying it hither" for current audiences. Kroskrity describes this coda-like component: "The last criterion involves situating the narratives in known geographical locales…elaborating or editing episodes as part of recipient designing, and other details that contribute to the audience's sense of immediacy by virtue of the narrator's reshaping of old texts to new contexts" (1985:196). In this sense, John is speaking the past to an imagined future, repeatedly creating a sense of immediacy for his current audience.

An additional formal characteristic of the speech genre of speaking the past at San Ramón Pueblo is the repetition of ceremonial kinship terms. In lines 8, 11, and 12, the author expands his definition of "all of the pueblo" in line 10 by including each of the kinship terms for children in the original Keiwa version, a formal mode of address that indexes all community members. In other speech forms, the generic term for "children" (gender marking is optional in San Ramón Keiwa) or the word meaning "relatives" would be used. John includes the terms for religious groups and clans as well, again utilizing more formal forms of address appropriate for the performance of this genre or ceremonial registers. In combination with this, he uses repetition to emphasize these terms (line 12), highlighting this feature of his performance. An additional formal facet of speaking the past that appears throughout this text is the use of a modal enclitic (most often translated as "so," "in order to," or "because") to highlight the utility of former practices (lines 18, 45, 46). John ends the story with a final formal component of this genre, the prototypical closing "That's the way," which also serves to emphasize the purported advantages of returning to previous ways of doing things.

The themes of John's dialogue are contained in the overarching story he recounts, told alternately by "old timers" and an "old man." The metaphor of an entire family eating from one bowl becomes a symbol for the whole village, allowing the narrator to make claims about the lack of focus on the collective good at San Ramón and the recent membership controversies. In addition, other parts of the story contribute to his focus on generosity and sharing. In lines 15–25, John presents a series of examples of ways in which community members at San Ramón Pueblo used to work together, including group projects such as plastering walls, cutting alfalfa, and working cows, and he nests these collective activities within the larger metaphor of sharing a meal from a communal bowl. He begins the section by moving the narrative back into the past and emphasizing the importance of "helping each other" (line 15), repeating this emphasis explicitly at the end of several of the contained vignettes (lines 18, 22, 25). This nested, parallel structure allows him to emphasize the ways that people in the community used to help one another without having to be asked, a quality whose absence in current San Ramón life he sees as a moral shortcoming.

Genre and Lexicography

Comparing this example of speaking the past with many of the dictionary example sentences makes apparent the presence of both formal characteristics and other aspects of this speech form. At times, truncated versions of this genre appear in single sentences. For example, each afternoon when I was working at the tribal library with the dictionary committee, children arrived for the after-school program when the bus dropped them off at the pueblo. They would often greet members of the language program with "Hi" or "How are you?"—prompting the language committee members to instruct the children on appropriate forms of address by recounting stories of how things used to be, including how children used to use forms of address that the adults feel "show respect." A miniature version of such a story was created for a dictionary example sentence:

> (4.3)   *Children used to say Tata and Nana.*

Shortened forms of this genre also appear over several entries, and some were even created in consecutive order, as seen in examples 4.4 and 4.5, which were written for the entries "to smoke" and "to listen," respectively. These words appeared in alphabetical order in the SIL lexicon, resulting in the consecutive creation of these example sentences for the San Ramón dictionary:

> (4.4)   *They used to smoke us with cedar a long time ago.*

> (4.5)   *That's why you better listen.*

The author is describing a way that children were punished when he was growing up, by being held over a cedar fire until their eyes watered (4.4), a practice that seems likely to produce the desired result, which is expressed in the accompanying directive (4.5). In the first sentence of the couplet, the habitual past aspectual marker is used, which contrasts with the subjunctive form used to issue the directive in the second sentence. As a couplet, this illustrates the relationship between speaking the past and carrying it hither in the aesthetics of Pueblo storytelling. Both the realized and the hoped for, the perfective and the imperfective, are united in a single "chronotope" (Bakhtin 1981:84): a moral, Pueblo space/time where ideal visions of community can be realized.

Elements of this speech genre also appear in examples created in isolation. Here, the dictionary's authors recount traditional technologies by using the habitual past aspectual form:

> (4.6)   *They used to make wine out of grapes.*

> (4.7)   *They used to make bracelets out of turquoise.*

> (4.8)   *We used to cross the river with a dugout.*

> (4.9)   *Both of us used to go out and hoe.*

Another means used by speakers to locate the action of the narrative in the past, a word that translates as "a long time ago," is also present in isolated example sentences:

> (4.10)   *A long time ago they used to eat blackbirds.*

> (4.11)   *A long time ago we didn't have spoons and forks.*

The dictionary authors also draw sharp distinctions between the past and the present in individual sentences (examples 4.12 and 4.13), and they foreground the moral failings or wastefulness of the present (4.14 and 4.15), both of which are generic features of speaking the past.

> (4.12)   *It used to be like that, now it's different.*

(4.13)   It's been a long time, but we used to have ditches with dirt.

(4.14)   Now marriages don't last, they split right away.

(4.15)   Now they grind coffee seeds with electricity.

The preponderance of directives in the San Ramón Keiwa dictionary example sentences also points to a reliance on the genre of speaking the past as a discursive resource for the creation of new texts. Using subjunctive or future tense/aspect markers (examples 4.16 and 4.17), authors bring the discourse into the present tense, explicitly stating the moral lessons that this genre is designed to communicate, carrying it hither.

(4.16)   Young people should always be respectful.

(4.17)   When you are given words of advice, take them.

In the example sentences, the multiple generic resources available to Keiwa speakers when constructing local morality tales are repurposed, and nowhere is this more evident than in the strict distinctions between past and present that are drawn.

Additionally, as in longer examples of this generic form, the dictionary authors use the modal enclitic "in order to" to explicitly state a moral position and to explain the logic behind local practices:

(4.18)   Gather the wood so we can put it in the wagon.

(4.19)   I sent him to get wood so I could make bread.

(4.20)   We went out to pray, to ask for health and longevity.

Emphasizing the importance of helping other community members is another way the authors utilize generic conventions associated with speaking the past to carry it hither. The following sentence illustrates the use of this resource:

(4.21)   When it came to cutting wheat, we helped each other.

          (Notes: Your machine was the community that came over to help you, and
          you in turn were part of that machine.)

This is another example of the moral point being stated baldly outside the Keiwa and English example sentences. Again, what is being communicated is not grammatical regularity, but the features of a local speech genre and the moral lesson contained within.

Perfectibility, Correction, and Refinement

The life of *The Bowl Story* did not end after John recorded the dialogue and we finished the transcription and translation. First, he spent time "correcting" (as he said) the written version: fixing spelling mistakes and adding or subtracting nasal vowel diacritics from my typed transcription. During this process, he was not interested in replaying the original recording; if there was a question about a particular sound or expression, he used his knowledge as a Keiwa speaker of what it "should" be. He eliminated false starts and what he thought were needless repetitions in his initial recorded version, similar to the editing strategies and ideologies employed by the newly literate Tzotzil Maya speakers whom Haviland (1996) describes. After these changes were made and I typed up a revised copy, he said that he wanted to continue working on the story. I asked whether he wanted to make a new recording, but he declined: "[You] could just write it, and we could add it to what we already had."

The process of creating the many subsequent versions of this text took place over the next several days and resembled aspects of the dictionary editing sessions, although the focus was much more concentrated. We would start by John speaking Keiwa as I transcribed the additions to the text. I would then read the story back to him, and he would provide a free translation, which I then transcribed in English. I would then type up the additional lines, which John would insert into the story, all the while refining the content and tweaking spelling, word choice, and story structure. The final version of *The Bowl Story* still opens with the metaphor of eating from one piece of pottery and still adheres to the formal conventions of the genre, but it has been transformed into a different text with additional content.

(4.22) The Bowl Story (*final revision of English translation*)

1   The old timers, a long time ago, used to say
2   When we ate we used to sit on the floor
3   We used to eat from one pottery
4   Just by dipping the bread in the bowl
5   That's the way they used to eat
6   Once an old man said
7   The day is coming when we will no longer eat out of one pottery
8   Everyone will have their own little pottery bowl
9   Some will still be sitting on the floor
10 Some will be sitting someplace else
11 Some won't be there (at home)
12 When that happens, we won't care for each other as much
13 If we all have our own little bowls and we are eating like that
14 We won't recognize each other as brothers and sisters, or as husbands and wives
15 Husbands and wives won't be living together anymore
16 Siblings will not get along with each other
17 They won't help each other like now
18 All of the Pueblo
19 Male children, female children, groups, clans
20 will also not care for each other as much
21 There will be greed
22 There will be stinginess
23 There will be jealousy
24 There will be divisiveness
25 But it's really still up to us
26 That's why we need to think about this carefully
27 Let's help each other
28 Let's take care of each other
29 That's the way it's supposed to be
30 I still remember we all used to help each other
31 If somebody was plastering their house
32 Fixing their house
33 The neighbors would come over to help
34 The person that owned the house
35 The homeowner would then get ready and fix lunch for the helpers

36 And also they used to cut alfalfa and haul bales
37 Also, if the neighbor saw, he came to help
38 When they were working domestic livestock
39 if they were branding them they also used to help each other
40 Everyone also used to help each other
41 And now, just as he was saying
42 We don't eat together anymore
43 We do not care for each other
44 And that's the way it's getting to be
45 Some of our people are more greedy and stingy
46 They are getting more jealous
47 We don't help each other like we did a long time ago
48 We used to take care of each other
49 When children were playing
50 Anybody could advise them
51 They used to correct them
52 And now if anybody advises them, corrects them
53 And now if the children are corrected, their mothers and fathers don't like it
54 That's the way we're going now
55 Maybe we need to be careful
56 Let's not let our good fortune, financially, ruin our way of life
57 So that once again we can be together
58 So everybody in the community is of use and worth, is a contributor, of one mind, heart, and effort
59 Now we're seeing divisions among ourselves
60 It is not necessary for us to be so stingy
61 There's plenty for everybody, and there will be even more if we share
62 And it will even be better and we'll see again the village that used to be
63 So we will help each other
64 So we won't be jealous

65 That's the way it needs to be
66 The chiefs and the council members are supposed to take care of the Pueblo and its members
67 That's why, whenever there are things, like food, like corn, like wheat, like fruits and vegetables, like jewelry, like money, like loud purchases
68 Whatever there is
69 It is said whatever it is that we have, the people take what they want first
70 Afterwards, whatever is left, if anything is left, the chiefs then take it
71 That's what they used to say.
72 If the Hopis hadn't adopted us where would we be?
73 They gave us land to settle on
74 We were there for more than fifty years
75 When we returned, we built the village called San Ramón Pueblo.
76 Maybe because we lost some of our dances
77 Other villages gave us some
78 The buffalo's dance
79 The one that comes to see life at the village
80 That we call ours
81 Came from ██████████████
82 The eagle's dance
83 The one that comes to see life at the village
84 Also came from over there
85 Also the buffalo's dance that includes wildlife from the plains and the mountains
86 Came from ██████████████ Pueblo
87 They gave these beautiful dances to us
88 If we don't take care of them, respect them
89 It is said, if we don't live the way we should, they can take them back
90 That's what they used to say

In this expanded version of *The Bowl Story*, John preserves the use of the habitual past marker (lines 1–3, 30, 33, 35–37, 39, 40, 47, 48, 50, 51, 71, 90) but uses imperfect and future aspectual forms to a greater degree than in the first draft in order to contrast current practices at the pueblo with the ways things used to be (lines 7–12, 14–17, 20–24, 42–46, 52–56, 61–64). He also emphasizes sharing and working together, through increased use of the modal enclitic "in order to" (lines 57, 58, 63, 64). He retains the ritual kinship terms that appeared in the first draft but reduces the repetition of the recorded version, and he changes the ending by using a contracted form of the closing word in the Keiwa version. The force of these changes, and indeed of the entire text, is enhanced by the use of a four-part parallel structure throughout the piece, which can be seen in individual lines (14, 19) but most pointedly in the series of invoked predictions (lines 21–24). Connecting the piece poetically to the Pueblo conception of the "fourth world" (Courlander 1987), the present world into which the Pueblo people emerged, *The Bowl Story* shares a reliance on the use of this numerical motif with many other ceremonial forms.

Although John eliminated redundancies, the text grew from fifty-four to ninety lines. One addition is the use of first-person plural forms and subjunctive aspectual markers to issue directives to community members (lines 27, 28) that outline the theme clearly ("Let's help each other," "Let's take care of each other"). John's most substantial additions in the final draft are three vignettes: descriptions of the role of chiefs and council members in the distribution of local resources (lines 66–70); the history of the flight to the Hopi reservation (lines 72–74); and the provenance of and proper attitude toward several sacred dances (lines 76–89). At first glance, these may seem like offhand additions, simply padding the story by expressing the interests of an individual author. However, as in the Western Apache speech genre "speaking with names" (Basso 1996), John ties moral lessons to each of these stories as part of his greater rhetorical goal. Instead of linking these tales to a spatial and geographic cosmology, as seen in the Western Apache example, John augments his text with three historical events at San Ramón Pueblo that carry particular moral lessons. He leaves it to his ratified audience to correctly recontextualize such accounts and to correctly infer their indexical meanings, the same semiotic approach the authors took in writing the dictionary example sentences. Additionally, these stories themselves are connected to the Pueblo fourth world. The use of the three vignettes, in some ways, casts the present as a time yet to be perfected; relying on processes of "manifesting" (Whorf 2012[1956]) and continual refinement, the implied fourth story—the one still being lived at San Ramón Pueblo—can be perfected.

The first story—the assertion that chiefs and council members should put the village first before thinking of their own needs—refers to a recent historical event at San Ramón: the decision to exclude women married to non–San Ramón men, including their children, from the membership rolls. Instead of openly criticizing the current leadership, John frames his commentary on fairness inside the "story world" (Hill and Zepeda 1993). This rhetorical move is apparent in line 71, where he attributes authorship to the old-timers, whom he has not invoked since the beginning the story, thus distancing himself personally from a controversial stance. Because every family at San Ramón has been affected by this decision, its relationship to the description of resource distribution in *The Bowl Story* would be immediately evident to any tribal member. The moral is clear, as are the reasons for not stating it outright: by excluding some people from membership, the tribal leaders have failed in their roles. They are not considering the good of the entire village, in John's opinion, but are acting in their own interests and those of their immediate family members. This view has the potential to cause trouble for John if tribal officials hear or read about it in a more direct manner, making it necessary for him to present his critique more covertly.

The second story John includes in the final version of *The Bowl Story* concerns a more distant historical event. Following the Pueblo Revolt of 1680 and the subsequent Spanish reconquest, many Pueblo communities, including San Ramón, sought refuge on Hopi lands (Liebmann 2008; Simmons 1979). San Ramón Pueblo was repopulated in the 1700s, but many people still talk about the event, expressing intensely conflicted feelings. Although they are proud to have been part of the only indigenous group in North America to successfully overthrow the Spanish, considerable anxiety remains about "losing" the fight to control their lands and the subsequent flight to First Mesa. There are still proscriptions against certain clans and groups visiting Hopi, and when asked why, community members at San Ramón always vaguely refer to problems that arose when they "lived over there."[1] John's three-line addition foregrounding the generosity of the Hopi people criticizes such practices and the defensive stance they index. This fits into his larger rhetorical goal of highlighting the importance of sharing and collectivity but also refers to the tensions between San Ramón Pueblo and neighboring reservations. The result is a constant shifting between pan-pueblo displays of unity and inter-pueblo factionalism.

John's final additional vignette, in lines 76–89, also speaks to regional tensions by invoking the provenance of several sacred dances performed at San Ramón Pueblo, dances that John is "exposing" as originating outside San Ramón. Despite its small size, San Ramón Pueblo enjoys the regional status of "keeping" particular dances—having knowledge of the appropriate songs, dress, and movements that make it possible for performances to be done in a certain way to achieve specific goals. Community members speak with pride about this custodial role and claim that many dances would be lost without their knowledge and without their sharing it with neighboring pueblos. Like the flight from Hopi, however, this aspect of life is tinged with regret because many tribal members are increasingly unable to produce the linguistic, musical, or visual elements of such performances. This mixture of pride and anxiety surrounding the stewardship of dances is evident during feast days. Many tribal members remark worriedly that "there are so many people from other pueblos dancing" but also acknowledge that such large numbers are necessary to do the dance properly and obtain the desired results. Again, there is tension between expressing pan-clan, pan-Pueblo identities and expressing an individualized, unitary Pueblo stance, echoing the larger goal of John's narrative.

All three of these vignettes are included to emphasize the role of sharing and the importance of unity in the current sociopolitical situation. The efficacy of such stories as part of the genre of speaking the past depends on a community member's knowledge of the pueblo's history and each vignette's significance and on his skill in recontextualizing each story within the larger text. As in Basso's Western Apache examples, the "subtle and subterranean affair" (1996:81) that John performs is a "call to memory and imagination" (91) in the service of the larger function of speaking the past. Although the genre depends on the invocation of past practices, it is essentially about affecting action in the future, specifically, collective action that will ideally produce a particular version of the Keiwa language and the San Ramón community.

The time spent producing multiple drafts and improving the entire story highlights the importance of John's text itself, which simultaneously points out the purpose of the genre: to emphasize proper moral behavior, how to "live the way we should" (line 89) through sharing resources and being generous. The fact that he devoted so much time and energy to getting the story "perfect," as he described it, while ignoring the other recordings produced for the language program also underscores its importance. Like secrecy practices, the processes of editing and perfecting elevate the importance of texts, both the content they contain and their value as cultural objects in their own right. As we worked together to produce and type the text, John frequently brought up the membership controversy and the potentially harmful effects of casino wealth. He said, "We should just give those guys [the leadership] what they want! They could take as much as they wanted, and the rest of us could live off what was left. There is plenty for everybody."

The focus on continual perfectibility, as seen in the creation and editing of *The Bowl Story*, is present in other emergent uses of written texts and in verbal and nonlinguistic semiotic practices at San Ramón Pueblo. For example, the authors of the dictionary have decided to wait indefinitely to print a "final" version, choosing instead to move words and example sentences in and out of the text and to create a list of material deemed incorrect or inappropriate. At the pueblo Head Start, at community events, and in private homes, adults continually regulate the dress, behavior, and language of children and, in the case of elders, younger tribal members. Such repetitive, collective socialization practices are mentioned in *The Bowl Story*; John laments a time "when children were playing, anybody could advise them, they used to correct them" (original version, example 4.2, lines 38–40). In *Pueblo Mothers and Children* (1991[1919]), Parsons identifies similar examples of child rearing among the Tewa, Laguna, Zuni, and Acoma tribes. Returning to the feast day example, during nonlinguistic, "public" cultural practices, we can identify similar sensibilities among all of the Rio Grande Pueblos.

Like the content of John's text, the circulation of the finished *Bowl Story* was calibrated to honor such proprietary ideals. After he completed the final version, he asked me to print several copies, along with an accompanying English translation. He then met individually with a handful of people in the community who "might learn to see things" his way, referring to the membership struggles, and gave them single copies of the text. Since then, he has asked for additional copies of the written text several times but has showed no interest in revisiting the original recorded version or making improvements using nonwritten tools. This text has been distributed only in written form, to targeted individuals, with a total print run of no more than ten copies. Here, writing surfaces as a new technology of perfectibility at San Ramón Pueblo, enabling multiple revisions of indigenous language texts and allowing for a new material manifestation of culture, whose circulation can (and must) be managed and controlled.

Literacy, Perfectibility, and Control

When we consider the installation of the new dance boss alongside the creation, content, and circulation of *The Bowl Story*, it is apparent that both examples are part of a "representational economy" among the Rio Grande Pueblos and at San Ramón more specifically (Keane 2003, 2007). Describing this analytic, which allows for comparison across semiotic modalities, Keane says, "More generally, different kinds of practices and institutions affect one another within a representational economy, but it is the logic of a semiotic ideology that helps brings the effects into alignment" (2007:20). In the present example, the semiotic ideology of Pueblo propriety mediates between events, interactions, texts, and other types of cultural practice at San Ramón Pueblo, aligning seemingly unrelated forms through a focus on perfectibility, indirectness, and control and through the continual production and reception of signs indexing such values.

Keane's approach points to one way of formulating a more nuanced understanding of Pueblo secrecy and literacy in that the emphasis on information control can be productively compared to processes of perfectibility. The presence of multiple dance bosses, who continualy correct both dancers and audience, resembles the multiple editing sessions devoted to *The Bowl Story* and to the dictionary example sentences. In turn, these examples of refinement align with rules against accessing religious or linguistic knowledge, using recording equipment without permission, and sharing certain information outside one's clan. Both secrecy and perfectibility work to assert the existence of valued cultural property rightfully controlled by ratified community members. Perfectibility resembles aspects of Pueblo secrecy and other proprietary practices in that it allows for the owners of cultural objects, including indigenous language texts, to exert greater control over them. The amount of time and care that is directed toward the continued perfecting of cultural forms and controlling their circulation indirectly asserts the importance of the social work being done, whether through a ritual performance or the creation of a pedagogical text. Therefore, secrecy is not merely exclusionary, but intensely inclusionary in that practices of information control cordon off areas of knowledge for special treatment. Knowledge is not buried, but perfected and veiled.

The implications of applying processes of refinement to the new realm of indigenous language literacy at San Ramón extend beyond theorizing Pueblo secrecy.

By following Collins's (1995) point that literacies need to be studied ethnographically, we can see the specificity of the San Ramón case, but we must also keep in mind one facet of the technology of literacy that exists across all contexts: it allows you to revise. In US educational contexts, students are told that writing is 99 percent revision, but in the majority of social scientific studies of circulation, literacy is characterized as the often anonymous circulation of identical texts, like Anderson's novels and newspapers or Habermas's political tracts. In new forms like *The Bowl Story*, literacy allows for the active, ongoing regulation of appropriate performances of language use while allowing tribal members to perfect their visions of community and personhood. Like *The Bowl Story* and the visions of citizenship and community it depicts, written materials in this community are endlessly perfectible works, worthy of large amounts of time, attention, and negotiation. The ongoing negotiations and revisions that in fact constitute these unfinished texts highlight the special relationship between perfectibility, propriety, and literacy in this case. People are invested not only in harnessing or shaping cultural property in the form of indigenous language texts but also in constantly making them better.

A critique of the formation of publics arises centering on this depiction of literacy as a technology of refinement and control rather than of anonymous circulation. The problem with Anderson, Habermas, and others is that they lead us to imagine written language as a collection of fixed forms. Having missed that literacy is not only about completion but also about revision, theories of the public sphere and the creation of groups rest on narrowly characterized understandings of circulation, authorship, and permanence. An ideology of continual perfectibility, whether evidenced in Pueblo ceremonies or in written languages, relies on cultural projects never truly being complete, but always manifesting, and reflects different understandings of citizenship and political participation that rely on known but indirectly addressed individuals rather than on anonymous publics for their realization.

Pueblo literacy appears paradoxical only if you fall into the ideological trap of thinking that unfettered, "public" circulation is what writing is all about. Studying Pueblo literacy ethnographically and looking at indigenous texts as examples of material culture show that this technology can also be about collaboration and control. Writing can hold cultural knowledge still for a long enough time that community members can work on it together and circulate it among appropriate people and in precise contexts in order to, in this example, affect political goals. This political project involves addressing known private spheres rather than unknown publics. Thus, writing becomes another tool at San Ramón Pueblo that is constitutive of community through its adherence to proprietary practices. *The Bowl Story*, the dictionary, and other new texts can accomplish these and other types of social work only by remaining continuously unfinished, perfectible works.

five
The Hopeful Nostalgia of Language Revitalization Movements

> What seems most likely is that producers of the counter-discourse recognize that the discourse of "nostalgia" is in fact a pragmatic claim on the present, using "pastness" as a "naturalizing" ideological strategy: rhetorically, the claim is that those practices which are most like those of the past are the most valuable. The counter-discourses, then, constitute a pragmatic claim on the future, when everyone will have an equal chance for education and a decent life.
>
> —*Jane Hill, "Today There Is No Respect"*

Jane Hill's 1992 essay on Mexicano language ideologies details how "pure" forms of indigenous languages are presented as embodiments of values that some community members feel are lost: respect, hard work, and fair access to resources. In the village she describes, Spanish has come to be associated with societal fragmentation, disrespect, and laziness. Employing specific syntactic and generic features, discourses of nostalgia are used primarily by elites, with women and other non-elites more often utilizing counterdiscourses that critique romanticized visions of the past.

Nostalgic discourse is a central part of San Ramón Pueblo's language revitalization efforts. This became especially clear to me when I was working on my spoken Keiwa. The first aspectual forms that I could consistently use correctly were those marking perfective and habitual perfect forms, which are handy for translating example sentences but not for talking about my day or where to get dinner later. As the examples in chapters 3 and 4 illustrate, Keiwa authors rely on nostalgic stances as part of crafting pedagogical and political texts.

Unlike in Hill's study, however, San Ramón nostalgia is not a straightforward example of some speakers focusing on the past and others on the future. Although "pastness" is indexed in numerous ways in San Ramón writings and in everyday conversations, the fact that written materials are being produced in order to encourage greater use of the Keiwa language situates this project as essentially forward thinking. My colleagues at the pueblo would often remark on the importance of "getting everything down" so that "the language will be around long after [they are] gone," again and again connecting the greater use of Keiwa to changes at the pueblo while lamenting that "things have really changed" there. This contrast caused me to wonder why a project whose goals were to encourage future language use and the health of the community focused primarily on the past.

In this chapter, I attempt to answer this question by advancing a new understanding of language revitalization movements. I argue that previous depictions of these social projects—so common in Indian Country—have failed to take into account critical aspects of the efforts to promote indigenous language use, aspects that are revealed through looking at such nostalgic motifs. To more fully understand the implications of language revitalization, the reasons for its ubiquity, and the social meanings surrounding these endeavors, I examine anthropological works on nostalgia, hope, and faith while drawing on ethnolinguistic examples from San Ramón. The similarities between these topics and language revitalization movements in Pueblo contexts and elsewhere include their focus on lack, their distinctly utopian character, the difficulty in evaluating their "success" or end point, and their iterative, ritualistic contours. These similarities are especially revealing in the San Ramón case in that they highlight the reasons behind the Keiwa authors' preference for focusing on the past, their visions of San Ramón community and identity, and the continuous perfectibility surrounding literacy and other social processes. The San Ramón authors invoke the past in order to bring about a refined, imagined future characterized by widespread fluency in Keiwa and the wholeness of the community. In imagining the fourth world invoked in *The Bowl Story*, nostalgic discourse becomes another resource for refinement, enabling people to perfect their language and community by temporally removing themselves from the unfinished, contested present.

Paradoxical Nostalgia

During the three summers that I helped to teach the young adult Keiwa class with John, I started every morning at Michelle's house for coffee. Our routine consisted of sitting on the glider in her front yard while playing with her dogs, Chopper and Fatty Girl, enjoying the sun and the stunning view of San Ramón Mountain. Whereas John was my Keiwa teacher, it was Michelle who taught me the history of the pueblo, a task just as complex as trying to understand verbal morphology or pronounce ejective consonants. Over the years, she patiently described extended families and how they were connected to other pueblos. As we would sit and talk about friends and family, Michelle's talk would move deftly back and forth, connecting stories of events that happened when she was a child or when her grandmother was young to people I knew from working in the community.

The old San Ramón church stands directly in front of Michelle's house, framed by the mountain. One morning as we were sitting outside, I asked her about the church and how the tribe made the switch to using "the new one," an impressive adobe building built at the end of the twentieth century with gaming revenues. "Oh, you know, they had too much money and didn't know what to do with it," she said, referring to the tribal leadership. She continued:

> I really preferred the old church—I have so many memories there! Plus, it used to be the diocese for the area for a while in the seventeen or eighteen hundreds after the church in Coronado burned down, so lots of Spanish people went to church there. I remember this one time when I was really little, we got a new saint, and we were all slowly walking past it during church. I didn't know what to do, so I asked Grandma, and she said, "Adore him!" [*Urgent whisper*] So I—when it was my turn—instead of making the sign of the cross, I gave the saint a kiss right on the face! Grandma was, like, "Oh my God!" but I didn't know what she meant by "Adore him." It was hilarious.

This story *was* especially hilarious for both of us since we knew how devout her grandmother was, and we laughed over Michelle planting a kiss on the saint. She went on:

> So, yeah, I really like the old one better, but you know, they've got to show off, putting it [the new church] right there by the highway. Another example of—what is it they say?—absolute power corrupts absolutely? There was some talk about turning it into a museum, which would be cool, I guess, but we already have enough on our hands with language, you know? Who's gonna run the museum?

We glided along, finishing our coffee and looking at the old church while Fatty Girl patrolled the yard and Michelle finished her cigarette. "Time to head out," she said, standing up, and we walked to the library.

Although older people at San Ramón are far more likely to utilize nostalgic stances, Michelle's story about the old church unites many features of such discourses at the pueblo. Specifically, she refers to multiple temporalities, differences between collective and individual experiences, and themes of rupture and loss. Also present in the telling of her story is the productive power of nostalgia, the ability of social actors to use backward-facing stances to, in this case, construct a political critique. Not only emblematic of nostalgic discourses at San Ramón, these features also appear in discussions of nostalgia in other contexts.

Nostalgic discourses do not consist solely of backward-facing stances or the exclusive use of descriptions of the past. Nor are they necessarily formally analogous, since examples from different speech communities or individuals use varied approaches to invoking the past. In "Nostalgia—A Polemic," Kathleen Stewart describes the diverse and temporally complex features of such discourses, defining nostalgia as "an essential narrative function of language that orders events temporally and dramatizes them in the mode of 'things that happened,' that 'could happen,' that 'threatened to erupt at any moment'" (1988:227). Rather than assume that nostalgia is simply a collection of past images and memories, Stewart asserts that nostalgia is "a cultural practice, not a given content; its forms, meanings, and effects shift with the context—it depends on where the speaker stands in the landscape of the present" (227). Stewart shows that although the past and future are highlighted as part of this discursive practice, any nostalgic depiction hinges (and comments) on present conditions, which is certainly a central feature of *The Bowl Story* and Michelle's description of the old church. Moore's description of memorializing stances toward indigenous language writing locates a similar temporal variability: "Here the written marks can be 'read' as indexical signs pointing back toward an original oral/aural utterance—itself an emblem of its context, a swatch of a sociocultural order—or forward, to a next re-utterance or re-animation" (2006:298). At San Ramón and elsewhere, written materials, engaged with regeneratively, are both presupposing and creative indexicals (Silverstein 1976), used in the imagining of a pre-contact language (and its accompanying context) and possible future iterations of other linguistic forms (and their associated contexts). Nostalgic discourses depend on a similar semiotic logic, presupposing former contexts while making possible or envisioning possibilities for future signification.

In Svetlana Boym's book *The Future of Nostalgia* (2001) and a related article (2007), she summarizes the temporal aspect of nostalgia, connecting it to the collective nature of such discourses: "Nostalgia, in my view, is not always retrospective; it can be prospective as well. The fantasies of the past, determined by the needs of the present, have a direct impact on the realities of the future. Unlike melancholia, which confines itself to the plains of individual consciousness, nostalgia is about the relationship between individual biography and the biography of groups or nations, between personal and collective memory" (2007:8). Although individuals certainly utilize discourses of nostalgia at San Ramón Pueblo, these are, as Boym argues, largely a way of depicting collective experience. This is evident in Michelle's story. While much of her account takes place in the past, the funny anecdote about kissing the saint is not held up as an example of a longed-for and lost object but is just a beloved family story about specific people we both know. What is being positioned as exemplary in her discourse is the prior instantiation of community itself or the former tribal leadership. Here, contrasts between past and present are not constructed to incite personal improvement or salvation (although I am sure she would never kiss the saint again), but to encourage the improvement and salvation of the entire pueblo.

If, as Stewart asserts, nostalgia does not consist of a "given content" (1988:227), what makes San Ramón written materials nostalgic? Hill carefully shows how the nostalgic Mexicano discourse consists of "multiplex signs" (1992:267, citing Briggs 1988), co-occurring topics, grammatical constructions, and lexical preferences that, when aggregated, produce a recognizable way of speaking. The San Ramón case can be typified in a similar manner. As I have shown, in the dictionary example sentences, the authors tend to describe past practices, local genealogies, or the history of the pueblo. At the level of the lexicon, care was taken to remove any loanwords from other Pueblo languages or from Spanish, English, or Navajo, maintaining a code in keeping with the depiction of a pre-contact past. Throughout this document and in other pedagogical materials, such as *The Bowl Story* and the adult curriculum, there is a preference for using past aspectual forms to describe how things "used to be" done. Voicing strategies in these same documents ascribe authorship and authority to "old-timers" or "elders." Meanwhile, the forward-looking aspect of nostalgia is invoked by addressing imagined future speakers of the language and by aligning the reinstatement of past practices, linguistic or otherwise, with a vision of the pueblo in the immediate future. Future and subjunctive aspectual marking is employed to make predictions about the state of the pueblo or to support particular types of behavior. Both forward- and backward-looking stances are also invoked metaprag- matically when the Keiwa authors comment on "saying things the way they used to be said" or hope that "things will turn around when more of [their] people can speak Keiwa." Thus, nostalgic discourses are employed to construct a Bakhtinian chrono- tope enveloping the entire pueblo at a prior time and, it is implied, in a projected future.

As evidenced by the use of perfective aspectual forms in the dictionary exam- ple sentences, in other written materials, and in Michelle's story, nostalgic forms at San Ramón are preferred across different contexts. Still, students in the sum- mer language program avoided the use of nostalgic forms in Keiwa and in English when writing pedagogical texts. Even those community members, such as John, who favored such stances would comment on nostalgia's potentially negative effects, saying, "Well, maybe it's time to write about things happening *now*," when work- ing on language materials. Boym argues that nostalgia can in fact be dangerous, potentially leading to unrealistic thoughts and actions: "The danger of nostalgia is that it tends to confuse the actual home and the imaginary one. In extreme cases it can create a phantom homeland, for the sake of which one is ready to die or kill" (2007:9). She devotes a section of her book to describing historical attempts to "cure" nostalgics, but she and other theorists also point out that nostalgia can be productive. Stewart describes the potential for nostalgia to be a galvanizing force: "If cultural hegemonies and resistances are interpretive practices based in social uses rather than fixed contents of ideas, th[e]n a similarly alternat[ive], allegorical reading is also pos- sible through other, less obviously contentious forms of nostalgia" (1988:233). Fredric Jameson, writing on Walter Benjamin's use of nostalgia in his social and literary criticism, makes a related comment: "But if nostalgia as a clinical motivation is most frequently associated with Fascism, there is no reason why nostalgia conscious of itself, a lucid and remorseless dissatisfaction with the present on the grounds of some remembered plenitude, cannot furnish as adequate a revolutionary stimulus as any other" (1972:82). In these works, there is a distinction between the rampant, unexamined examples of looking backward and the potential for using pastness as the basis of a critique of the present, which is also found in ethnolinguistic examina- tions of nostalgia (Hill 1992) and in literary critiques (Ladino 2004). In other words, looking back can be agentive, a productive way to mobilize political support based on a remembered or imagined past.

It is precisely this active aspect of looking back that Boym (2001, 2007) clarifies in her discussion of the two types of nostalgia—the reflective and the restorative—a distinction that also informs the difference between the invocation of individual and collective memories or of imagined pasts at San Ramón. As Boym describes these terms (which are not necessarily mutually exclusive or oppositional), reflective nostalgia occurs at the individual level and is expressed through recognition of the vast space between the present and the past. Nostalgics of this type do not actively try to bring back aspects of the past but find affective meaning in the recognition of loss and symbols of this gulf. Often associated with melancholic states, this is the type of nostalgia that historically had to be cured or corrected in order to avoid extreme interiority and sadness. Restorative nostalgia, however, "does not think of itself as nostalgia, but rather as truth and tradition" (Boym 2007:13). It is "at the core of recent national religious revivals" and consists of "two main plots—the return to origins and the conspiracy" (13).

This second sense of nostalgia, the restorative, and its manifestation as a return to origins are what should inform the understanding of language revitalization movements. At San Ramón and likely in many other Native North American communities, restorative nostalgia is seen in descriptions of returning to precolonial or pre-casino eras, although these two temporal bookmarks are often used together as nostalgic motifs. As Boym describes, nostalgia for these previous eras "builds on the sense of loss of community and cohesion and offers a comforting collective script for individual longing" (2007:8). The centrality of both precolonial and pre-casino discourses to the construction of nostalgic discourses at the pueblo points to their effectiveness as collective scripts; they serve as discursive resources in numerous contexts and for myriad goals. Concomitantly, Boym's distinction aligns with Moore's description of regenerative and memorializing discourses. In both cases, the past (or indigenous language writing) is seen as either a means of connecting to the sublime through a sense of irreparable loss or a means of enacting social and linguistic change, which can be manifested through the discourses of individual actors but is at the same time connected to collective visions of the past and its utility. This is not to argue that reflective nostalgia or memorializing stances are not felt or performed by people at San Ramón but that it is the collective, productive aspect of nostalgia that is such an integral part of language revitalization projects.

At San Ramón Pueblo and elsewhere, nostalgia not only is about co-present temporalities and the potential for productivity but also concerns the discursive use of experiences of loss. For my colleagues and friends at the pueblo, such loss was usually expressed in terms that were material, for example, losing land due to the encroachment of Albuquerque, Rio Rancho, and Santa Fe; affective, as seen in the feeling of losing Indian identity as a result of recent membership policies; or linguistic, which was present in discussions of not being able to speak and understand Keiwa as people did in the past. Many of these motifs of loss were apparent during one ceremonial dance I attended at the pueblo. I sat with an elderly friend, Ellen, under a shade structure on the plaza, chatting about the dancers, practicing my Keiwa, and gossiping. At one point, the conversation turned to the half-completed houses facing us and the tribal council's decision to refurbish all of the houses in the old village using suburban-style balloon frame construction. Ellen emphatically disagreed with this development, saying disgustedly, "It wasn't like this before. They should have left the houses like they were. They could have repaired them, but to make people move out while they redo them? All of the houses will look exactly alike! They look like the houses they have built on our land! We might as well be white people."

Nostalgic discourses that hinge on experiences of loss are also frequently used by non-Pueblo tribal employees. For example, the Lands Department at San Ramón has been working with tribal attorneys for years to challenge state and federal decisions that have ceded land and water rights to non-Pueblo towns and cities that abut the reservation. Mirroring the strategies used by indigenous and non-indigenous people to encourage support for language revitalization programs that Hill (2002) depicts, the loss of land and water rights is described using enumeration (how many square miles have been lost, how many acre feet of water have been lost) and hyperbolic valorization ("the spiritual inheritance of Pueblo people, their land and water"). These various senses of loss intermingle and overlap as part of local nostalgic discourses and emerge as productive resources in extra-Pueblo contexts as well.

Central to the depictions of loss in nostalgic talk is the sense of fragmentation of self and community. Stewart shows this in her description of the impoverished residents of a Kentucky town. Bringing in Edward Said's (1984) work on exiles, she states, "They live in the bodily realization of knowing one life and also another life that displaces the first. Theirs is at each moment [a] double vision—two cultures differentiated through the lived experience of loss" (Stewart 1988:236). Boym (2001, 2007) also sees rupture as a potential harbinger of nostalgia, arguing that such discourses appear at times of crisis. Her primary example is the collapse of the Soviet Union and the nostalgia for life under communism that accompanied this change. Gaming has successfully reversed poverty and ameliorated the lack of political power at San Ramón Pueblo; nonetheless, it is a rupture. The immense changes wrought by economic success happened in a very short period of time. The shift from a "locals only" bingo hall to a huge resort occurred so quickly that all but the youngest residents of the pueblo have experienced substantial economic and social changes. Housing patterns, educational opportunities, the ability to participate in religious activities—these and all other aspects of pueblo life have been altered by gaming.

Read through the lens of nostalgia, language revitalization can be seen as both a symptom and a cure, a way to diagnose the amount of cultural loss and a way to reinstate what has gone missing, what has been taken, and what is seen to be vital to the health of the community. The push to reinvigorate the use of Keiwa at the pueblo is a way to draw distinctions between temporalities that are experienced, related, or imagined and is a way to picture the possibility of reversing radical changes. Stewart observes, "the nostalgic desires to turn history into private or collective mythology, to revisit time like space, *refusing to surrender to the irreversibility of time that plagues the human condition*" (1988:236, emphasis added). Thus, nostalgia is another form of perfectibility, in this case, temporal perfectibility. Like other Pueblo practices of refinement, past practices, including speaking Keiwa, and their related contexts are shown to be very important because Pueblos spend a lot of time talking about them, often nostalgically. Language revitalization movements, like nostalgic discourses, are essentially metapragmatic processes, "interpretive practices" (Stewart 1988:233) that look back lucidly (to borrow Jameson's term) in order to perform social critique and enact change.

Hope, Faith, and Language Revitalization Movements

Although Keiwa authors and speakers display a preference for the use of perfective forms and nostalgic genres, the ethnographic and linguistic examples I have presented also display a focus on imminent events. However, just as nostalgic discourses are not entirely about the past, hopeful discourses are not strictly about the future, and both often occur at times of great social upheaval, simultaneously grounding them in the present. Following Wallace's (1956) model of cultural revitalization movements, anthropologists have long been interested in "examples of rapid, intentional attempts to restructure culture and society, documented in classic studies of nativistic movements, millen[n]ialism, messianic sects, apocalyp[t]icism, 'Cargo Cults,' and utopian communities" (Liebmann 2008:360). Considering language revitalization movements as a previously unexplored corner of this continuum connects the work on hope and faith with a literature that heretofore has largely concentrated on raising awareness and designing language programs.[1] Like cargo cults or the Ghost Dance, attempts to promote the use of indigenous languages are often seen by practitioners as "successful" despite the lack of quantifiable results or the predictions about language "death" made by academics and media figures.

Language revitalization efforts share many traits of cultural revitalization movements, nicely summarized by Liebmann (2008), including a focus on purism (seen at San Ramón in the practice of removing loanwords from the dictionary); revivalism and innovation surrounding cultural practices (the attempt to reintroduce previous practices and technologies while also introducing Keiwa literacy); and the centrality of objects in both reflecting and constituting such programs (the way that written materials have been perfected and controlled like other valued cultural objects). Although a complete survey of the notion of hope in the philosophical and anthropological literature is outside the scope of this book, this topic highlights issues not often associated with language phenomena, illustrating the hopeful nature of San Ramón literacy and language revitalization.

Vincent Crapanzano's 2003 essay "Reflections on Hope as a Category of Social and Psychological Analysis" outlines the history of examining the idea of hope and the way hope differs from other affective and political stances, including desire and utopianism. Drawing on a substantial number of examples in theology, philosophy, and anthropology, Crapanzano looks at hope from the following perspectives: understandings in Christian theology; phenomenological descriptions and critiques (using Whorf as an example); its social determinants; its communicative etiquette (citing work with cancer patients and apartheid era South Africans); and its role, along with desire, in cargo cults (2003:5–25). One of his stated goals is to augment the relatively few studies that take hope seriously "as a category of both experience and analysis" (4).

One contribution of his survey is to highlight the notions of agency and action in examples of hopeful social projects. Crapanzano discusses how hope has often been seen as passive, a stance consisting only of waiting for a desired, yet unlikely, outcome. He shows, however, that action is inextricably built into hopeful projects: "Both hope and desire have to be understood as precipitates of interaction or interlocution" (Crapanzano 2003:6). He acknowledges that hope, like nostalgia, can lead to paralysis or lack of action, as exemplified by white South Africans waiting for some kind of social change during apartheid. But hope also requires a different understanding of agency: "Hope depends on some other agency—a god, fate, chance, an other—for its fulfillment. Its evaluation rests on the characterization—the moral characterization—of that agency" (6). As with nostalgia, there is a moral component in such hopeful, agentive waiting, as well as "enormous political and economic potential" (8) in such processes.

The relationship between hope and agency is also tackled by Hirokazu Miyazaki in *The Method of Hope* (2006) and a related essay (2000). Miyazaki helps to further an understanding of hope and faith by comparing "a range of rituals performed by Fijian Christians" (2000:32), including gift exchanges, forms of Christian worship, and petitions to the Indonesian government for land. All of these activities are essentially hopeful, involving outcomes that are unlikely to match stated goals or that require a large amount of trust between groups and individuals for their success. Miyazaki has developed what he calls a "method of hope" (2006), a model that explains both the contours of hope and the ways it is replicated by social actors.

Miyazaki's contribution to understanding the relationship between hope and action centers on what he calls "the abeyance of agency." Describing this concept vis-à-vis gift exchange, he says, "Fijian gift giving…entails a moment in which gift givers place their own agency in abeyance and the subsequent moment in which gift receivers recuperate their gift givers' agency" (Miyazaki 2000:39). In order to reduce the risk of an unsuccessful gift exchange, participants put their agency on hold at certain points during the ritual, distancing themselves from their own ability to affect the outcome. This also comes into play when people wait for replies from government agents and in other hopeful projects that he analyzes.

Both of these understandings of agency help to explain the complexity inherent in the language revitalization efforts at San Ramón Pueblo and elsewhere. The moral imperative of reintroducing Keiwa at the pueblo is emphasized in discussions about language learning, connecting the drive to learn the language with being an American Indian, a good citizen, and a community member. The agency involved in participating in or advocating for language learning is intimately connected to local moral standards, is constitutive of being a good person, and serves as a means of discussing others' relative (im)morality. This moral agency is seen in *The Bowl Story* and in numerous dictionary entries, including the following sentences, which are discussed earlier as examples 2.31 and 2.33:

(5.1)   *If you can't speak Indian, at least try.*

(5.2)   *Always speak in Indian. I will try.*

The imagined language learner here is directly instructed to try to speak Keiwa, and these sentences appear alongside sentences that encourage learners to go to church, to help with community projects, and to be generous.

Some community members do seem to be hopefully waiting for changes to come to the pueblo and for more people to begin speaking the language, but many actively engage in the project by teaching, by studying, or simply by talking about Native language. To reach the hoped-for outcome, however, will take the combined efforts of numerous individuals at San Ramón and perhaps at other Keiwa-speaking pueblos. The enormity of the task necessitates individual and collective actors placing their agency as language teachers and learners in abeyance, tacitly acknowledging their lack of control over the direction the entire community is taking. However, because the future of the language and the pueblo is of such great importance, the chance that Keiwa will be lost or that greed will continue are possibilities too terrible for people *not* to hope for the antidotes of increased fluency and community harmony.

In another correlation with nostalgic discourses, understanding the relationship between language revitalization and hope also involves describing how temporality is characterized and utilized as part of hopeful social projects. Crapanzano describes the temporal zone of hope as being located in the "mediate future," which "lies between the zone of the immediate future, characterized by expectation and activity, and the zone of the remote future, characterized by prayer and ethical action" (2003:9). Expanding on this liminal temporality, he discusses how hope necessarily calls into effect a time that will never be: "Hope, particularly in its abstract form, always invokes an ever further horizon—a beyond of a mysterious, transcending (if not transcendental) nature. We may call it divine, but despite our yearning, we can never really know it" (10). This mirrors Moore's (2006) characterization of the sublime, the lost landscape of pre-contact languages and peoples, which is chased by indigenous language writing through a memorializing orientation toward indigenous language texts.

Miyazaki describes a similar view of time, using the examples of petitions and rituals. He characterizes hope as existing in "a delicate balance between future-oriented openness [and] anticipation of the moment at which their self-knowledge would be finally proven and closed" (Miyazaki 2006:82). At San Ramón Pueblo, actors' agencies must be placed in abeyance in order for hope to be achieved and replicated, but to do this, time itself must be displaced as well. To hope for increased Keiwa fluency is to skirt the current state of language use in the community and the difficulty of increasing the number of speakers. In a sense, this is the inverse of utilizing Hill's (2002) discourse of enumeration in that it avoids the invocation of shrinking numbers of speakers, rates of transmission, and so forth. Displacing the object of hope also downplays the hard work of learning a language (occurring in the here and now or in the immediate future) by focusing on the mediate future—a time when all the hard work will have resulted in more speakers of San Ramón Keiwa— and the accompanying context in which such a change is possible.

Temporality also figures in Miyazaki's depiction of how hope re-creates itself and how hopefulness becomes an ongoing stance: "In other words, hope was replicated from one moment to the next. And this replication was mediated by the recurring impulse to reintroduce a retrospective perspective to the present. From this perspective, we can understand that the method of hope consists in replicating the (immediate or distant) past" (2006:128). In addition to describing the constant temporal work that must be done to produce hope, this echoes Crapanzano's point that hope is necessarily interactional, taking place within and across encounters between social actors and groups. This interactional dimension of hope, combined with the idea of radical temporal rupture, also places the hopeful project of language revitalization in dialogue with work on religious conversion in the anthropology of Christianity (Cannell 2006; Handman 2010; Hanks 2010; Harding 1987; Robbins 2004, 2007).

In "Continuity Thinking and the Problem of Christian Culture" (2007), Joel Robbins details the problems for anthropological theory that result from privileging views of culture that emphasize continuity over abrupt change. Looking at religious conversion among Papuans, he examines "before-and-after" (11) events that irrevocably shift the focus of an individual's life or a community's history, identifying "similarities between the rupturing of temporal continuity in conversion and in millennial imaginings" (12). One reason for this likeness that he identifies is an analogous conception of time: "Something does not just happen in time but rather happens to it. One temporal progression is halted or shattered and another is joined. It is this kind of thinking about the possibility of temporal rupture that allows people to make claims for the absolute newness of the lives they lead after conversion and of the ones they hope they will lead in the millennial future" (12). As evidenced by nostalgic discourses at San Ramón, this is precisely the kind of temporal shift that language revitalization movements aim to facilitate. Courtney Handman points this out in her study of conversion: "People are engaged in projects of modeling transformation for themselves" (2010:576). Producing indigenous language texts and reintroducing spoken Keiwa are "central ritual enactments of models of change" (577), like the sermons Handman analyzes that draw distinctions between the community in the present and preconversion. Rewriting Keiwa example sentences is an example of one such enactment, as people work together to perfect entries that will hopefully bring about changes from English to Keiwa, from diluted to pure, from profane to sacred, and from splintered to whole.

Concerning such enactments as part of cultural revitalization movements, both Crapanzano and Miyazaki assert that hope is essentially performative, involving ritually enacted stances that mirror or make possible the realization of hoped-for outcomes. As Miyazaki explains, "the method of hope, in other words, is a performative inheritance of hope" (2006:128). This involves the creation of new contexts, spaces where it becomes possible, for example, for avenging ancestors to reappear, for airplanes and appliances to be provided, or for Keiwa to be spoken again at the pueblo. Thus, the stated outcomes necessarily involve even more than, in these cases, the reversal of death, material goods, or improved linguistic ability. Crapanzano says, "The objects of hope and desire are always more than themselves. They are multi-meaning symbols that have, in linguistic terms, enormous pragmatic force. They evoke a world, a society, a moral order, a psychology" (2003:19). He describes how those hoping for cargo were really hoping for "a new moral, social, and cultural order in which these objects figure" (20). This is similar to the San Ramón authors' assertions that fluency in Keiwa would necessarily lead to a community in which people help one another, are not greedy, and essentially inhabit an imagined pre-contact context. Widespread Keiwa fluency, it is thought, would create a community in which the correct "moral, social, and cultural order" could exist and readers/listeners could "live life the way it's supposed to be lived." Similarly, objects that are hoped for—such as a perfectly constructed dictionary—can be imagined as having a place in a community able to produce such a work and use it properly: limiting access to the Keiwa language and the cultural knowledge contained in the text and knowing enough about "being Indian" to correctly decode the veiled knowledge within.

Several aesthetic aspects of hope's performative, ritualistic character are especially salient when considering language revitalization projects: the iterative, repetitive nature of such projects; the adherence to generic rules as part of enacting hope; and the indeterminacy such rituals produce. In the examples Crapanzano and Miyazaki describe, participants in hopeful projects engage in processual, ongoing acts in the service of producing and replicating hope. The production and maintenance of hope require exacting, enduring action. In one example, Miyazaki describes how Fijians repeatedly petitioned the government for redress for land they lost, making numerous trips to the capital and taking great care in how they invoked in written and oral texts their ancestors' claims to the land. He argues that the hoped-for outcome was not simply recognition or gain but involved meeting the aesthetic criteria, again and again if necessary. He summarizes this process: "Getting the promised money depended on finding the correct manner by which to convey their grievances to the government. The promised money would be an effect of and response to the correct manner of presentation" (Miyazaki 2006:32). This adherence to the generic rules involved with presentation also occurs in Fijian gift-giving ceremonies, in which participants index an "aesthetics of completion" (Miyazaki 2000). The care that the dictionary's authors take in fashioning and refashioning example sentences or that John took in editing *The Bowl Story* is evidence of continuous processes that reflect favored generic features in their content and creation. Like practices of perfectibility, the emphasis in hopeful ritual acts is on the process rather than on a desired end point.

As part of Miyazaki's analysis, he cites Locke's definition of hope, which, along with deemphasizing agency, using repetition, and sticking to generic conventions, includes "indeterminacy as a condition of the possibility for hope" (2006:27). The transmission of linguistic knowledge shares many similarities with gift exchange, specifically, the management of risk through the creation of indeterminacy. In the San Ramón case and in other contexts where heritage language use is declining, the same kinds of risk exist concerning uptake by language learners and gift receivers. If learners are unable to devote enough time to practicing Keiwa, or if they cannot maintain their language ability by talking to other speakers, or if they do not have the fluency to speak the language with their children, the risk of English monolingualism always looms. As a result, learners and speakers rely on "multiple devices for creating the effect of indeterminacy" (84), including never commenting on the likelihood of eventual Keiwa reinstatement, spending time discussing preferred approaches to teaching and learning Keiwa as opposed to practicing the language, and commenting on other tribes' experiences with language loss and revitalization. Such practices displace the difficult task of promoting the use of Keiwa to the future and avoid some dimensions of the current context.

Finally, looking at the literature on hope also contributes to an understanding of why language revitalization has been portrayed in certain ways, both inside and outside the academy. Specifically, the relative focus on documenting referential aspects of languages, emphasizing the utility of "saving" indigenous languages, and relying on "experts" to speak for heritage learners resembles corollary discourses among theorists of faith and hope.[2] Crapanzano summarizes this proclivity: "Anthropologists have tended to focus on their concrete object and the instrumentality that arises from such a focus rather than on the metaphysics that prayer and magic presuppose, the horizon they postulate, and the mystery they call forth" (2003:23). According to his analysis, students of hope and faith have repeatedly explained supposedly irrational practices by highlighting material gain, community cohesion, or social function, echoing the discourses of hyperbolic valorization and enumeration (Hill 2002) through the idea that saving examples of linguistic diversity at the level of grammar or phonology is the best way to *measure* the social work performed or imagined by language revitalization program participants. This also shows the relative inability of granting agencies, academic institutions, and journalists to take seriously the need for language programs for community members, outside of simple instrumentality. "Their (primitive) response is 'emotional' rather than 'intellectual'" (2003:23), Crapanzano says of anthropological inquiries, which is similar to how some people view language activists when the latter try to explain the centrality of language revitalization efforts across Indian Country.

Conclusion

> We're losing our Indianness.
> No—that isn't happening.
> Yes.
>
> *—San Ramón adult curriculum*

This small Keiwa-English dialogue is the final part of the short introduction to the San Ramón adult curriculum. The authors "discuss some of the possible reasons behind obstacles to language learning, the history of Native language use in the United States, and ways to move beyond potential obstacles and historical patterns to promote language learning at San Ramón Pueblo" (San Ramón Language Committee 2007:3). Immediately before the dialogue, the curriculum authors state, "So, learning San Ramón Keiwa is both an educational and emotional process, because the language is an important part of the culture. Remember that revitalizing the language is possible if the community works together to move forward and support each other in learning the language" (5).

This short selection from a pedagogical volume encapsulates the discussion of language revitalization movements in this chapter. What is at stake here—the loss of Indianness itself—can be reversed if the entire community works to learn the Keiwa language. The potential obstacles to achieving this goal in the present, such as fear of making mistakes, shame, and lack of extracommunity support for Native languages, are recognized, but these are refuted in the final line. This refutation of loss, in the form of learning Keiwa ("Yes") is something that must be done continually, utilizing examples from the past to create radical transformation in the future. Thus, the invocation of the past as part of this and other language revitalization programs constitutes another example of perfectibility. Just as the Fijians whom Miyazaki describes continually petitioned the state about their land grievances, focusing on the form of their supplications and disregarding their past failures in order to win their case, radical temporal discontinuity and a new/old instantiation of the San Ramón community rely on repetition in the hopeful project that is the production of indigenous written materials.

s i x
As the Rez Turns

Propriety and Covert Political Action

> VIVIAN: Do you know my cousin? This is Skylar—she came home from school.
> She came to check out the rez for the summer.
>
> AUNT AND UNCLE: Oh that's good. When was the last time you were home?
>
> SKYLAR: I haven't been here since I was seven. So it's been about eleven years.
> It sure has changed.
>
> —*As the Rez Turns*

Like Skylar, a character in the soap opera *As the Rez Turns*, community members at San Ramón Pueblo often discuss the numerous changes that have occurred at the reservation during the past twenty years. In the "first Indian soap opera," written by students in the summer Keiwa language class, Skylar's vision of the rez is, of course, fictional; her commentary, however, seems accurate—at times, hilarious—to the young adults at San Ramón Pueblo who created her. In the tribal library, in the community Head Start building, and at feasts and parties, people talk about how incredibly different life was "before [they] had a casino" or "back when [they] all had to go to Indian school in Santa Fe." Community members identify many of these changes as positive, such as the greater number of people returning to the pueblo to live and work, the new educational opportunities that are available to tribal members, and their increased religious, cultural, and political autonomy. However, other evaluations of the past, such as those I describe in chapter 5, trigger a nostalgic look back to a time free of the contemporary kinds of conflict that have arisen at the pueblo: when "people weren't as greedy" or "no one argued over who was or wasn't San Ramón—you just knew."

As I have noted, discussions about what to write in Keiwa, who can write it, and how written materials should be circulated or controlled intersect with discussions about relative progress in the community. Some tribal members see literacy as a way to help retrieve some of the routines they think disappeared with the advent of the casino and greater self-determination. Others view certain writing practices as potentially harmful, hastening what they see as movement away from Pueblo values. New written materials, like *The Bowl Story* and the dictionary, often accomplish social work outside strictly pedagogical or archival pursuits, conveying much more than the grammatical regularities of the Keiwa language and instead focusing on the lived experience of people at San Ramón and the desired moral aspects of being Pueblo. Additionally, as I have shown, indigenous language texts serve as new forums for the discussion and critique of social and political issues.

As the Rez Turns was produced over two subsequent summers by the members of the San Ramón Pueblo young adult language program. Similar to the popular cultural forms that Philip Deloria describes in *Indians in Unexpected Places* (2004), this series of dialogues is an example of how Native Americans' active engagement with popular cultural forms—here, soap operas—is often perceived as anomalous, challenging extracommunity stereotypes of Native people. Deloria's concepts of "expectation" and "anomaly" can be applied to the present case to examine not only the extracommunity stereotypes that figure in the production of a community soap opera but also intracommunity hopes, since the text is designed for a San Ramón audience. Local expectations concerning how new texts should adhere to Pueblo language ideologies and which registers and genres should be represented in written materials created as part of the Keiwa language program also shaped the creation of this text, which at once adheres to and defies local assumptions. Deloria's analytic is a useful complement to Briggs and Bauman's (1992) analysis of intertextuality, which describes the ways that generic expectations can be variously exploited across occasions of use to either produce or diminish "intertextual gaps" to accomplish various goals. Both the entextualization processes and content of *As the Rez Turns* contain expected ways of using language that align this text with Pueblo and non-Pueblo models of interaction and personhood, and also with anomalous moves that emphasize the distance between local or nonlocal ways of speaking and aspects of the soap opera.

By challenging local expectations of how nonfluent speakers should approach indigenous language literacy, the authors of *As the Rez Turns* effectively assert the right to create cultural materials and use the Keiwa language in new ways, positioning themselves as creators, not just consumers, of indigenous language texts while deviating from a prototypical nostalgic focus by writing a contemporary story. Simultaneously, the authors of this series of dialogues crafted another, indirect challenge: this supposedly pedagogical piece emerges as a sharp critique of current events at San Ramón Pueblo, recalling Basso's (1996) analysis of the Western Apache use of stories and place names to mold indirect commentaries on local matters. The authors of *As the Rez Turns*, through their deployment of multiple stylistic and generic devices, have created a fictional space where they are able to comment to other community members and to one another regarding sensitive political and social issues at the pueblo, similar to the discursive moves employed by the dictionary authors and by John in

The Bowl Story. This text is an example of a Bakhtinian "complex" genre (Bakhtin 1986) in that its authors establish multiple connections to many types of texts, voice many kinds of subjectivities, and simultaneously address several local audiences, not least of which is the student authors themselves.

Including veiled critiques in a pedagogical text may seem unexpected in that it is potentially quite risky. However, such moves reflect Pueblo forms of political discourse and interaction that privilege avoidance and indirectness, providing another example of Pueblo propriety. Like *The Bowl Story* and other Keiwa texts, *As the Rez Turns* is an example of how ideologies are reinscribed in indigenous literacy practices. In this chapter, I examine the creation and content of *As the Rez Turns* in order to outline the interplay between anomaly and expectation both inside and outside San Ramón Pueblo, showing how a simple classroom exercise can accomplish myriad unforeseen forms of social work.

Entextualization and Voicing

After the "completion" of the dictionary and the adult curriculum, members of the San Ramón language program turned their attention to language instruction. The young adult summer classes were started in 2007 to coincide with the annual recreation program for elementary and middle school students. With state money earmarked for indigenous language education, students in the program were paid not only to attend Keiwa classes but also to lead language-learning activities with younger tribal members. Participants in the summer programs were seven to nine high school and college students (the number varied across summers), John, Michelle, a small rotating group of Keiwa speakers from San Ramón and one neighboring pueblo, and I. Aside from John, who is fluent and literate in Keiwa, the participants varied in their spoken and written Keiwa abilities. During the eight-week program, we would meet every weekday from nine until two in the tribal library. Each day, the young adult class would begin with a lesson on a phonological or grammatical aspect of Keiwa, followed by in-class exercises designed to practice verb conjugation, pronoun use, or pronunciation. Then, each student spent time with a fluent speaker or in pairs, practicing spoken Keiwa and language comprehension. These activities were interspersed with cultural events, such as attending ceremonial dances at other pueblos or traveling to the mountains to learn Keiwa words for local geographic sites, often in concert with the summer recreation program. Each day, the older students would lead language-based games with the younger summer program participants, including Keiwa versions of Red Rover, Twister, and bingo. To my surprise, the most popular activity started with a simple class assignment.

The creation of *As the Rez Turns* began when I asked the students and Michelle to write dialogues in English and then work with John and other fluent speakers to translate and transcribe the dialogues into Keiwa. This assignment was designed to practice translation, transcription, and conversation and to augment the growing collection of recorded and written Keiwa pedagogical materials. The students had the option to work alone or in groups. When one of the class members said that she wanted to work on a soap opera about "how it is around here," the other students immediately signed on to work on the project as a class. They started during one summer by establishing the plot and major characters and, when they returned the following summer, began work immediately on the project.

Although John and I contributed to *As the Rez Turns* as a translator and a scribe, respectively, we also completed our own versions of this class assignment. Predictably, the series of dialogues I created in English and then worked with John to translate into Keiwa closely resembled the pedagogical dialogues used in foreign language classes in the United States. Consisting of ordered exchanges between pairs of interlocutors, my contributions highlighted specific grammatical and phonological aspects of Keiwa that I wanted the students to practice, including person-marking strategies, verb conjugation, and contrasts between nasal and non-nasal vowels. John's dialogues, written in Keiwa and then translated into English, focused on the past and on cultural practices he felt most people had abandoned. This assignment was the source of *The Bowl Story* (chapter 4). The students' efforts resulted in the six dialogues that constitute *As the Rez Turns*. Thus, the three responses varied greatly in their goals, content, and generic and stylistic forms, despite the fact that they resulted from the same class assignment.

The final version of *As the Rez Turns* chronicles a classic love triangle between the characters Vivian, Chance, and Skylar, who are brought together at San Ramón Pueblo's annual ceremonial feast day. Melodrama ensues when it is revealed that Chance's secret college girlfriend, Skylar, is also a tribal member and a cousin of Vivian, his local romantic interest. Ki'i Moonlight, another central role, was designed for Michelle, who wanted her character to be "a wise old *ki'i* [pseudonym for grandmother] who still likes to party." Additional characters are other community members or people from other pueblos, with each role designed especially for one of the class members. Neither John nor I was assigned a speaking part, although the students intermittently discussed casting me as an extra, playing "the white friend" or "the person working at the casino." The narrative unfolds over six scenes that take place on or near San Ramón Pueblo: near the river after the feast, a party at the casino, a football game, a concert at the tribal venue, a meal at a local diner, and two private homes at the pueblo. Throughout the dialogues, the authors utilize aspects of numerous speech genres and registers, ranging from speech forms associated with American and Mexican soap operas to local patterns of interaction.

Much of the social work accomplished and imagined by the authors of *As the Rez Turns* took place in the group negotiations surrounding its creation, recalling Peterson's observation that Navajo filmmakers "often have a heightened awareness of representational practices and their implications" (2011:113), which elevates the importance of crafting the text for its authors. After a long day of wrestling with the complex pronominal system or practicing ejective consonants, working as a group on the soap opera dialogues became a time for the students to relax, be creative, and have fun without worrying about comprehension or saying something incorrectly. Students took turns as scribes at the board and mapped out the web of intrigue woven by Skylar, Vivian, and Chance. Patrons of the tribal library, where the language classes were located, often stopped by to see what the racket was all about, and the students would excitedly tell visitors about the "Keiwa soap opera" that they hoped to perform "in Indian" very soon for members of the community.

Most of these work sessions were devoted to humor. Students used their newly acquired Keiwa skills to construct puns and off-color remarks, to make up slang words, and to create neologisms. The soap became a tool for building solidarity and establishing in-group boundaries, resembling a genre of Pueblo clowning that uses wordplay to parody human behavior (Justin Richland, personal communication 2013). Its authors would tempt their peers and younger siblings, saying, "Maybe we could find a small part for you," and shrouded the enterprise in secrecy and import. The processes of entextualization surrounding the creation of *As the Rez Turns*, as well as the finished text itself, are emblematic of the co-constructed nature of the work, another example of processes of perfectibility pointing to highly valued activities at San Ramón Pueblo.

While the students debated plot devices and hashed out the details of each setting for the film version of the soap opera, they further refined aspects of the characters, many of whom came to closely resemble their intended animators. One student, Jordan, a classic rock fan, designed a party scene in which his character acted as the DJ; he even made a list of songs he was going to play. The fictional people in *As the Rez Turns* attend colleges with basketball teams that particular students admire; Michelle insisted that the character of Ki'i Moonlight not be portrayed as "too old and lame"; and the student playing Chance, the notorious cheater, repeatedly assured the class, "I would never act like this!" for fear he would be associated with his character's evil ways. Throughout the project, its authors engaged in processes of identification, alternately distancing themselves from or aligning themselves with their respective dramatic roles.

Also during these group conversations, students would directly challenge existing extracommunity stereotypes by mocking characteristics that non-Pueblo people might expect of characters in *As the Rez Turns*. For instance, in a discussion about the name for one of the minor characters, one of the students, Scott, said jokingly, "Well, why don't we just call him Buffalo Thunder!" and the class exploded in laughter in response to what they perceived as a stereotypical, unrealistic example of a local name. When discussing the music choices for certain scenes, one of the students rolled her eyes and exclaimed, "Anything but that awful flute music they always play," with "they" being the proprietors of restaurants and stores catering to tourists in New Mexico. Similarly, the students joked that characters in the soap opera could wear T-shirts with images of Kokopelli, the iconic Pueblo flute player,[1] since it was, after all, "a Native soap opera," their comments dripping with irony. While writing the dialogues, students frequently highlighted such "cheesy" uses of Native imagery in gaming and tourist projects, using them both as jokes and as critiques of those who employ stereotypical "Native" symbols.

Unlike many of the vignettes included in Deloria's analysis, San Ramón community members' critiques involving the (mis)use of indigenous languages or imagery are often directed at other area tribes and not at non-indigenous people. Scott's quip about Buffalo Thunder illustrates this point. This name is at once presented as an example of an overblown, non-indigenous, Hollywood-style term and as a subtle critique of a neighboring tribe, which named its casino Buffalo Thunder. Here, Scott is making fun of a laterally opposed group for capitalizing on outsider ideas about appropriate names for American Indian things. This is an interesting kind of identity management; a comment about "cheesiness" embodies a complex critique of otherness, distancing the authors of the text from both non-indigenous and Pueblo individuals. Crucially, this kind of identity work is not just about "Indian" versus "non-Indian" identity. Instead, it is about utilizing certain postures and calling out individuals who are not from San Ramón Pueblo in order to frame multiple kinds of belonging between and among American Indian groups, mirroring Basso's description of the complexity in insider-outsider relationships in *Portraits of the "Whiteman"* (1979). Invoking the possibility of a character named Buffalo Thunder calls to mind imagined, absent individuals, both Native and non-Native, who might expect or utilize such a name and compares them with those who would find such a name anomalous. Thus, the contrast between the cheesy Native imagery used in advertising and the complex identities of the students writing *As the Rez Turns* serves as a challenge to stereotypes and also to outsider depictions of Indian Country as homogeneous or the supposed uniformity of the Pueblo Southwest.

In addition to Deloria's framework, cheesiness can be theorized by looking at linguistic anthropological works on identification. During the processes of entextualization that yielded *As the Rez Turns*, its authors utilized both "authenticating" and "denaturalizing" discourses, opposing the "tactics of intersubjectivity" that Bucholtz and Hall (2004) identify among other dyadic semiotic processes used by interlocutors to index various stances and to constitute identities. Scott's denaturalizing move, which portrays those who employ exaggerated Native imagery as inauthentic, also recalls Hastings and Mannings' analysis of identity, the construction of which, they argue, relies as much on differentiation as it does on identification:

> These voices attributed to others—"anti-registers"—create monstrous or deviant figures of alterity, with respect to which the (normal) identity of the speaker emerges as a sort of unmarked ground to the figure of abnormal alterity. Where registers involve the asymptotic imitation, adoption, or appropriation of a figural voice, mockeries and say-fors involve sharp demarcations between one's own voice and the voice imitated: in the typical case, a stance of alterity is constructed between the interactants and some other(s), who may be present but are usually not. (Hastings and Manning 2004:304)

With the Buffalo Thunder quip, Scott distinguishes himself and the other authors from users of a cheesy "anti-register," casting recognizably indigenous but non–community members as "figures of alterity."

San Ramón Literacy: Challenging Expectations

In the San Ramón community, Deloria's framework of expectation and anomaly is also applicable, outlining the contrasts between ideologies regarding the appropriate use of indigenous language and anomalous aspects of *As the Rez Turns*. Simply by engaging in the project, the student authors assert their right to create cultural materials that will be used in the future with other Keiwa language classes, challenging the expectation that the purpose of the class is for students to receive, rather than create, indigenous language texts. In *As the Rez Turns*, the authors index different attitudes regarding the state of the community and challenge local language ideologies that privilege the primacy of the Keiwa language and foreground language purism. Additionally, the students display attitudes regarding the uses of humor and indigenous language that diverge from established uses of Keiwa, shedding light on the ideological relationship between levels of fluency and language appropriateness at San Ramón Pueblo.

Unlike John and other middle-aged and elderly community members, the authors of *As the Rez Turns* (with the occasional exception of Michelle) do not express nostalgia for a time before the tribe had a casino. The characters in the soap opera discuss tribal ventures and casino wealth freely, a trait not shared by the tribal members at San Ramón Pueblo who draw a sharp distinction between "before" and "after" this development and do not dwell on the economic benefits of gaming operations in everyday conversation. This is apparent in the introduction to scene 2, which takes place at an after-feast party in the casino:

> [*People are seated all around, eating and visiting. A DJ is playing music. Some people are dancing. Vivian and Skylar are talking at a table and an older couple stops by to say hi to Vivian.*]
>
> SKYLAR: Okay. Man, it's so cool you got me a room here! I think I'm gonna roll up there and check out the huge tub! I have to roll because I'm stuffed with crab legs. I can't believe the tribe paid for all this.
>
> VIVIAN: Okay, I'm gonna check out the scene. There's always all kinds of action for these tribal things. Yeah! Hey Skylar—
>
> SKYLAR: Yeah?
>
> VIVIAN: No parties and no diving either!

Exchanges like this, which depict affluence and economic security as uncontroversial aspects of life at the pueblo, appear throughout the dialogues. This challenges the indirect ways that older tribal members usually discuss casino wealth, which is typically presented not only as an organizing temporal framework for talking about the many changes that have taken place in San Ramón society but also as a possible explanation for negative developments. The student authors' neutral treatment of this issue signals an alternative depiction, echoing Jessica Cattelino's (2008, 2010) analyses of changing attitudes regarding value and wealth among the Florida Seminoles and the emergent ways that cultural difference is calibrated in the casino era. While it could appear that such exchanges constitute additional examples of veiled critiques, the fact that the students did not identify them as such while writing the story stands in contrast to the metapragmatic moves that accompanied other covert critiques.

This comfort with discussing casino wealth and the benefits of tribal programs is accompanied by another theme not shared by older tribal members and fluent Keiwa speakers: the ease with which the authors of *As the Rez Turns* deviate from dominant language ideologies that emphasize the importance of maintaining linguistic purism. This is evident when the characters combine secular and ceremonial topics in individual exchanges, as seen below:

> CHANCE: What a beautiful day, huh? I'm so tired. I'll bet your feet really hurt, 'cause you didn't wear shoes all day. I'm so proud of you. Want something cold to drink, babe?
>
> VIVIAN: Oh yeah, a beautiful hot day. Hopefully, our prayers will be answered.

Here, Chance and Vivian discuss the efficacy of ceremonial dances in the same conversation they discuss grabbing a drink. The deviation from linguistic purism is also evident at the level of register; characters use extremely informal language throughout the soap opera, even when discussing ceremonial practice, as seen when Chance addresses Vivian as "babe." Even in the original English version of the text, authors use Keiwa honorifics, kinship terms, and interjections and also use both English and American Indian names, displaying a preference for heterogeneity at the level of code. In an analysis of Navajo code mixing, Margaret Field (2009) finds a similar divergence from ideologies of purism, with younger speakers unproblematically employing English words and constructions even when speaking mostly in Navajo.

John's reaction to the exercise seemed to include concern about some of these uses of the Keiwa language, signaling that this text differed from the others that the students practiced or learned. Whereas the students and Michelle saw *As the Rez Turns* as a site for language play and camaraderie and looked forward to working on the project, John suggested doing other activities before eventually agreeing to translate for the group. Unlike his response to the grammatical lessons I designed or the other cultural activities the class engaged in, he chose not to sit in on these sessions and would use the time to catch up on other work and answer phone calls, joining the class only when the Keiwa translation was needed. From his adjoining office, he would remark, "You all are having too much fun," or ask, "What will people say when they hear you making all this noise?"

Although it might seem that John's reaction was the result of a generational difference characterized by language ideologies that portray certain subjects as inappropriate for speakers of indigenous languages, this is not strictly the case. He supported the soap opera project and acknowledged the need for exercises to encourage the students to practice pronunciation and transcription, repeatedly asserting, "It's time for them to write stories about what they are interested in." Nor did he object to the informal or racy content of the dialogues. While editing the Keiwa version, John would laugh to himself as he read through the script, and he suggested additional jokes and slang words in Keiwa that could be included, such as the words for "two-timer" and "skirt-chaser." At San Ramón Pueblo, the expectation of seriousness is not predicated on membership in a particular age cohort and does not center on the relative salaciousness of the content but depends on levels of Keiwa fluency. For John, joking *in* Keiwa is a comfortable activity, but joking about it or with it by those who do not fully embody the language is not. This appears to be a generational difference only because all fluent speakers of San Ramón Keiwa are late middle-aged or elderly. Creating a text outside these and other conventions allowed the students to assert their right to create their own linguistic materials and to use the Keiwa language in unexpected ways, like Deloria's subjects, problematizing notions of authenticity and modernity.

Intertextuality, Identification, and Simultaneity

In addition to challenging both extra- and intracommunity expectations regarding indigenous language use and depictions of indigeneity, *As the Rez Turns* is populated by characters who utilize multiple generic resources and numerous approaches to indexing identities. Many of the speech genres that the authors use are recognizable Pueblo speech genres or invoke place in a specifically local way, whereas others indicate extracommunity genres and locales. Some traits of the principal characters are embodied by the students in the class, who share their tastes, American Indian names, or ways of speaking; others are patently foreign. As several scholars have pointed out (Fox 2004; Keeler 2009; Samuels 2004), the job of the anthropologist is not to untangle what is local or authentic practice from what is foreign or borrowed but instead to describe the various practices of identification and how cultural forms indexical of various identity traits are produced and circulated. Like the San Carlos Apaches David Samuels describes, who engage in punning and other ambiguous practices in their language and expressive culture, the authors of *As the Rez Turns* "make full use of the indexical ambiguity, the simultaneity of the pointing gestures, at the heart of contemporary cultural identities on the reservation" (2004:8). Similar to the stereotypically Native and non-Native processes of identity formation that he describes among San Carlos musicians and community members, the soap opera exhibits the multiple resources available for the construction of San Ramón subjectivities, many of which refer to Anglo, Hispanic, and Pueblo practices. Simultaneously, the soap opera's authors distance themselves from the story by including personas, stances, places, and tastes that index extralocal identities.

Throughout the dialogues, characters anchor the text as a specifically San Ramón story by invoking local places and history. Characters either overtly reference local sites, such as Bailey's Diner (the setting for scene 4), or leave out information that would be necessary for a nonlocal audience to understand the dialogue, for example, using place names such as "the Clear" or "the Lakes," locations that are ambiguous for nonresidents. Specificity of place is also apparent in the focus on lineage and family, a dominant theme in the text. In the scene that follows, Skylar has just met an older couple at the casino party:

SKYLAR: They seem like nice people.

VIVIAN: They are. They were your Mom's favorite Aunt and Uncle. At least that's what my Dad told me. I should take you visiting. That way you can learn who your relatives are. It's important to know your relations, Skylar. I wouldn't want you to hook up with one of your cousins!

SKYLAR: Yeah, it's been so long and my Dad doesn't even know which kids belong to which parents.

VIVIAN: For real. I'll tell you who the cool ones are! Yeah!

Characters emphasize the importance of knowing the intricacies of San Ramón lineage throughout *As the Rez Turns*. In the following excerpt, Vivian and Chance study the pictures of community members, which are displayed in the casino buffet, and Vivian describes her long-lost cousin, Skylar:

VIVIAN: Yeah, she hasn't been here for a long time. You know that big picture of Nana Betty in this hallway? She looks almost the same as her. That's her great grandma.

CHANCE: You mean that one of her in the fancy white dress?

This scene not only is an invocation of San Ramón knowledge but also depicts actual interactions that regularly occur in the community. Every time the members of the language class would eat at the casino buffet, the students and John would point out the old pictures of the pueblo. Together, they would identify each person and explain how they were related to the individuals in the photographs.

The characters' speaking styles are also used to anchor the text locally. Throughout the dialogues, all the characters exhibit a fluent command of the latest San Ramón slang, peppering their exchanges with exclamations of "Ba(h),"[2] calling one another "cuz," and asking incredulously, "For real?" Although I do not represent them here, the characters, as voiced by the authors, also utilize local pitch accents, sociophonetic values that distinguish San Ramón English speakers from residents of other pueblos, as well as from Navajo, white, and Hispanic youth in New Mexico.

The characters in *As the Rez Turns* also emphasize markers of local identities, engaging in authenticating practices that allow them to identify as San Ramón and

Pueblo. In each scene, like this one at the football game at San Ramón's field, the characters discuss tribal affiliation:

VIVIAN: This is my friend, Peppa.

PEPPA: Hey, what's up?

JAMES AND CHANCE: S'up? Where you from?

PEPPA: Oh, I'm ████████████ [*name of pueblo obscured*]

CHANCE: Hey, you from ██████████? Do you know Tiffany?

PEPPA: Oh yeah, that's my cuz.

This is a prototypical introduction at San Ramón Pueblo. Many tribal members have parents from different pueblos, and all community members have extended family from other reservations. Initial interactions such as these identify the main characters as being from San Ramón and locate the secondary characters in relation to such local identities.

As the Rez Turns emphasizes locality most directly in its depiction of actual relationships at San Ramón Pueblo. Before Michelle joined the Keiwa language group, she worked for fifteen years in the tribal recreation program. In this capacity, she helped to design and lead after-school programs and served as a teacher and mentor for numerous children at the pueblo. Intergenerational friendships are not unusual at San Ramón Pueblo, but Michelle remains especially popular and many teenagers and young adults go to her for advice and support. The scenes featuring Ki'i Moonlight depict the types of interaction that Michelle has with younger community members. In the following scene, the character of Ki'i Moonlight is introduced:

VIVIAN: Look! There's Ki'i Moonlight, sitting by herself. Let's take her something to drink.

CHANCE: Hey Ki'i, how are you? Tired from dancing? We brought you something to drink.

KI'I MOONLIGHT: Oh thank you. Yes, I'm tired, but it's a good tired. When I was younger, we would dance all day, go home and change and then dance all night.

CHANCE: Oh Ki'i, I bet you can still go for it! There's Jared. I'm going to say hi. I'll be right back.

After seeing Michelle at a concert that was held at the tribal venue during the summer, the student authors incorporated the event into the soap opera:

CHANCE: Hey, Ki'i! How are you?

KI'I MOONLIGHT: Good. I'm doing good.

VIVIAN: I didn't know you liked Judas Priest.

KI'I MOONLIGHT: Are you kidding? I *love* Judas Priest! Woo! Rock on! Do you wanna stand next to me?

Indexing their particular locality by describing the personal attributes of the soap opera characters, the student authors have created a text with specifically San Ramón qualities. These are designed to be recognized as local, as descriptions of particular people. Any tribal member could read the scenes that feature Ki'i Moonlight and connect her to Michelle or know where Chance and Vivian are going when they "meet at the Lakes."

At the same time, the authors include pointedly nonlocal features throughout *As the Rez Turns*, referencing extracommunity speech genres, locations, and personas. This is most obvious in their choice of the soap opera genre as the organizing framework for the series of dialogues. By asserting that this is the "first Native soap opera," the students identify this genre as one originating outside the pueblo, a form they are borrowing and imbuing with local features. As evidenced by their choice of title, the students looked to American soap operas, but they also discussed Mexican telenovelas, which, as they said, were "really out there" as possible sources of inspiration. Like soaps and telenovelas, *As the Rez Turns* includes cases of mistaken identity, double-crossing, "evil" characters, and melodramatic confrontations. Rather than thinking of the dialogues as disparate texts used only to practice Keiwa, the authors emphasize the importance of the piece as a whole, both highlighting its social importance and aligning it with extralocal forms.

The students also cited pedagogical language dialogues as a generic influence. Every author had taken at least two years of foreign language classes in high school, and in the soap opera, they consciously included the features they had found most helpful as students. The authors admonished one another, "Make sure that one character doesn't get too many speaking parts, because we all have to practice," and, for the most part, penned exchanges between only two interlocutors. Although they did not aim to design dialogue that would impart particular grammatical or phonological lessons, they repeatedly invoked the opinion that this exercise was important in order to practice their Keiwa and recognized that the texts would be used for this purpose by future language students. Although their approach to constructing teaching materials is indicative of the students' participation in the US education system, it references an additional language ideology at San Ramón Pueblo: the emphasis on the utility of language. Across generations, contexts, and linguistic codes, community members emphasize the "perlocutionary effects" of language use rather than its grammatical or referential attributes (Austin 1962). This can be seen in the circulation of *The Bowl Story*, discussions of the efficacy of carefully crafted example sentences, and the preference for using the modal enclitic meaning "in order to" or "because." Again and again, the reasons for engaging in practices felt to be central to a San Ramón subjectivity, especially speaking Keiwa, are explicitly highlighted in written and spoken texts.

At many points in *As the Rez Turns*, the invocation of local and nonlocal speech genres and registers occurs almost simultaneously. For example, the students insisted that each of the main characters be given an "Indian name" and an "English name," which mirrors the situation of most individuals at the pueblo. After intense discussion, the students chose the names Vivian, Chance, Skylar, and Peppa for the main characters. The students viewed the names either as hyper-Anglo (in the case of the first three choices) or as associated with hip-hop culture (in Peppa's case). One of the students said about Chance's name, "Like anyone around here would *ever* be named something like *that*!" The class roared when he emphasized this instance of indexing otherness through the invocation of particular types of outsiders, the humor lying in the immense distance between local identities and cheesy, over-the-top, soap-worthy names. Like the Buffalo Thunder joke Scott made, complex voicing strategies were used to create characters born out of non-Native visions of indigeneity.

After choosing the English names, the students selected Keiwa names in close consultation with John. The name they chose for Vivian was one that John said had not been used for years, and Chance's name was the American Indian name of one student's favorite uncle. After lengthy discussions with John, the students chose a name for Skylar that employed a Keiwa word for "sky," although John laughingly admitted that "it didn't really sound like a name." The name for Michelle's character is also local and nonlocal, combining the Keiwa word for grandmother (ki'i, a pseudonym) with a dramatic moniker, Moonlight, that the students thought sounded appropriately soapy.

The simultaneous indexing of locality and otherness also occurred in the construction of the personas of characters in *As the Rez Turns*. Whereas some characters exhibit qualities that the authors closely associate with their future animators, as in the case of Ki'i Moonlight, others have personality traits that are consciously opposed to those of their animators, preventing the audience from fully aligning the characters with the students inhabiting the roles. Christine was one of the quieter students in the class, a quality almost always shared by Peppa, the role she plays in the soap opera. However, the stage directions in the scene set at the football game describe Peppa scanning the crowd, looking for a fight, an ironic joke embedded in the larger work. By the end of the summer, the students would pretend to quake with fear when Christine entered the classroom, shouting, "Watch out! Peppa gonna brawl!" Like the use of both American Indian and hyper-white names, the simultaneity of indexing localness and otherness contributes to the authors' ability to include political and social commentaries in *As the Rez Turns*. Here, metapragmatic regimentation produces multiple "orders of indexicality" (Silverstein 2003) that allow for oppositional, sometimes ironic, meanings.

Liminality and Indirect Political Discourse

Meeting local thematic, generic, and stylistic expectations and exemplifying distinctly San Ramón stances and subjectivities while referencing and critiquing genres, styles, and vocabularies associated with non-Pueblo popular cultural forms partially obscures the pointed social commentary, which would otherwise be impossible, embedded in *As the Rez Turns*. The myriad interdiscursive and intertextual links between this work and others, including American and Mexican soap operas, local ways of speaking, and the personal histories of community members at San Ramón as embodied by specific characters in the text, create a liminal space similar to Pueblo clowning, in which the authors comment on sociopolitical developments by using complex voicing strategies.

I am not utilizing the concept of liminality to describe a place between stages in an established life cycle cline (Turner 1967), a physical space (De Meis 2002), or a social/sexual category (Besnier 1994, 1997; Hall 2005).[3] Instead, I see it as a discursive space that is neither an exact representation of life at San Ramón Pueblo nor a depiction that is not still fiercely local. The possibilities for critique and protest that exist in discursive spaces not regulated by strict adherence to particular speech genres are often seen in new uses of language—here, indigenous language literacy—that are in the process of being institutionalized and regulated due to their status as in-between states. By inhabiting such a space, the authors of *As the Rez Turns* have crafted a text whose stated use is to practice the Keiwa language and contribute to the growing archive, but it actually functions as a comedy of manners containing pointed political commentary.

One way that the authors critique the current political situation at San Ramón Pueblo is by making veiled prognostications about the state of the community. The ominous warning issued by Aunt and Uncle to Skylar is an example of this tactic, which appears throughout the dialogues:

> SKYLAR: I haven't been here since I was seven. So it's been about eleven years. It sure has changed.
>
> VIVIAN: Gosh, has it been that long?
>
> AUNT AND UNCLE: Yeah, it really has changed. More than you will ever know. Well, we're gonna go see what we do. Take care. [*They go dance.*]
>
> SKYLAR: See you.

When reading this scene aloud, the students playing the parts of Aunt and Uncle darkly intoned "More than you will ever know" in unison while staring pointedly at the student playing Skylar. One time after they finished reading the line, Michelle said, "Yeah, no kidding," which elicited nods from all the students. Though negative depictions of the community were never made explicit in the dialogues, each member of the class knew that what was being criticized was the recent change in tribal membership policy. That Michelle and the other class members were indirectly criticizing tribal membership policy as part of this and other exchanges while writing the soap opera was confirmed by subsequent conversations I had with participants about the project. When discussing the text, the authors certainly comment on the humorous or ironic aspects of the work, but they also never fail to identify it as a critique.

The characters in *As the Rez Turns* do address specific aspects of the membership policy, highlighting the impact that the recent changes have had on particular individuals and families at the pueblo. Since the new membership decisions have been put into place, it has become harder for parents to enroll their children, with the standards for enrollment varying across, and sometimes within, families. The following excerpt from a conversation between Vivian and Ki'i Moonlight addresses this issue:

VIVIAN: Ki'i, are you okay? You look like you were sure thinking hard about something.

KI'I MOONLIGHT: Na. For the most part I'm just tired.

VIVIAN: So what's the other part?

KI'I MOONLIGHT: I was thinking about my grandkids and their situation. It's a pity. I was trying to think what I could do to help make things better.

VIVIAN: Poor Ki'i. You want me to come over tomorrow and we can talk about it?

KI'I MOONLIGHT: Oh, ba. That's okay. That's what my therapist is for. Yeah! Thanks for asking. Look, here comes Chance! You guys go jam, or whatever.

This fictional conversation closely parallels the difficulty Michelle is having ensuring that her own grandchildren are enrolled at the pueblo. When I brought this up with her and the class, Michelle was adamant in her decision to include this vignette. "We should put more stuff like that in here," she said. "The whole thing should be stuff like that." This metapragmatic statement makes clear that the authors were conscious of the text's status as a political tract, one that allowed the members of the group to surreptitiously compare their respective political views while addressing an imagined audience of community members and future language learners.

As the Rez Turns' position as a comedy of manners designed to convey specific social critiques is also apparent in the overall narrative arc, which traces Chance's descent from a confident two-timer to a single outcast. In the authors' gender commentary, a cheater is shamed, and kinship and lineage win out in the end. Chance's fall begins when Vivian sees him kissing Skylar at a local diner:

VIVIAN: What in the world was that about?

CHANCE: What are you talking about? It was nothing…

VIVIAN: Then why did she kiss you? You do know that's my cousin.… Right?

CHANCE: Shut up…for real? Since when? Well, she's just some girl I know from school…that's all.

VIVIAN: Since when? Since forever! Looks like more than a friend to me and everyone else at the table.

CHANCE: What's it to you? What do you care?

VIVIAN: Well, because I was your girlfriend, but you can forget about that. You're just a shithead anyway!

CHANCE: Well, Skylar is way better than you anyway, so forget you!

VIVIAN: I'm done with you. Get out of my face!

Chance's fate is sealed when Skylar finds out about his relationship with Vivian, and she confronts him during the final scene, which takes place at a community get-together:

SKYLAR: So what's up with you and her?

CHANCE: Not a damn thing.

SKYLAR: Oh, I know you're lying. My cousin told me all about you two.

CHANCE: Oh babe, I am so, so, so sorry. Can you please forgive me?

SKYLAR: You hurt me so bad. It hurt my feelings when I found out the truth!

CHANCE: Man, I'm really sorry. Now I know why you look so familiar. I never snapped. Then I looked at that picture of your great grandma.

SKYLAR: Oh well, too bad! [*She walks over to Vivian and Vivian's new guy, James.*] Hey! Don't worry, cuz. I got your back. No worries, there's plenty more fish in the sea.

VIVIAN: Cool, cuz. Oh, this is James. James, this is my cousin, Skylar.

[*Scene fades.*]

By punishing the fictional Chance, the authors indirectly express opposition to the recent membership policies, decisions that have predominantly affected women and children at San Ramón. Like Pueblo ideals regarding misfortune and punishment, which are manifested in clowning and other practices, those who do not adhere to received values suffer known or unknown consequences. After the class finished writing the last scene in the soap opera, they congratulated one another on the finished product. "There are so many guys like that around here," Christine said, and the other students, male and female both, nodded in agreement.

Expectation, Anomaly, and Pueblo Propriety

Expectation and anomaly inform my analysis of this text at many levels. First, let us consider extracommunity expectations with respect to the title of the work. Certainly, it is funny because it is a clever send-up of a popular soap opera, but do our reactions contain implicit ideas about what kinds of speech genres and representations indigenous people should be producing? In this case, the students are reframing outsiders' expectations of the kinds of cultural material Native people should be creating, by writing a text populated by characters who are not relegated to a mythic past (Deloria 2004) but are actively engaged with modernity in all its trashy glory. To the students at San Ramón, it is not anomalous to move between expected categories, such as ceremonial/secular, indigenous/non-indigenous, and traditional/modern, as evidenced by their willingness to utilize seemingly oppositional styles and genres associated with both sides of these dichotomies.

Local expectations also serve as resources for the construction of a liminal discursive space, and the authors simultaneously maximize and minimize the distance between local and nonlocal genres, individuals, conversations, places, and events. Potentially controversial critiques are possible only because of the rampant, competing, interdiscursive and intertextual connections to established ways of speaking and being. Bakhtin's observations regarding the unique features of the novel genre mirror the characteristics of *As the Rez Turns*: "Authorial speech, the speeches of narrators, inserted genres, the speech of characters are merely those fundamental compositional unities with whose help heteroglossia can enter the novel; each of them permits a multiplicity of social voices and a wide variety of their links and interrelationships" (1981:263). The unexpected use of these novelistic features in a pedagogical language text creates a semifictional place containing grandmothers, tribal rolls, and cousins, along with therapists, heavy metal concerts, and mistaken identities. The San Ramón students, like the indigenous people whose lives Deloria chronicles, are taking advantage of a "moment of paradox and opportunity" (2004:225) when the students' facility in indexing multiple genres coincides with still evolving approaches to indigenous language literacy.

The critique that the authors offer, however, is not a straightforward example of "weak" factions voicing critiques against "dominant" groups (Scott 1985), nor is it merely an example of emergent youth cultural forms. Daniel Suslak observes in his study of language use and generational difference among the Mixe people, "There exists a tendency to describe youth cultural practices and ways of speaking as irrepressibly hybrid and to imply that hybridity is inherently creative and counterhegemonic" (2009:206). *As the Rez Turns* is indeed hybrid in that it does not adhere to dominant language ideologies privileging language purism. But it serves as an example of a Bakhtinian (1981) "complex genre," and contains themes that are patently counterhegemonic in their critique of the San Ramón Pueblo political elite; the strategies that the authors employ as part of their political treatise are not. As evidenced by other practices with writing I detail in this book, forms of interaction that rely on audiences' ability to correctly identify veiled indexical references are prototypical forms of sociality in Pueblo contexts. In writing *As the Rez Turns*, the students utilized the extant forms of co-created, indirect political discourse, similar to the dictionary example sentences and *The Bowl Story*. Whereas the authors' choice of genre is perhaps anomalous, the approaches they employ are decidedly local and expected.

In this way, the soap opera is not an odd form at all in its use of indirection created by the lamination of multiple, anomalous frames, ranging from the world of the absurdly fictional ("Like anyone around here would *ever* be named something like *that*!") to the established and familiar. *As the Rez Turns* is thus, in many ways, a very conservative comedy of manners. Its authors manage to reinforce and uphold the norms of Pueblo propriety even as (perhaps precisely because) they call everything else into question through oblique and fictional references.

s e v e n
Conclusion

After finishing *As the Rez Turns*, the language students and teachers went to the casino buffet for lunch to celebrate a successful summer. While filling our plates with everything from pizza to posole, we practiced asking one another to pass the salt and other table etiquette and talked about the ways the students could keep practicing their Keiwa when they returned to school. The tribe was footing the bill for our lunch, and one of the students suggested that we write a thank you note to the tribal leaders as our last Keiwa exercise. John was skeptical. "You never know what might set them off," he warned. "I'm not so sure about the idea." Eventually responding to the students' enthusiasm, he helped them to draft a short thank you note in Keiwa, which the students transferred to a large poster board and delivered to the tribal offices.

John's hesitancy was prescient. Apparently, in the next council meeting, the governor raised several political issues and connected them to literacy, calling for the end of writing the Keiwa language. Members of his staff were sent to the library to collect copies of the curriculum and other written materials and then went to Michelle's house and collected her verb flash cards. After several weeks, Michelle called me to break the difficult news that during the meeting, the governor had made another decision: to stop working with non–community members on language revitalization. Trying to comfort me, she said, "Don't worry about it, Erin. It won't be forever. It's not really about language—he was just making a power play." When I spoke to

John about what had happened, he agreed, but he was also feeling really down. "We never should have let the kids send that letter," he said regretfully. Shortly after the incident, he resigned as director of the language program.

The way these decisions played out resembles other incidents of information control at San Ramón Pueblo. Like the seldom checked sign-out sheets for the adult curriculum or John's ability to deliver his original congressional testimony, only cursory efforts were made to truly eradicate writing. Outside of the initial sweep by the governor's staff, no written materials were confiscated. I was never contacted by tribal officials to produce my archive of language materials, although I have since repatriated all the digital materials to John. After a few months, Michelle restarted work on the language program, practicing Keiwa with students in the after-school program and getting adult classes going again. John serves as one of the volunteer teachers. Michelle tells me that writing is still part of these efforts, with people using their own orthographies or asking her "how she would spell it," resulting in her using the alphabet developed by the language committee. The tribal librarian, a non–community member with a master's in linguistics, has also been tasked with contributing to language efforts.

For a year, John and I did some work with another pueblo to start its own language program, utilizing our experiences at San Ramón to help the pueblo develop its own alphabet and teaching materials, a project I am still involved with. Michelle continues to give me frequent reports on the San Ramón political climate, assuring me that things will change eventually, and I continue to answer language questions from individual tribal members who attend UNM. As I was finishing this book manuscript, I saw a harbinger of change in the political climate circulating on Facebook among my San Ramón friends: a picture of Ethan and his daughter holding a sign with a Keiwa greeting on *Good Morning, America*. The post had been "liked" more than one hundred times.

Whatever the future of San Ramón writing, this study is an ethnographic snapshot of an experiment with tribally sanctioned, indigenous language literacy, with both local and comparative implications. Like works by other anthropologists and historians working in Indian Country, this book illustrates the problems of relying on fixed oppositions when describing contemporary Native communities. Demarcations like traditional-modern, speaker-nonspeaker, enrolled-unenrolled, and literate-illiterate fail to map onto San Ramón people's lived experiences and potentially cloud analyses of Pueblo and New Mexican cultural and linguistic practices.

Methodologically, this work signals a departure from previous descriptions of Southwest tribes by virtue of my sometimes bifurcated attention: contributing to an indigenous language program while conducting an ethnographic study, producing curricula and descriptive materials while omitting tokens of the language of study, respecting the importance of concealment while trying to crack open the secret of Pueblo secrecy itself. My methods have yielded specific kinds of data, certainly, but also reflect San Ramón sociality. The appropriateness of long-term, careful, iterative projects and the conveyance of cultural knowledge through inference and circumlocution are aspects of San Ramón social life in many contexts, a fact I hope I have adequately conveyed.

This book also can inform understandings of information control in Pueblo and non-Pueblo milieus. Through presenting ethnographic examples from San Ramón and comparing them with previous works on secrecy, I show how the logic of information control in Pueblo contexts mirrors other cultural practices that aim to refine and perfect. Spending the time to control access to cultural knowledge and to align the divulgence of valued information with valued contexts positions everything associated with and contained in controlled texts, interactions, and objects as precious and whole. This indicates larger entities to be perfected as well. Luhrmann states, "The secretive world may be seen as an ideal, which the constraints of an outer society—a false, phenomenal world—forbid. The result of this confluence of characteristics is that the group is defined as safe, good, and pure" (1989b:159). Pueblo secrecy creates the possibility of uniqueness, safety, and purity at every level—individual, linguistic, and tribal; this secrecy is made possible by concealment practices that in their ideal manifestations are never finished. Secrets are shown to be important by being constantly talked about and continuously veiled.

This analysis also extends beyond Pueblo contexts. After looking closely at one example of Pueblo information control—limiting access to indigenous language materials—the incredibly fruitful and polyvalent nature of secrecy is apparent. Masco reminds us, "Secrecy...is also wildly productive: it creates not only hierarchies of power and repression, but also unpredictable social effects, including new kinds of desire, fantasy, paranoia, and—above all—gossip" (2002:451). In contexts ranging from formal, generically regimented projects like the San Ramón dictionary to looser, less regulated, emergent uses of Keiwa like *As the Rez Turns*, practices of concealment engender awe of the magnificence and elusiveness of Keiwa alongside incredible anxiety about not being able to produce faultless examples of the language. Secrecy can enable community members to feel a deep sense of belonging because of being the only ratified owners of the Keiwa language and its new, material manifestations. Secrecy also calls into question their own subjectivities and the future of the community through instances such as having their flash cards confiscated or their membership status questioned. In a broader context, in the current climate of increased circulation of information, the flexible yet powerful resource of secrecy is poised to become an even more recognizable social force. Privacy debates such as the controversies surrounding government surveillance are heating up at the same time individuals and institutions invest millions to increase certain types of visibility through global-level advertising. The power of discretionary practices has never been more salient.

Describing this mutable, intensely dynamic aspect of secrecy is part of explaining why the actions Pueblo language activists are taking to preserve Keiwa are not paradoxical. My ethnographic work at San Ramón proves that each example of lexicography, language revitalization, and literacy comes with its own history and its own consequences. Pulling apart assumptions about these three common processes has yielded counterexamples to the ways that they are commonly discussed. Dictionaries, however mundane they may seem, are never neutral works. The grammatical, poetic, and generic choices the San Ramón authors made in the creation of their text not only position it as a means of conveying important cultural information to imagined future Keiwa speakers but also accomplish this goal while adhering to local proprietary ideals.

All language revitalization movements are not uniform. The approaches that communities take to reintroduce indigenous languages have been shown to differ widely, but they also deviate from one another in their very goals. The texts created at San Ramón Pueblo do not communicate grammatico-semantic regularity but index preferred ways of being through the use of nostalgic yet hopeful discourses. The entire pueblo is the object of hopeful care and refinement, and learning Keiwa—or even talking about it—is another way to ritually perfect the community and ensure its future moral health. It is my intention that the examples I have presented communicate the incredible variety in lexicographic and revitalization pursuits and demonstrate how outlining differences and similarities can inform understandings of the groups that engage in such projects.

It is in the examination of literacy comparatively, however, that the San Ramón case is especially valuable. Like dictionaries and language renewal programs, writing practices often seem commonplace, established, and unworthy of considering their implications, especially when so many new technologies demand our analysis and attention. However, when we start to disassemble the trope of the ability of written materials to circulate anonymously without constraint, it becomes clear how entrenched these ideas are and how often they are connected to ideas about informed, democratic groups. One way we tell ourselves that we are politically active is by virtue of being members of reading publics, but alongside this way of participating are other, more circumscribed ways of enacting political subjectivities. The San Ramón example proves not only that writing is used in different ways—to establish value, control group membership, indirectly craft social critiques, and ritually refine language and community—but also that the implications of various literacy practices differ. Instead of the circulation of texts yielding anonymous reading publics who are able to imagine themselves as cohesive polities, the limited circulation of San Ramón texts produces targeted, known audiences whose political participation is expressed in indirect ways. Because writing in Western contexts has been typified as centering on circulation, not circumscription and refinement, analyses of literacy have ignored how writing practices can contribute to the establishment and continuance of extremely limited, private spheres, which are no less political but are indicative of very different visions of citizenship, subjectivity, and participation. Like the San Ramón linguistic and cultural practices analyzed here, my ongoing examination of Pueblo languages, writing, and communities will always remain essentially unfinished, reflecting its imperfect but captivating nature.

This is not the only way, I hope, that academic pursuits will dialogue with the example of San Ramón secrecy and indigenous language literacy. As other scholars have pointed out (Jones 2014; Mahmud 2012), secrecy as a topic and as a practice has been foundational to the discipline of anthropology: "Dynamics of concealment and revelation are central to anthropological theory, epistemology, and methods" (Jones 2014:9). The received view that through ethnographic fieldwork and engagement with theoretical writings, we are able to arrive at persuasive conclusions depends on the idea of revealing previously hidden truths. By not including the content of San Ramón secrets but focusing on the conditions of their production, I aim to direct any sense of incompleteness that the reader might feel at not having access to Keiwa examples toward questioning such codified approaches to knowledge production and the relative merit we, as anthropologists and linguists, assign to types of cultural and linguistic knowledge. In other words, I hope that recognizing secrecy's central but often unspoken place in anthropological inquiry leads to questioning why certain kinds of knowledge tend to be privileged for academic and popular consumption at the potential expense of eliding other forms of cultural and linguistic practice.

My decision to conceal secrets in this book also performs its very argument, making clear through avoidance and indirectness the politics of language that I describe. This book is intertextually linked to the San Ramón dictionary, *The Bowl Story*, *As the Rez Turns*, and the other Keiwa texts I discuss in it. It was produced using similar tactics of suggestion and inference to convey my arguments, attempting to extend this view of knowledge and property into other contexts. In addition to enacting for readers the logic of Pueblo secrecy, this relates to a facet of anthropological knowledge production. In *Time and the Other* (1983), Fabian argues that the temporal disjuncture between ethnographic fieldwork and anthropological writing contributes to the depiction of the subjects of anthropological inquiry as always inhabiting a time before. This observation is of special concern, considering that such depictions have led to the relegation of Native North Americans to a mythic past, a social imaginary that continues to influence public policy and popular opinion. Such a "denial of coevalness" (Fabian 1983:32), or "allochronism," has also led to a temporal disjuncture that solidifies the subject-object distinction in research, relegating some people to always being the static studied and others the objective experts occupying the present. Although this artifact results from the very intellectual and methodological traditions Fabian rightly criticizes, the textual choices I have made regarding how to represent Keiwa language practices extend the continued force of ongoing San Ramón proprietary practices. I hope that I have contributed to the possibility of a sense of coevalness by enacting Pueblo views of knowledge production and the control of cultural property, respecting the people who have more frequently been the objects, not the subjects, of anthropological analysis.

Notes

Chapter 1. Introduction

1. The terms "tribe" and "community" are used interchangeably in this book, reflecting the use of these terms at San Ramón Pueblo. "Tribal membership" or "tribal enrollment" refers to an individual's inclusion on the membership rolls.

2. Molly Mullin's 2001 study of the development of "multicultural" Santa Fe contains a history of the Santa Fe Indian Market. The market's website is www.swaia.org.

3. For works that focus on particular aspects of Pueblo religious and political organization, see Ortiz 1969, 1972; Parsons 1917, 1920, 1925, 1929, 1932, 1933, 1939, 1940, 1970, 1974a, 1974b; Sando 1992; Trimble 1993.

4. For information on Kateri prayer circles and her 2012 canonization, see http://conservation.catholic.org/kateri.htm.

5. There is a rich and growing literature on the history of the use of blood quantum as a determinant of tribal membership and on the growth of racial ideologies in Indian Country. See Barker 2005, 2011; Kauanui 2008; Strong and Van Winkle 1996; Sturm 2002; Wolfe 2001, 2006.

6. Joanne Barker's 2011 work contains an excellent analysis of this case and its impacts on debates about recognition and American Indian identity.

7. See Trujillo 2009 for more on these and other racial, historical, and ethnic designations in New Mexico.

8. The Pueblo Revolt was a successful, organized uprising against the Spanish colonists

in 1680. After twelve years of self-rule, the Pueblos were reconquered by the Spanish, who reestablished political and religious control of the area.

9. Keith Basso's work with the Western Apaches in Arizona (1979, 1996) details the centrality of place in notions of indigeneity.

10. The Indian Pueblo Cultural Center, a pan-Pueblo meeting place, museum, and restaurant in Albuquerque, devotes a section of its website to educating visitors and instructing them on proper etiquette during feast days: http://www.indianpueblo.org/19pueblos/etiquette.html.

11. For comprehensive studies of Native American boarding schools, see Archuleta, Child, and Lomawaima 2000; Coleman 1993; Ellis 1996; Peshkin 1997.

Chapter 2. Ideology, Literacy, and Secrecy

1. For more information on the introduction of modern Hebrew, which is often held up in the language revitalization literature as a "successful" project, see Hoffman 2004 and Kuzar 2001.

2. See Besnier 1995 and Collins and Blot 2003 for discussions of the universalist models of literacy and their critics.

3. For an excellent, much more extensive treatment of the anthropological literature on secrecy, see Jones 2014.

4. The work done on pre-contact Pueblo religion supports the claim that the strict demarcations between clans, moieties and pueblos pre-date European contact and repression. See, for instance, Liebmann 2008 and Sando 1992.

5. Marx and Muschert's piece is firmly grounded in quantitative sociological methods and ideas about truth and visibility that do not apply cross-culturally, but it is a useful survey of what kinds of topics concern scholars of secrecy. They assert that "much of the writing on secrecy can be found within four topical groups": studies of the interpersonal processes and qualities of secrecy; studies of secrecy and openness in government, policing, and business; studies of space and concealment; and secret societies (Marx and Muschert 2009:3). They also define the scope of secrecy inquiries as "a family of concepts encompassing personal, group and organizational information—e.g., privacy and publicity, public and private, personal and impersonal data, surveillance and surveillance neutralization, secrecy, confidentiality, anonymity, pseudo-anonymity, identifiability, and confessions" (6).

6. Again, Jones 2014 is especially useful regarding the relationship between anthropology and secrecy.

7. On politeness, see Brenneis 1978; Gagné 2010; Goody 1978; Hill 1980; and numerous articles in *Language in Society*. On indirectness and concealment, see Abu-Lughod 1986; Brody 1991; Caldeira 1988; Ewing 2006; Kuipers 1986; Mahmud 2012; Mannheim and Van Vleet 1998; Piot 1993. On avoidance registers, see Basso 1996; Dixon 2002; Haviland 1979a, 1979b. On the deliberate structuring of information in texts and use of intertextual gaps, see Bauman 2004, 2005; Briggs and Bauman 1992; Handman 2010; Hill 2005; Hill and Irvine 1993; Irvine 1979; Kroskrity 2009b; Silverstein 2005.

Chapter 3. Setting an Example

1. For a much more extensive discussion of the numerous lexicons I surveyed for this project, see Debenport 2009:ch. 3.

2. The dictionary committee members also decided not to credit the SIL dictionary authors or tribal members from the Keiwa-speaking pueblo that produced it. A copy of the SIL dictionary was given to a community member at San Ramón in confidence, and it is felt that because this individual might get into trouble with tribal authorities for sharing language materials, no mention should be made of the original lexicon.

3. Whereas people at San Ramón readily highlight the educational and professional accomplishments of family members, colleagues, and friends, emphasizing one's own individual accomplishments is frowned upon. To claim authorship for an indigenous language text would be doubly inappropriate because the language is most frequently characterized as a collectively held ability and/or cultural property.

4. Those involved with the language program have started to plan continuing education workshops on the San Ramón Keiwa alphabet in response to Head Start employees' requests for training after the language program posted signs in Keiwa in their classrooms. Interestingly, only nontribal members requested these trainings, most likely reflecting tribal members' fear of being disenrolled.

5. It is interesting that dictionaries retain their stodgy reputations even as games like Balderdash, Scrabble, and Bananagrams enjoy record popularity. This only proves that it is not the collecting and knowledge of words and their meanings that people perceive as tiresome but that lexicography as an endeavor is seen as exceedingly tedious, associated with nonleisure activities and nonrecreational spaces.

6. I do not include statistical data on pronoun usage in San Ramón dictionary example sentences because of the constant process of editing, changing, and creating illustrative material. Instead, I discuss the preferred constructions that authors used throughout the creation of the document.

7. The San Ramón saying associated with this directive is "The same man whose new horse you envy today might give you a ride tomorrow."

8. This is likely related to the Spanish word meaning "field" or "clearing."

9. Until recently, community members were also given names that they used in noncommunity or nonceremonial contexts, usually common Spanish or American English names. Some parents have begun to give their children only an Indian name, and in some cases, they consult with members of the language program before deciding on the spelling.

10. See Fowles 2013 for a discussion of Pueblo rituals and "doings."

Chapter 4. Perfecting Texts, Perfecting Community

1. The importance that the Pueblo Revolt still holds for contemporary Pueblo people cannot be overstated, and it impacts political and social relationships between individuals and among these tribes. For example, the people at Ysleta del Sur Pueblo, the sole Pueblo tribe located outside New Mexico, in El Paso, Texas, are still castigated for not returning to New Mexico following the violence of reconquest. Ysleta del Sur was not admitted to the All Indian Pueblo Council until 2009.

Chapter 5. Hopeful Nostalgia

1. For a complete review of the language revitalization literature, see Debenport 2009.

2. Many theorists have taken up the task of describing the dominant discourses present in

discussions about language shift, including Errington 2003; Hill 2002; Moore 2006; Muehlmann 2008; and Whiteley 2003. I survey several of these in my dissertation (Debenport 2009).

Chapter 6. As the Rez Turns

1. Although Kokopelli is recognized as a religious deity in Pueblo, specifically, Hopi, culture and history, stylized depictions of the flute-playing figure are also popular images in the southwestern United States, used as decoration on everything from garage doors to greeting cards. For an ethnographic and historical account of the Kokopelli image, see Malotki 2000.

2. "Ba" and "bah" are interjections translated as the English terms "whatever," "right," or, in some non-ironic cases, "well," as in "Oh well." I am unsure of the exact etymology but would venture a guess that the term stems from the Keiwa word for "and," which is often used as a discourse marker in spoken Keiwa.

3. Although I utilize the concept of liminality to look at different phenomena than Besnier does, his depictions of liminality as closely connected to performance also apply to the present case.

References

Abu-Lughod, Lila. *Veiled Sentiments: Honor and Poetry in a Bedouin Society.* Berkeley: University of California Press, 1986.

Agha, Asif. "Voice, Footing, Enregisterment." *Journal of Linguistic Anthropology* 15, no. 1 (2005): 38–59.

Ahearn, Laura M. *Invitations to Love: Literacy, Love Letters, and Social Change in Nepal.* Ann Arbor: University of Michigan Press, 2001.

Ahlers, Jocelyn C. "Framing Discourse: Creating Community through Native Language Use." *Journal of Linguistic Anthropology* 16, no. 1 (2006): 58–75.

Anderson, Benedict R. O'G. *Imagined Communities: Reflections on the Origin and Spread of Nationalism.* London: Verso, 1991.

Anthes, Bill. *Native Moderns: American Indian Painting, 1940–1960.* Durham, NC: Duke University Press, 2006.

Archuleta, Margaret, Brenda J. Child, and K. Tsianina Lomawaima. *Away from Home: American Indian Boarding School Experiences, 1879–2000.* Phoenix, AZ: Heard Museum, 2000.

Austin, J. L. *How to Do Things with Words.* Cambridge, MA: Harvard University Press, 1962.

Bakhtin, M. M. *The Dialogic Imagination: Four Essays.* Edited by Caryl Emerson. Translated by Michael Holquist. Austin: University of Texas Press, 1981.

———. *Speech Genres and Other Late Essays.* Edited by Caryl Emerson and Michael Holquist. Translated by Vern W. McGee. Austin: University of Texas Press, 1986.

Barker, Joanne. "For Whom Sovereignty Matters." In *Sovereignty Matters: Locations of Contestation and Possibility in Indigenous Struggles for Self-Determination*, edited by Joanne Barker, 1–32. Lincoln: University of Nebraska Press, 2005.

———. *Native Acts: Law, Recognition, and Cultural Authenticity.* Durham, NC: Duke University Press, 2011.

Barrett, Rusty. *From Drag Queens to Leathermen: Language, Gender, and Gay Male Subcultures.* New York: Oxford University Press, forthcoming.

Basso, Keith H. *Portraits of the "Whiteman": Linguistic Play and Cultural Symbols among the Western Apache.* Cambridge: Cambridge University Press, 1979.

———. "Speaking with Names." In *Wisdom Sits in Places: Landscape and Language among the Western Apache*, 71–104. Albuquerque: University of New Mexico Press, 1996.

Bauman, Richard. "Genre." In *Key Terms in Language and Culture*, edited by Alessandro Duranti, 79–81. Malden, MA: Blackwell, 2001.

———. *A World of Others' Words: Cross-cultural Perspectives on Intertextuality.* Malden, MA: Blackwell, 2004.

———. "Commentary: Indirect Indexicality, Identity, Performance." *Journal of Linguistic Anthropology* 15, no. 1 (2005): 145–150.

Bauman, Richard, and Charles Briggs. "Language Philosophy as Language Ideology: John Locke and Johann Gottfried Herder." In *Regimes of Language: Ideologies, Polities, and Identities*, edited by Paul V. Kroskrity, 139–204. Santa Fe, NM: SAR Press, 2000.

———. *Voices of Modernity: Language Ideologies and the Politics of Inequality.* Cambridge: Cambridge University Press, 2003.

Bender, Margaret Clelland. "From 'Easy Phonetics' to the Syllabary: An Orthographic Division of Labor in Cherokee Language Education." *Anthropology & Education Quarterly* 33, no. 1 (2002a): 90–117.

———. *Signs of Cherokee Culture: Sequoyah's Syllabary in Eastern Cherokee Life*. Chapel Hill: University of North Carolina Press, 2002b.

Benveniste, Emile. *Problems in General Linguistics*. Coral Gables: University of Florida Press, 1971.

Besnier, Niko. "Polynesian Gender Liminality through Time and Space." In *Third Sex, Third Gender: Beyond Sexual Dimorphism in Culture and History*, edited by Gilbert H. Herdt, 285–328. New York: Zone, 1994.

———. *Literacy, Emotion, and Authority: Reading and Writing on a Polynesian Atoll*. Cambridge: Cambridge University Press, 1995.

———. "Sluts and Superwomen: The Politics of Gender Liminality in Urban Tonga." *Ethnos* 62, nos. 1–2 (1997): 5–31.

Blommaert, Jan. "Artefactual Ideologies and the Textual Production of African Languages." *Language and Communication* 28, no. 4 (2008): 291–307.

Blommaert, Jan, and Jef Verschueren. *Debating Diversity: Analysing the Discourse of Tolerance*. London: Routledge, 1998.

Boym, Svetlana. *The Future of Nostalgia*. New York: Basic, 2001.

———. "Nostalgia and Its Discontents." *Hedgehog Review* 9, no. 2 (Summer 2007): 7–18.

Brandt, Elizabeth. "Sandia Pueblo: An Ethnolinguistic Investigation." PhD diss., Southern Methodist University, 1970.

———. "On Secrecy and the Control of Knowledge." In *Secrecy: A Cross-cultural Perspective*, edited by Stanton K. Tefft, 123–146. New York: Human Sciences Press, 1980.

Brenneis, Donald. "The Matter of Talk: Political Performances in Bhatgaon." *Language in Society* 7 (1978): 159–170.

Briggs, Charles L. *Competence in Performance: The Creativity of Tradition in Mexicano Verbal Art*. Philadelphia: University of Pennsylvania Press, 1988.

Briggs, Charles L., and Richard Bauman. "Genre, Intertextuality, and Social Power." *Journal of Linguistic Anthropology* 2, no. 2 (1992): 131–172.

Brody, Jill. "Indirection in the Negotiation of Self in Everyday Tojolab'al Women's Conversation." *Journal of Linguistic Anthropology* 1, no. 1 (1991): 78–96.

Brown, Penelope, and Stephen C. Levinson. *Politeness: Some Universals in Language Usage*. Cambridge: Cambridge University Press, 1987.

Bucholtz, Mary, and Kira Hall. "Theorizing Identity in Language and Sexuality Research." *Language in Society* 33, no. 4 (2004): 469–515.

Caldeira, Teresa Pires Do Rio. "The Art of Being Indirect: Talking about Politics in Brazil." *Cultural Anthropology* 3, no. 4 (1988): 444–454.

Calhoun, Craig J. *Habermas and the Public Sphere*. Cambridge, MA: MIT Press, 1992.

Cannell, Fenella. *The Anthropology of Christianity*. Durham, NC: Duke University Press, 2006.

Cattelino, Jessica R. *High Stakes: Florida Seminole Gaming and Sovereignty*. Durham, NC: Duke University Press, 2008.

———. "The Double Bind of American Indian Need-Based Sovereignty." *Cultural Anthropology* 25, no. 2 (2010): 235–262.

Chafe, Wallace L. *Discourse, Consciousness, and Time: The Flow and Displacement of Conscious Experience in Speaking and Writing*. Chicago: University of Chicago Press, 1994.

Clifford, James. *The Predicament of Culture: Twentieth-Century Ethnography, Literature, and Art*. Cambridge, MA: Harvard University Press, 1988.

Cody, Francis. "Linguistic Anthropology at the End of the Naughts: A Review of 2009." *American Anthropologist* 112, no. 2 (2009): 200–207.

Coleman, Michael C. *American Indian Children at School: 1850–1930*. Jackson: University Press of Mississippi, 1993.

Collins, James. "Literacy and Literacies." *Annual Review of Anthropology* 24, no. 1 (1995): 75–93.

———. *Understanding Tolowa Histories: Western Hegemonies and Native American Responses*. London: Routledge, 1997.

———. "The Ebonics Controversy in Context: Literacies, Subjectivities, and Language Ideologies in the

United States." In *Language Ideological Debates*, edited by Jan Blommaert, 201–234. Berlin: De Gruyter, 1999.

Collins, James, and Richard K. Blot. *Literacy and Literacies: Texts, Power, and Identity*. Cambridge: Cambridge University Press, 2003.

Colwell-Chanthaphonh, Chip. "Sketching Knowledge: Quandaries in the Mimetic Reproduction of Pueblo Ritual." *American Ethnologist* 38, no. 3 (2011): 451–467.

Comaroff, John L., and Jean Comaroff. *Ethnicity, Inc.* Chicago: University of Chicago Press, 2009.

Courlander, Harold. *The Fourth World of the Hopis: The Epic Story of the Hopi Indians as Preserved in Their Legends and Traditions*. Albuquerque: University of New Mexico Press, 1987.

Cowell, Andrew. "Arapaho Imperatives: Indirectness, Politeness and Communal 'Face.'" *Journal of Linguistic Anthropology* 17, no. 1 (2007): 44–60.

Crapanzano, Vincent. "Reflections on Hope as a Category of Social and Psychological Analysis." *Cultural Anthropology* 18, no. 1 (2003): 3–32.

Deacon, Desley. *Elsie Clews Parsons: Inventing Modern Life*. Chicago: University of Chicago Press, 1997.

Debenport, Erin. "'Listen So You Can Live Life the Way It's Supposed to Be Lived': Paradoxes of Text, Secrecy, and Language at a New Mexico Pueblo." PhD diss., University of Chicago, 2009.

———. "As the Rez Turns: Anomalies within and beyond the Boundaries of a Pueblo Community." *American Indian Culture and Research Journal* 35, no. 2 (2011): 87–109.

Deloria, Philip Joseph. *Indians in Unexpected Places*. Lawrence: University Press of Kansas, 2004.

De Meis, Carla. "House and Street: Narratives of Identity in a Liminal State among Prostitutes in Brazil." *Ethos* 30, nos. 1–2 (2002): 3–24.

Dixon, Robert M. W. *Australian Languages: Their Nature and Development*. Cambridge: Cambridge University Press, 2002.

Donellan, Keith. "Reference and Definite Descriptions." *Philosophical Review* 75, no. 3 (1966): 281–304.

Dozier, Edward P. "Resistance to Acculturation and Assimilation in an Indian Pueblo." *American Anthropologist* 53, no. 1 (1951): 56–66.

———. *The Pueblo Indians of North America*. 1970. Prospect Heights, IL: Waveland, 1983.

Durkheim, Emile. *The Division of Labor in Society*. 1893. Translated by W. D. Halls. New York: Free Press, 1997.

Eckert, Penelope, and John R. Rickford. *Style and Sociolinguistic Variation*. Cambridge: Cambridge University Press, 2001.

Eisenlohr, Patrick. "Language Revitalization and New Technologies: Cultures of Electronic Mediation and the Refiguring of Communities." *Annual Review of Anthropology* 33, no. 1 (2004): 21–45.

Ellis, Clyde. *To Change Them Forever: Indian Education at the Rainy Mountain Boarding School, 1893–1920*. Norman: University of Oklahoma Press, 1996.

Errington, Joseph. *Shifting Languages: Interaction and Identity in Javanese Indonesia*. Cambridge: Cambridge University Press, 1998.

———. "Getting Language Rights: The Rhetorics of Language Endangerment and Loss." *American Anthropologist* 105, no. 4 (2003): 723–732.

Ervin-Tripp, Susan. "Is Sybil There? The Structure of Some American English Directives." *Language in Society* 5, no. 1 (1976): 25–66.

Ewing, Katherine Pratt. "Revealing and Concealing: Interpersonal Dynamics and the Negotiation of Identity in the Interview." *Ethos* 34, no. 1 (2006): 89–122.

Fabian, Johannes. *Time and the Other: How Anthropology Makes Its Object*. New York: Columbia University Press, 1983.

Field, Margaret C. "Changing Navajo Language Ideologies and Changing Language Use." In *Native American Language Ideologies: Beliefs, Practices, and Struggles in Indian Country*, edited by Paul V. Kroskrity and Margaret C. Field, 31–47. Tucson: University of Arizona Press, 2009.

Fowles, Severin. *An Archaeology of Doings: Secularism and the Study of Pueblo Religion*. Santa Fe, NM: SAR Press, 2013.

Fox, Aaron A. *Real Country*. Durham, NC: Duke University Press, 2004.

Frawley, William, Kenneth C. Hill, and Pamela Munro, eds. *Making Dictionaries: Preserving Indigenous Languages of the Americas*. Berkeley: University of California Press, 2002.

Frege, Gottlob. *Translations from the Philosophical Writings of Gottlob Frege*. 1892. Edited by Peter Geach and Max Black. Oxford: Blackwell, 1952.

Gagné, Nana Okura. "Reexamining the Notion of Negative Face in the Japanese Sociolinguistic Politeness of Request." *Language and Communication* 30, no. 2 (2010): 123–138.

Gal, Susan. "A Semiotics of the Public/Private Distinction." *Differences* 13, no. 1 (2002): 77–95.

Garroutte, Eva Marie. *Real Indians: Identity and the Survival of Native America*. Berkeley: University of California Press, 2003.

Goffman, Erving. "On Face-Work: An Analysis of Ritual Elements of Social Interaction." *Psychiatry: Journal for the Study of Interpersonal Processes* 18, no. 3 (1955): 213–231.

———. "Footing." *Semiotica* 25, nos. 1–2 (1979): 1–30.

Goody, Esther N. *Questions and Politeness: Strategies in Social Interaction*. Cambridge: Cambridge University Press, 1978.

Goody, Jack, and Ian Watt. "The Consequences of Literacy." In *Literacy in Traditional Societies*, edited by Jack Goody, 27–68. Cambridge: Cambridge University Press, 1968.

Grice, H. P. "Logic and Conversation." In *Syntax and Semantics*, vol. 3, edited by P. Cole and J. Morgan, 22–40. New York: Academic, 1975.

Guthrie, Thomas. "Dealing with Difference: Heritage, Commensurability and Public Formation in Northern New Mexico." *International Journal of Heritage Studies* 16, no. 4 (2010): 305–321.

Habermas, Jürgen. *The Structural Transformation of the Public Sphere: An Inquiry into a Category of Bourgeois Society*. Cambridge, MA: MIT Press, 1989.

Haeri, Niloofar. *Sacred Language, Ordinary People: Dilemmas of Culture and Politics in Egypt*. New York: Palgrave Macmillan, 2003.

Hall, Kira. "Intertextual Sexuality: Parodies of Class, Identity and Desire in Liminal Delhi." *Journal of Linguistic Anthropology* 15, no. 1 (2005): 125–144.

Handman, Courtney. "Events of Translation: Intertextuality and Christian Ethnotheologies of Change among Guhu-Samane, Papua New Guinea." *American Anthropologist* 112, no. 4 (2010): 576–588.

Hanks, William F. "Discourse Genres in a Theory of Practice." *American Ethnologist* 14, no. 4 (1987): 668–692.

———. *Converting Words: Maya in the Age of the Cross*. Berkeley: University of California Press, 2010.

Harding, Susan F. "Convicted by the Holy Spirit: The Rhetoric of Fundamental Baptist Conversion." *American Ethnologist* 14, no. 1 (1987): 167–181.

Harrington, John P. "Notes on the Piro Language." *American Anthropologist* 11, no. 4 (1909): 563–594.

———. "A Brief Description of the Tewa Language." *American Anthropologist* 12, no. 4 (1910a): 497–504.

———. "An Introductory Paper on the Keiwa Language, Dialect of Taos, New Mexico." *American Anthropologist* 12, no. 1 (1910b): 11–48.

———. "Tewa Relationship Terms." *American Anthropologist* 14, no. 3 (1912): 472–498.

Hastings, A., and P. Manning. "Introduction: Acts of Alterity." *Language and Communication* 24, no. 4 (2004): 291–311.

Haviland, John B. "Guugu Yimidhirr Brother-in-Law Language." *Language in Society* 8, nos. 2–3 (1979a): 365–393.

———. "How to Talk to Your Brother-in-Law in Guugu Yimidhirr." In *Languages and Their Speakers*, edited by Timothy Shopen, 160–239. Cambridge, MA: Winthrop, 1979b.

———. "Text from Talk in Tzotzil." In *Natural Histories of Discourse*, edited by Michael Silverstein and Greg Urban, 45–80. Chicago: University of Chicago Press, 1996.

Hill, Jane H. "Culture Shock, Positive Face, and Negative Face: Being Polite in Tlaxcala." *Central Issues in Anthropology* 2, no. 1 (1980): 1–13.

———. "The Grammar of Consciousness and the Consciousness of Grammar." *American Ethnologist* 12, no. 4 (1985): 725–737.

———. "'Today There Is No Respect': Nostalgia, 'Respect' and Oppositional Discourse in Mexicano (Nahuatl) Language Ideology." *Pragmatics* 2, no. 3 (1992): 263–280.

———. "'Expert Rhetorics' in Advocacy for Endangered Languages: Who Is Listening, and What Do They Hear?" *Journal of Linguistic Anthropology* 12, no. 2 (2002): 119–133.

———. "Intertextuality as Source and Evidence for Indirect Indexical Meanings." *Journal of Linguistic Anthropology* 15, no. 1 (2005): 113–124.

Hill, Jane H., and Judith T. Irvine, eds. *Responsibility and Evidence in Oral Discourse*. Cambridge: Cambridge University Press, 1993.

Hill, Jane H., and Ofelia Zepeda. "Mrs. Patricio's Trouble: The Distribution of Responsibility in an Account of Personal Experience." In *Responsibility and Evidence in Oral Discourse*, edited by Jane H. Hill and Judith T. Irvine, 197–225. Cambridge: Cambridge University Press, 1993.

Hill, Kenneth C., Ekkehart Malotki, Mary E. Black, and the Hopi Dictionary Project. *Hopi Dictionary: A Hopi-English Dictionary of the Third Mesa Dialect with an English-Hopi Finder List and a Sketch of Hopi Grammar/Hopìikwa Lavàytutuveni*. Tucson: University of Arizona Press, 1998.

Hinton, Leanne, and Kenneth L. Hale, eds. *The Green Book of Language Revitalization in Practice*. San Diego, CA: Academic, 2001.

Hinton, Leanne, and William Weigel. "'A Dictionary for Whom': Tensions between Academic and Non-academic Functions of Bilingual Dictionaries." In *The Green Book of Language Revitalization*, edited by Leanne Hinton and Ken Hale, 155–170. San Diego, CA: Academic, 2001.

Hoffman, Joel M. *In the Beginning: A Short History of the Hebrew Language*. New York: New York University Press, 2004.

Hull, M. "The File: Agency, Authority, and Autography in an Islamabad Bureaucracy." *Language and Communication* 23, nos. 3–4 (2003): 287–314.

———. *Government of Paper: The Materiality of Bureaucracy in Urban Pakistan*. Berkeley: University of California Press, 2012.

Irvine, Judith T. "Formality and Informality in Communicative Events." *American Anthropologist* 81, no. 4 (1979): 773–790.

———. "When Talk Isn't Cheap: Language and Political Economy." *American Ethnologist* 16, no. 2 (1989): 248–267.

———. "'Style' as Distinctiveness: The Culture and Ideology of Linguistic Differentiation." In *Style and Sociolinguistic Variation*, edited by Penelope Eckert and John R. Rickford, 21–43. Cambridge: Cambridge University Press, 2001.

Irvine, Judith T., and Susan Gal. "Language Ideology and Linguistic Differentiation." In *Regimes of Language: Ideologies, Polities, and Identities*, edited by Paul V. Kroskrity, 35–84. Santa Fe, NM: SAR Press, 2000.

Jackson, Howard. *Lexicography: An Introduction*. London: Routledge, 2002.

Jaffe, Alexandra. "The Second Annual Corsican Spelling Contest: Orthography and Ideology." *American Ethnologist* 23, no. 4 (1996): 816–835.

———. *Ideologies in Action: Language Politics on Corsica*. Berlin: De Gruyter, 1999.

Jameson, Fredric. *Marxism and Form: Twentieth-Century Dialectical Theories of Literature*. Princeton, NJ: Princeton University Press, 1972.

Jones, Graham. *Trade of the Tricks: Inside the Magician's Craft*. Berkeley: University of California Press, 2012.

———. "Secrecy." *Annual Review of Anthropology*. Special issue, *Risk* (November 2014).

Kauanui, J. Kēhaulani. *Hawaiian Blood: Colonialism and the Politics of Sovereignty and Indigeneity*. Durham, NC: Duke University Press, 2008.

Keane, Webb. "Semiotics and the Social Analysis of Material Things." *Language and Communication* 23, nos. 3–4 (2003): 409–425.

———. *Christian Moderns: Freedom and Fetish in the Mission Encounter*. Berkeley: University of California Press, 2007.

Keeler, Ward. "What's Burmese about Burmese Rap? Why Some Expressive Forms Go Global." *American Ethnologist* 36, no. 1 (2009): 2–19.

Kripke, Saul. *Naming and Necessity*. Cambridge, MA: Harvard University Press, 1980.

Kroskrity, Paul V. "Growing with Stories: Line, Verse, and Genre in an Arizona Tewa Text." *Journal of Anthropological Research* 42, no. 2 (1985): 183–199.

———. *Language, History, and Identity: Ethnolinguistic Studies of the Arizona Tewa*. Tucson: University of Arizona Press, 1993.

———. "Arizona Tewa Kiva Speech as a Manifestation of a Dominant Language Ideology." In *Language Ideologies: Practice and Theory*, edited by Bambi B. Schieffelin, Kathryn Ann Woolard, and Paul V. Kroskrity, 103–122. New York: Oxford University Press, 1998.

———. "Language Ideologies in the Expression and Representation of Arizona Tewa Ethnic Identity." In *Regimes of Language: Ideologies, Polities, and Identities*, edited by Paul V. Kroskrity, 329–360. Santa Fe, NM: SAR Press, 2000.

———. "Embodying the Reversal of Language Shift: Agency, Incorporation, and Language Ideological Change in the Western Mono Community of Central California." In *Native American Language Ideologies: Beliefs, Practices, and Struggles in Indian Country*, edited by Paul V. Kroskrity and Margaret C. Field, 190–212. Tucson: University of Arizona Press, 2009a.

———. "Narrative Reproductions: Ideologies of Storytelling, Authoritative Words, and Generic Regimentation in the Village of Tewa." *Journal of Linguistic Anthropology* 19, no. 1 (2009b): 40–56.

———. "Growing with Stories: Ideologies of Storytelling and the Narrative Reproduction of Arizona Tewa Identities." In *Telling Stories in the Face of Danger: Language Renewal in Native American Communities*, edited by Paul V. Kroskrity, 151–183. Norman: University of Oklahoma Press, 2012a.

Kroskrity, Paul V., ed. *Telling Stories in the Face of Danger: Language Renewal in Native American Communities*. Norman: University of Oklahoma Press, 2012b.

Kroskrity, Paul V., and Margaret C. Field, eds. *Native American Language Ideologies: Beliefs, Practices, and Struggles in Indian Country*. Tucson: University of Arizona Press, 2009.

Kuipers, Joel C. "Talking about Troubles: Gender Differences in Weyewa Speech Use." *American Ethnologist* 13, no. 3 (1986): 448–462.

Kuzar, Ron. *Hebrew and Zionism: A Discourse Analytic Cultural Study*. Berlin: De Gruyter, 2001.

Ladino, Jennifer. "Longing for Wonderland: Nostalgia for Nature in Post-frontier America." *Iowa Journal of Cultural Studies* (2004): 5, no.1 88–109.

Landau, Sidney I., et al., eds. *Cambridge Dictionary of American English*. Cambridge: Cambridge University Press, 2000.

Leap, William. "Keiwa Noun Class Semology: A Historical View." *Anthropological Linguistics* 12 (1970a): 38–45.

———. "The Language of Isleta, New Mexico." PhD diss., Southern Methodist University, 1970b.

Liebmann, Matthew. "The Innovative Materiality of Revitalization Movements: Lessons from the Pueblo Revolt of 1680." *American Anthropologist* 110, no. 3 (2008): 360–372.

Lippi-Green, Rosina. *English with an Accent: Language, Ideology, and Discrimination in the United States*. London: Routledge, 1997.

Luhrmann, T. M. "The Magic of Secrecy." *Ethos* 17, no. 2 (1989a): 131–165.

———. *Persuasions of the Witch's Craft: Ritual Magic in Contemporary England*. Cambridge, MA: Harvard University Press, 1989b.

Mahmud, Lilith. "'The World Is a Forest of Symbols': Italian Freemasonry and the Practice of Discretion." *American Ethnologist* 39, no. 2 (May 2012): 425–438.

Malinowski, Bronislaw. *Argonauts of the Western Pacific: An Account of Native Enterprise and Adventure in the Archipelagoes of Melanesian New Guinea*. London: Routledge, 1922.

Malotki, Ekkehart. *Kokopelli: The Making of an Icon*. Lincoln: University of Nebraska Press, 2000.

Mannheim, Bruce, and Krista Van Vleet. "The Dialogics of Southern Quechua Narrative." *American Anthropologist* 100, no. 2 (1998): 326–346.

Martin, Bill, and Eric Carle. *Brown Bear, Brown Bear, What Do You See?* New York: Holt, 1996.

Marx, Gary T., and Glenn W. Muschert. "Simmel on Secrecy: A Legacy and Inheritance for the Sociology of Information." In *Soziologie als Möglichkeit: 100 Jahre Georg Simmels Untersuchungen über die Formen der Vergesellschaftung* [The Possibility of Sociology: 100 Years of Georg Simmel's Investigations into the Forms of Social Organization], edited by Cécile Rol and Christian Papilloud, 217–236. Wiesbaden, Germany: VS Verlag für Sozialwissenschaften, 2009. http://www.users.miamioh.edu/muschegw/FinalFormMarxMuschert%20Version%203%20PDF.pdf, 1–16.

Masco, Joseph. "Lie Detectors: On Secrecy and Hypersecurity in Los Alamos." *Public Culture* 14, no. 3 (2002): 441–467.

———. *The Nuclear Borderlands: The Manhattan Project in Post–Cold War New Mexico*. Princeton, NJ: Princeton University Press, 2006.

———. "'Sensitive but Unclassified': Secrecy and the Counterterrorist State." *Public Culture* 22, no. 3 (2010): 433–463.

Mauss, Marcel. *The Gift: Forms and Functions of Exchange in Archaic Societies*. New York: Norton, 1967.

Milroy, James, and Lesley Milroy. *Authority in Language: Investigating Language Prescription and Standardisation*. 3rd ed. London: Routledge and Kegan Paul, 1998.

Mithun, Marianne. *The Languages of Native North America*. Cambridge: Cambridge University Press, 2001a.

———. "Who Shapes the Record: The Speaker and the Linguist." In *Linguistic Fieldwork*, edited by Paul Newman and Martha Susan Ratliff, 34–54. Cambridge: Cambridge University Press, 2001b.

Miyazaki, Hirokazu. "Faith and Its Fulfillment: Agency, Exchange, and the Fijian Aesthetics of Completion." *American Ethnologist* 27, no. 1 (2000): 31–51.

———. *The Method of Hope: Anthropology, Philosophy, and Fijian Knowledge*. Stanford, CA: Stanford University Press, 2006.

Moore, Robert. "Disappearing, Inc.: Glimpsing the Sublime in the Politics of Access to Endangered Languages." *Language and Communication* 26, nos. 3–4 (2006): 296–315.

Muehlmann, Shaylih. "'Spread Your Ass Cheeks' and Other Things That Should Not Be Said in Indigenous Languages." *American Ethnologist* 35, no. 1 (2008): 34–48.

Mullin, Molly H. *Culture in the Marketplace: Gender, Art, and Value in the American Southwest*. Durham, NC: Duke University Press, 2001.

Munn, Nancy D. *The Fame of Gawa: A Symbolic Study of Value Transformation in a Massim (Papua New Guinea) Society*. Cambridge: Cambridge University Press, 1986.

Nevins, Eleanor. "Learning to Listen: Coming to Terms with Conflicting Discourses of 'Language Loss' among the White Mountain Apache." *Journal of Linguistic Anthropology* 14, no. 2 (2004): 269–288.

Norcini, Marilyn. *Edward P. Dozier: The Paradox of the American Indian Anthropologist*. Tucson: University of Arizona Press, 2007.

Ortiz, Alfonso. *The Tewa World: Space, Time, Being, and Becoming in a Pueblo Society*. Chicago: University of Chicago Press, 1969.

———. *New Perspectives on the Pueblos*. Albuquerque: University of New Mexico Press, 1972.

Parsons, Elsie Worthington Clews. *Notes on Zuñi*. Lancaster, PA: Pub. for American Anthropological Association, 1917.

———. *Notes on Ceremonialism at Laguna*. New York: Trustees, 1920.

———. *The Pueblo of Jemez*. New Haven, CT: Pub. for Dept. of Archaeology, Phillips Academy, Andover, Massachusetts, by Yale University Press, 1925.

———. *The Social Organization of the Tewa of New Mexico*. Menasha, WI: American Anthropological Association, 1929.

———. "Isleta, New Mexico." In *Annual Report of the Bureau of American Ethnology to the Secretary of the Smithsonian Institution*, 193–466. Washington, DC: Bureau of American Ethnology, 1932.

———. *Hopi and Zuñi Ceremonialism*. Menasha, WI: American Anthropological Association, 1933.

———. *Pueblo Indian Religion*. Chicago: University of Chicago Press, 1939.

———. *Taos Tales*. New York: American Folklore Society and J. J. Augustin, 1940.

———. *Isleta Paintings*. Edited by Esther Schiff Goldfrank. Washington, DC: Smithsonian Institution Press, 1962.

———. *Taos Pueblo*. New York: Johnson Reprint, 1970.

———. *A Pueblo Indian Journal: 1920–1921*. Millwood, NY: Kraus, 1974a.

———. *The Pueblo of Isleta*. Albuquerque, NM: Calvin Horn, 1974b.

———. *Pueblo Mothers and Children: Essays*. Edited by Barbara A. Babcock. 1919. Santa Fe, NM: Ancient City Press, 1991.

Pecos, Regis, and Rebecca Blum-Martinez. "The Key to Cultural Survival: Language Planning and Revitalization in the Pueblo de Cochiti." In *The Green Book of Language Revitalization*, edited by Leanne Hinton and Ken Hale, 75–82. San Diego, CA: Academic, 2001.

Peshkin, Alan. *Places of Memory: Whiteman's Schools and Native American Communities*. Mahwah, NJ: Erlbaum, 1997.

Peterson, Leighton. "'Reel Navajo': The Linguistic Creation of Indigenous Screen Memories." *American Indian Culture and Research Journal* 35, no. 2 (2011): 111–134.

Piot, Charles D. "Secrecy, Ambiguity, and the Everyday in Kabre Culture." *American Anthropologist* 95, no. 2 (1993): 353–370.

Povinelli, E. A. "Settler Modernity and the Quest for an Indigenous Tradition." *Public Culture* 11, no. 1 (1999): 19–48.

Putnam, Hilary. "The Meaning of 'Meaning.'" In *Mind, Language and Reality, Philosophical Papers*, vol. 2, 215–271. Cambridge: Cambridge University Press, 1975.

Rice, Keren, and Leslie Saxon. "Issues of Standardization and Community in Aboriginal Language Lexicography." In *Making Dictionaries: Preserving Indigenous Languages of the Americas*, edited by William Frawley, Kenneth C. Hill, and Pamela Munro, 122–154. Berkeley: University of California Press, 2002.

Robbins, Joel. *Becoming Sinners: Christianity and Moral Torment in a Papua New Guinea Society*. Berkeley: University of California Press, 2004.

———. "Continuity Thinking and the Problem of Christian Culture: Belief, Time, and the Anthropology of Christianity." *Current Anthropology* 48, no. 1 (2007): 5–38.

Rodríguez, Sylvia. *The Matachines Dance: Ritual Symbolism and Interethnic Relations in the Upper Río Grande Valley*. Albuquerque: University of New Mexico Press, 1996.

Romaine, Suzanne. "Signs of Identity, Signs of Discord: Glottal Goofs and the Green Grocer's Glottal in Debates on Hawaiian Orthography." *Journal of Linguistic Anthropology* 12, no. 2 (2002): 189–224.

Rosa, Jonathan. "Looking like a Language, Sounding like a Race: Making Latina/o Panethnicity and Managing American Anxieties." PhD diss., University of Chicago, 2010.

Rosaldo, Michelle. "The Things We Do with Words: Ilongot Speech Acts and Speech Act Theory in Philosophy." *Language in Society* 11, no. 2 (August 1982): 203–237.

Royce, Anya Peterson. *Anthropology of the Performing Arts: Artistry, Virtuosity, and Interpretation in a Cross-cultural Perspective*. Walnut Creek, CA: AltaMira, 2004.

Russell, Bertrand. "On Denoting." *Mind* 14 (1905): 479–493.

Said, Edward. "Reflections on Exile." *Granta*, no. 13 (Autumn 1984): 159–172.

Samuels, David William. *Putting a Song on Top of It: Expression and Identity on the San Carlos Apache Reservation*. Tucson: University of Arizona Press, 2004.

Sando, Joe S. *Pueblo Nations: Eight Centuries of Pueblo Indian History*. Santa Fe, NM: Clear Light, 1992.

San Ramón Language Committee. "Adult Language Curriculum." Unpublished, 2007.

Santa Fe New Mexican. "Pueblo Votes to Change Membershp Rules." April 30, 2012.

Schieffelin, Bambi. "Introducing Kaluli Literacy: A Chronology of Influences." In *Regimes of Language: Ideologies, Polities, and Identities*, edited by Paul V. Kroskrity, 293–322. Santa Fe, NM: SAR Press, 2000.

Schieffelin, Bambi B., and Rachelle Charlier Doucet. "The 'Real' Haitian Creole: Ideology, Metalinguistics, and Orthographic Choice." In *Language Ideologies: Practice and Theory*, edited by Bambi B. Schieffelin, Kathryn Ann Woolard, and Paul V. Kroskrity, 285–316. New York: Oxford University Press, 1998.

Schieffelin, Bambi B., and Perry Gilmore, eds. *The Acquisition of Literacy: Ethnographic Perspectives*. Norwood, NJ: Ablex, 1986.

Scott, James C. *Weapons of the Weak: Everyday Forms of Peasant Resistance*. New Haven, CT: Yale University Press, 1985.

Silverstein, Michael. "Shifters, Linguistic Categories, and Cultural Description." In *Meaning in Anthropology*, edited by Keith H. Basso and Henry A. Selby, 11–55. Albuquerque: University of New Mexico Press, 1976.

———. "Language Structure and Linguistic Ideology." In *The Elements: A Parasession on Linguistic Units and Levels*, edited by Paul R. Clyne, William F. Hanks, and Carol L. Hofbauer, 193–247. Chicago: Chicago Linguistic Society, 1979.

———. "Monoglot 'Standard' in America: Standardization and Metaphors of Linguistic Hegemony." In *The Matrix of Language: Contemporary Linguistic Anthropology*, edited by Donald Brenneis and Ronald Macaulay, 284–306. Boulder, CO: Westview, 1996.

———. "Whorfianism and the Linguistic Imagination of Nationality." In *Regimes of Language: Ideologies, Polities, and Identities*, edited by Paul V. Kroskrity, 85–138. Santa Fe, NM: SAR Press, 2000.

———. "The Whens and Wheres—as Well as Hows—of Ethnolinguistic Recognition." *Public Culture* 15, no. 3 (2003): 531–557.

———. "Axes of Evals." *Journal of Linguistic Anthropology* 15, no. 1 (2005): 6–22.

———. "Old Wine, New Ethnographic Lexicography." *Annual Review of Anthropology* 35, no. 1 (2006): 481–496.

Silverstein, Michael, and Greg Urban, eds. *Natural Histories of Discourse*. Chicago: University of Chicago Press, 1996.

Simmel, Georg. "The Sociology of Secrecy and of Secret Societies." *American Journal of Sociology* 11 (1906): 441–498.

Simmons, Marc. "History of Pueblo-Spanish Relations to 1821." In *Handbook of North American Indians*, vol. 9: *The Southwest*, edited by William C. Sturtevant, 178–193. Washington, DC: Smithsonian Institution Press, 1979.

Speirs, Randall. "Some Aspects of the Structure of Rio Grande Tewa." PhD diss., State University of New York, Buffalo, 1966.

———. "Number in Tewa." In *Studies in Linguistics in Honor of George L. Trager*, edited by M. Estellie Smith, 479–486. The Hague: Mouton, 1972.

Spicer, Edward Holland. *Perspectives in American Indian Culture Change*. Chicago: University of Chicago Press, 1961.

Stewart, Kathleen. "Nostalgia—A Polemic." *Cultural Anthropology* 3, no. 3 (August 1988): 227–241.

Strawson, P. F. "On Referring." *Mind* 59 (1950): 320–344.

Strong, Pauline Turner, and Barrik Van Winkle. "'Indian Blood': Reflections on the Reckoning and Refiguring of Native North American Identity." *Cultural Anthropology* 11, no. 4 (1996): 547–576.

Sturm, Circe. *Blood Politics: Race, Culture, and Identity in the Cherokee Nation of Oklahoma*. Berkeley: University of California Press, 2002.

———. *Becoming Indian: The Struggle over Cherokee Identity in the Twenty-First Century*. Santa Fe, NM: SAR Press, 2011.

SturtzSreetharan, Cindi L. "'I Read the Nikkei, Too': Crafting Positions of Authority and Masculinity in a Japanese Conversation." *Journal of Linguistic Anthropology* 16, no. 2 (2006): 173–193.

Suslak, Daniel F. "The Sociolinguistic Problem of Generations." *Language and Communication* 29, no. 3 (2009): 199–209.

Sweet, Jill D. *Dances of the Tewa Pueblo Indians: Expressions of New Life*. 1985. Santa Fe, NM: SAR Press, 2004.

TallBear, Kim. *Native American DNA: Tribal Belonging and the False Promise of Genetic Science*. Minneapolis: University of Minnesota Press, 2013.

Trager, Felicia H. "Picuris Pueblo, New Mexico: An Ethnolinguistic 'Salvage' Study." PhD diss., State University of New York, Buffalo, 1968.

Trager, George. "The Language of the Pueblo of Taos." *Maître Phonétique* 56 (1936): 59–62.

———. "The Historical Phonology of the Keiwa Languages." *Studies in Linguistics* 1, no. 5 (1942): 1–10.

———. "The Kinship and Status Terms of the Keiwa Languages." *American Anthropologist* 45, no. 4 (1943): 557–571.

———. "An Outline of Taos Grammar." In *Linguistic Structures in North America*, edited by C. Osgood, 184–221. New York: Wenner-Gren, 1946.

———. "Taos I: A Language Revisited." *International Journal of American Linguistics* 14, no. 3 (1948): 155–160.

———. "Taos II: Pronominal Reference." *International Journal of American Linguistics* 20, no. 3 (1954): 173–180.

———. "Taos III: Paralanguage." *Anthropological Linguistics* 2, no. 2 (1960): 24–30.

———. "Taos IV: Morphemics, Syntax, Semology in Nouns and in Pronominal Reference." *International Journal of American Linguistics* 27, no. 3 (1961): 211.

Trimble, Stephen. *The People: Indians of the American Southwest*. Santa Fe, NM: SAR Press, 1993.

Trujillo, Michael L. *Land of Disenchantment: Latina/o Identities and Transformations in Northern New Mexico*. Albuquerque: University of New Mexico Press, 2009.

Turner, Victor W. *The Forest of Symbols: Aspects of Ndembu Ritual*. Ithaca, NY: Cornell University Press, 1967.

Wallace, Anthony F. C. "Revitalization Movements." *American Anthropologist* 58, no. 2 (1956): 264–281.

Warner, Michael. *The Letters of the Republic: Publication and the Public Sphere in Eighteenth-Century America*. Cambridge, MA: Harvard University Press, 1995.

———. "Publics and Counterpublics." *Public Culture* 14, no. 1 (2002a): 49–90.

———. *Publics and Counterpublics*. New York: Zone, 2002b.

Watkins, Laurel J., and Parker McKenzie. *A Grammar of Kiowa*. Lincoln: University of Nebraska Press, 1984.

Waugh, Earle H. "Foreword." In Nancy LeClaire and George Cardinal, *Alberta Elders' Cree Dictionary/Alperta Ohci Kehtehayak Nehiyaw Otwestamakewasinahikan*, edited by Earle H. Waugh. Edmonton: University of Alberta Press, 1998.

Weiner, Annette B. *The Trobrianders of Papua New Guinea*. New York: Holt, Rinehart and Winston, 1988.

Whiteley, Peter. "Do 'Language Rights' Serve Indigenous Interests? Some Hopi and Other Queries." *American Anthropologist* 105, no. 4 (December 2003): 712–722.

Whorf, Benjamin A. *Language, Thought, and Reality*. 1956. Cambridge, MA: MIT Press, 2012.

Wilson, Chris. *The Myth of Santa Fe*. Albuquerque: University of New Mexico Press, 1997.

Wolfe, Patrick. "Land, Labor, and Difference: Elementary Structures of Race." *American Historical Review* 106, no. 3 (2001): 866–905.

———. "Settler Colonialism and the Elimination of the Native." *Journal of Genocide Research* 8, no. 4 (2006): 387–409.

Zagona, Karen T. *The Syntax of Spanish*. New York: Cambridge University Press, 2002.

Index

"A Semiotics of the Public/Private Distinction" (Gal), 49

Acoma Pueblo, 4, 102

address, forms of, 72, 82, 90–91, 95–96

African languages, 62

agency, 25, 42, 113–114, 117

Agha, Asif, 79–80

agriculture, 9. *See also* traditional: technologies

Ahlers, Jocelyn, 43

Albuquerque, 8–11, 14, 17, 19–20, 42, 51–52, 66, 89, 110, 144n10

Anderson, Benedict, 7, 104

Apache, 17, 31, 100, 120, 127, 144n9

Arabic, 37

Arapaho, 48

Arizona, 4, 8, 28, 33, 43, 80, 93, 144n9

As the Rez Turns soap opera, 26, 40, 49, 92, 139, 141; challenges expectations, 125–127, 134–135; challenges stereotypes, 120, 123–124; creation of, 119–123; critiques current events, 120–121, 131; and entextualization processes, 120, 123–124; humor in, 123–125, 127, 131–134, 136; and indigenous identity, 127–131; influences on, 130, 132; and liminality, 132, 135, 146n3; political/social commentary of, 132–135

assimilation, 18, 20, 37, 42, 67

audience, 7, 25–26, 49–50, 56, 59, 72–75, 133, 135, 140

authenticity, 15, 29, 32, 40, 43, 46, 63, 75, 77, 84, 89, 124, 127

authority, 7, 26, 29, 56, 59, 67, 72–74, 76, 87–88, 93, 109

authorship, 6–7, 59, 90, 104, 109, 145n3. *See also* San Ramón dictionary: authors

avoidance practices, 7–8, 17–18, 20, 32–33, 48–49, 52, 121, 141

Axelrod, Melissa, 21, 30, 39

Bakhtin, M. M., 84, 109, 121, 135

Barrett, Rusty, 56–57

Basso, Keith, 102, 120, 124, 144n9

Bauman, Richard, 84–85, 88, 120

Becoming Indian (Sturm), 18

Bender, Margaret, 39–40

Benveniste, Emile, 67, 71–72

Blommaert, Jan, 62

blood quantum, 13, 16, 143n5

Blum-Martinez, Rebecca, 35–37

Bowl Story, The, 120–122, 135, 141; circulation of, 102–103, 130; moral agency in, 114; and nostalgia, 106, 108–109; and pedagogical dialogues, 91–95; perfectability/refinement of, 97–104, 117; recording of, 91–92, 97–98, 102

Boym, Svetlana, 108–111

Brandt, Elizabeth, 20

Briggs, Charles, 85, 88, 108, 120

Brown Bear, Brown Bear, What Do You See?, 38

Bucholtz, Mary, 17, 124

Cambridge Dictionary of American English, 68, 71

cargo cults, 113, 116

casinos, 9, 40, 52, 89, 110, 122, 128; display cultural objects, 10–11; economic benefits of, 14, 125; and economic competitiveness, 31; harmful effects of, 14, 21, 102, 120, 126; Keiwa names at, 50–52; and life before/after, 119–120, 125–126; and Native imagery, 124; and San Ramón dictionary, 75; and tribal membership, 13–14. *See also* gaming revenues

Catholicism, 12, 18–19

Cattelino, Jessica, 10, 21, 126

ceremonial practices, 3–4, 11, 100, 135; control of, 12, 19; curing ceremonies, 81; dialogues about, 126; and kinship terms, 93, 95; and language programs, 20, 25; language spoken during, 19, 28–30, 32, 48, 79–80, 90; and outsiders, 42, 89–90; and perfectibility, 104; performing of, 8–9, 78, 90; and San Ramón dictionary, 32, 64, 66–67, 71, 78, 80–83; and secrecy, 4, 17, 42; and tribal membership, 16–17; words associated with, 80–84; and writing languages, 37. *See also* dances; kiva; religious practices

Chafe, Wallace, 38

charter schools, 11

Cherokees, 15, 18, 39–40

children: adoption of, 8, 16; after-school programs for, 10, 16, 19, 21, 31, 95, 129, 138; and forms of address, 95–96; kinship terms for, 93, 95; learn Keiwa at home, 37; learn Keiwa at school, 38; rearing of, 90, 102; summer language programs for, 55–56, 91, 119–121, 137; and tribal membership, 13–14, 100, 133–134

Christianity, 5, 113, 115. *See also* Catholicism; missionaries

citizenship, 91, 104, 114, 140

Clifford, James, 43

Cochiti Pueblo, 35–37

Cody, Francis, 28

Collins, James, 6, 35, 61, 104

colonial-era documents, 61–63, 87

Comaroff, John and Jean, 13

community, 7, 9–10, 12, 104, 110, 111

concealment practices, 6–7, 41–43, 45–49, 52, 138–139, 141

"Continuity Thinking and the Problem of Christian Culture" (Robbins), 115

Converting Words (Hanks), 63

Coronado district, 11, 107

Cowell, Andrew, 48

Crapanzano, Vincent, 112–118

Cree dictionary, 55, 63

cultural: activities, 13; autonomy, 119; concepts, 76; definitions, 16–17, 75; deterioration, 37; identities, 127; inappropriateness, 59; legitimacy, 31; loss, 21; order, 116; persecution, 18; practices, 64, 138; projects, 104; revitalization, 63, 112, 116; traditions, 32–33, 36, 89–90; uniqueness, 59; values, 69

cultural knowledge, 4, 11, 76, 141; access to, 41, 81, 116; circulation of, 5, 7–8, 24, 41, 45, 88, 104, 139; communication of, 32, 49, 77, 139; control of, 24–25, 41–42, 48, 67; controlling access to, 4, 7, 17–18, 22, 36, 40, 139; dissemination of, 7, 40, 48; and producing value, 45–46, 62; and San Ramón dictionary, 28, 58, 64–65, 73; sharing of, 20, 41–42, 48; teaching of, 6

cultural objects, 104, 112, 134; caretakers of, 46, 103; control/circulation of, 6–7, 46, 63, 90, 103, 141; displayed at casinos, 10–11; value of, 46, 102; written texts as, 6, 32, 84, 104

cultural practices, 112; communication of, 64–65, 93–95; loss of, 101, 122; and moral decline, 92–93; and nostalgia, 107–108; obsolete/past, 92, 94–95, 98–100, 102; and outsiders, 89–90; and San Ramón dictionary, 67, 69, 74–76; secrecy of, 64; youth, 135

"dance bosses," 90, 103

dances, 11–12, 17, 66, 80–81, 89–90, 99–101, 111, 121, 126

Deacon, Desley, 4

Deloria, Philip, 120, 124–125, 127, 135

democracy, 7, 49, 61, 140

Democratic Party, 12

diacritics, 22, 39, 97

dialects, 18, 28–29, 31, 55, 60–61, 68, 71

dictionaries, 6, 56–63, 68, 71, 74, 82–83, 85–88, 91,

140, 145n5. *See also* lexicographic traditions; lexicons; San Ramón dictionary

difference, 29, 31, 34, 38, 40, 61, 63

digital language materials, 5

"Discourse Genres in a Theory of Practice" (Hanks), 85

discretionary practices, 20, 41, 45, 50, 139

disenrollment, 8, 13–16, 18, 45, 47, 59, 100–101, 145n4

Eckert, Penelope, 79

economic: change, 111; competition, 31; consequences, 13–14; development, 9–10; power, 72; prosperity, 20, 111; security, 125; ventures, 4, 10

education, 11, 13–14, 16, 18–19, 23, 32, 38, 111, 119, 145n3

Education Department, 21, 30, 33–34, 42, 59

Egypt, 37

Eisenlohr, Patrick, 28

electronic media, 51–52

English, 51, 92; and *The Bowl Story*, 91, 98–99, 102; dictionaries, 56, 68, 71–72; loanwords, 31, 82, 109; replaces Native languages, 18–20, 29, 42, 117; and San Ramón dictionary, 60, 66, 69, 79, 97, 118; at San Ramón Pueblo, 28–30, 127; standardization of, 61; translations, 24, 45, 121–122

enregisterment, processes of, 80, 82, 84

entextualization, 28, 70, 76, 88, 120, 123–124

Ervin-Tripp, Susan, 72–73

Fabian, Johannes, 141

faith, 26, 106, 112–113, 117

feasts/feast days, 9, 11–12, 17, 23, 78, 89–90, 101–102, 119, 122, 144n10

federal funding, 42

federal Indian schools, 11, 18–20, 37, 68

Field, Margaret, 126

Fijians, 90, 113, 116–118

film/television industry, 11

First Mesa (Hopi reservation), 28, 101

Florida, 10, 21, 126

"fourth world," 100, 106

Frawley, William, 63

Freemasons, 41

Future of Nostalgia, The (Boym), 108

Gal, Susan, 28–29, 37, 49

gaming revenues, 14, 18, 91; fund buildings, 9–10, 107; harmful effects of, 21, 102, 111; positive aspects of, 9–10, 111. *See also* casinos

Garroutte, Eva Marie, 15–16, 18

gender, 75, 79, 95, 133

geography, 8, 19–20, 121

gift exchange, 90, 113, 116–117

Goffman, Erving, 73

grammatical: aspect, 26, 56, 77–79, 86, 94–95, 99–100; constructions, 32, 61, 63–78, 86, 108; information, 60; regularities, 32, 56, 76–77, 79, 120; standardization, 61; structures, 6, 24–25, 32, 38, 44, 62; tense, 26, 56, 77–78, 86, 94, 97

Great Britain, 61

greed, 14, 94, 98–99, 114, 116, 119

greetings, 19, 33, 42–43, 55, 92

Habermas, Jürgen, 7, 49, 104
Haeri, Niloofar, 37
Hall, Kira, 17, 124
Handman, Courtney, 115
Hanks, William, 62–63, 85
Hastings, A., 124
Haviland, John, 98
Head Start program, 9, 11, 19, 23, 31, 33–34, 38, 45, 51, 102, 119, 145n4
health care/benefits, 11, 13–14
Hill, Jane, 33, 37, 43, 105, 108, 111
Hill, Kenneth, 63
Hinton, Leanne, 63
Hispanic communities, 4, 10–11, 15, 20, 127
honorifics, 82, 126
hope, 16, 26, 56, 67, 78, 106, 112–118, 120, 140
Hopi, 8, 28, 35–36, 41, 90, 99–101, 146n1
Hotel Santa Fe, 50
House Committee on Education hearing, 42–44
housing, 8–9, 12–14, 111
humor, 34, 123–125, 127, 131–134, 136
Hurricane Katrina relief, 10

ideologies, 15–16, 25–26, 41, 58, 143n5. *See also* language ideologies
Ilongots, 73
Indian Health Service, 14
Indian Pueblo Cultural Center, 52, 144n10
Indians in Unexpected Places (Deloria), 120
indigeneity, 15, 40, 43, 127, 131, 144n9
indigenous identity, 24, 40, 101, 106, 124; collective, 7, 31, 33, 74; construction of, 16–17; definitions of, 15–16; individual, 18, 33; and language use, 20, 22, 28–29, 32–34, 43, 52, 114; loss of, 110, 118; in *As the Rez Turns*, 127; and San Ramón dictionary, 63, 65, 68, 73, 77–78, 88; and tribal affiliation, 128–129
indigenous language literacy, 4, 7, 12, 25–27, 35–41, 53, 85, 87, 90–91, 104, 120–121, 132, 135, 138–139. *See also* San Ramón literacy
indigenous language texts, 6, 108; access to, 38–39, 45; circulation of, 7, 44–46, 49, 51, 53, 88, 91, 140; control over, 7, 23, 112; controlling access to, 46, 49, 52; creators of, 120, 125, 132, 145n3; critique social/political issues, 120, 132–134; as cultural objects, 6, 32, 84, 104; and Indian identity, 52; limiting access to, 7, 20, 44–46, 48, 91–92, 139; and memorialization, 38–39; negative consequences of, 59; perfecting of, 102–104, 112; production of, 115, 118; by religious organizations, 35; scarcity of, 46, 61, 83; and secrecy, 22, 44–46; value of, 7, 46
indigenous languages, 5; appropriate use of, 49, 52, 71, 104, 124–125; controversy about, 35–36; declining use of, 60; discourse about, 91; documenting of, 63; endangered, 43, 61, 84; and forced assimilation, 18, 20; increased interest in, 21; limiting circulation of, 20, 42–43, 46; loss of, 19–20, 26, 37, 42–43, 63, 110–111, 117; oral vs. written, 36; policies for, 14, 18, 21, 23, 43; preservation of, 63, 117; programs for, 20, 35–37, 42–43, 117; promoting use of, 106,

112, 118; public use of, 50–52; social value of, 40; teaching of, 36, 46, 61; uniqueness of, 59
indirectness, 4, 7, 18, 32–33, 48–49, 52, 88, 91, 103–104, 120–121, 125–126, 132, 134–136, 140–141
information control, 7, 18, 24–28, 26, 33, 35, 41–43, 45, 49, 53, 103, 138–139
Institute of American Indian Arts, 11
interactional practices, 48–49, 52–53, 70, 71, 77, 115, 120–122
interactional texts, 73–74, 83
intermarriage, 8, 13–14, 16, 100, 129
internet, 46, 52, 57
intertextuality, 120, 127, 141
Irvine, Judith, 27, 29, 79, 81–82
Isleta Paintings (Parsons), 3–5, 7

Jameson, Fredric, 109, 112
Jones, Graham, 41, 45

Kauanui, J. Kehaulani, 16
Keane, Webb, 103
Keiwa alphabet, 31, 39, 46, 52, 59, 61, 138, 145n4
Keiwa language, 24, 74, 102; access to, 41, 47; appropriate use of, 26, 28–30, 32–34, 37, 42–44, 50, 52, 66, 125; in ceremonial contexts, 28–30, 37; circulation of, 44–46; decline in, 117–118; fluent speakers of, 18–19, 23, 30, 38, 43, 56, 73, 106, 115–116, 121, 125–127; future learners/speakers of, 38–39, 44, 59–61, 71, 82–84, 88, 106, 109, 125, 130, 133, 140; importance of, 67, 71, 114, 118; and indigenous identity, 14, 16, 31, 73; limiting access to, 46–48, 59, 116, 139; preservation of, 38, 64, 67, 83, 106, 139; promoting use of, 42–43, 117; public use of, 50–52; punished for speaking, 19–20; recording of, 91–92, 97; and secrecy, 12, 42, 44–46; social values of, 29–30; standardization of, 5, 31, 61–62; teaching of, 18, 32, 37–40, 42, 44–46, 51–52, 59, 60, 114, 117, 121–122, 130; uses of, 19–20, 32–33, 52, 120, 139; word lists of, 55–57. *See also* San Ramón dictionary; speaking: Keiwa; writing: of Keiwa
Keiwa language classes: adult curriculum for, 40, 44–46, 91–95, 109, 117, 138; for children, 55–56; for young adults, 26, 46–47, 51, 91, 106, 119–121
Keres, 8, 18, 24, 36, 50–51
Kewa (Santo Domingo) Pueblo, 50–51
kinship terms, 93, 95, 100, 126
Kiowa-Tanoan languages, 18, 24
kiva, 4, 80; ceremonies held in, 16–17; and San Ramón dictionary, 66, 81; "talk," 28–31, 81
Kleindedler, Steve, 25, 57
knowledge: collective, 65–66; forbidden, 7; local, 35, 60, 88; perfected/veiled, 103; privileged, 141; production, 141; religious, 37, 103; secret, 12, 45, 48; shared, 7; specialized, 82, 101–102; stereotyptic, 56, 75–76; systems of, 38
Kokopelli, 123, 146n1
Kroskrity, Paul, 25, 28–30, 32–33, 70, 80, 90, 93–95
K'uuyemugeh (Cuyamungue) Pueblo, 50–51

Lachler, Jordan, 21

Pueblo Revolt, 16, 28, 63, 101, 143n8, 145n1

Putnam, Hilary, 75

Real Indians (Garroutte), 15

refinement, 7, 21, 87, 90–91, 97–98, 100, 103–104, 106, 112, 139–140

"Reflections on Hope as a Category of Social and Psychological Analysis" (Crapanzano), 112

registers, 6, 28, 46, 56, 61–62, 76, 79–84, 88, 95, 120, 122, 126, 130

religious: autonomy, 119; conversion, 115; deity, 146n1; knowledge, 37; leaders, 29, 36, 70, 80, 90; observances, 9; organization, 20; persecution, 18; traditions, 36

religious practices, 8–9, 20, 33, 95, 103; control of, 11, 13; and gaming revenues, 111; knowledge of, 12; and language programs, 20; and language texts, 5; and language use, 29–30, 32, 46; and literacy, 38; and political system, 11–13; pre-contact, 144n4; at Pueblos, 12, 17; secrecy of, 12, 42; shrines/sites for, 47; and speaking Keiwa, 19; words associated with, 81–84; and written language materials, 36. *See also* ceremonial practices

Rice, Keren, 62

Rickford, John, 79

Rio Grande Pueblos, 3, 7–10, 18–20, 35, 101–103. *See also* Pueblo

Rio Grande valley, 8, 17, 78

ritual performances, 28–29, 47, 60, 66, 81, 90, 103, 114

Robbins, Joel, 115

Romance languages, 78

Rosaldo, Michelle, 73

Said, Edward, 111

Samuels, David, 127

San Carlos Apaches, 127

San Ramón church, 9–10, 18, 106–108

San Ramón dictionary, 5, 19, 44, 91, 120, 139, 141; audiences for, 72–75, 80–81, 91; circulation/use of, 74, 82–84, 88, 91; editing of, 91, 98, 102–104, 115–116, 145n6; English gloss for, 24, 31, 63, 69–70, 74–75, 78; entries for, 31, 63, 82, 85–86; and everyday conversations, 79, 83–84, 88; goals/purpose of, 57, 60–61, 63–64, 80, 83, 85; illustrative material for, 22–26, 32, 60, 64–65, 81, 84, 88, 145n6; importance of, 26, 56, 80, 83; introductory material in, 59–60, 87–88; and lemmata, 59–60, 63–64; meetings for, 30–32, 82–83; orthography for, 21–22, 31, 39, 50, 61; paradoxical nature of, 6, 22, 64; and sensitive information, 57, 60, 80–81, 116; and SIL dictionary, 31, 57–58, 83, 145n2; social/political ramifications of, 82; and standardizing Keiwa, 61–62; value of, 7, 25; and word lists, 55–57

San Ramón dictionary: and appropriate ways of speaking, 39; authors, 30, 34, 39–41, 61, 64; as authorities, 59, 73, 75–76, 87–88; on cardinal directions, 66, 80; on ceremonial practices, 66–67, 69, 71, 80–84, 88; critique particular people, 70, 76–77; on cultural practices, 22, 58, 64–65, 74–77; directives of, 58, 69–70, 73–74, 76–78, 96–97;

example sentences, 6, 22–26, 31, 56, 91; exhibit cultural knowledge, 65–67, 69, 73, 76–77, 140; fear reprisals, 40–41, 59; and first-person forms, 65–69, 71–76, 78; on geography/plants/animals, 66, 74–75; goals of, 38, 63–64, 71, 80, 83; index community, 66, 88; as informal conversations, 83–84; life histories of, 68–69; on local practices/technologies, 65–71, 73–77, 96–97; methods of, 21–23, 26, 31–32, 57–58, 81, 87, 100, 117; as mini-dialogues, 70–71, 118; moral agency in, 114; nostalgic stance of, 105, 109; obfuscate ceremonial information, 81, 84; on obsolete/past practices, 65, 69, 78, 96–97, 108–109; perfecting of, 115–117; on political/social issues, 76, 80, 135; and preaching words, 32, 66, 80, 82; preferences of, 25, 64, 68, 71, 73, 76–80, 84, 145n6; pressures faced by, 82; on San Ramón history, 64–65, 67, 108; and second-person forms, 69–76, 78; and sensitive information, 22, 32, 49, 60, 64, 80–81; on sociopolitical issues, 74, 85; and specialized vocabularies, 66; stylistic resources of, 82–84; and third-person constructions, 74–77; uniqueness of, 71–73

San Ramón language program, 3–5, 23–24, 26, 61, 145n4; and casino signs, 50; committee of, 44–45; and communally held beliefs, 32; contributors to, 16, 46; controls curricula circulation, 44–46; creation of, 18; and disenrolled tribal members, 47; importance of, 19; lack of support for, 70; learning materials for, 5, 91, 114, 121, 125, 127, 130, 132, 135, 137, 140, 145n2; as social movement, 26; staff of, 25, 59

San Ramón literacy, 5–7, 25–27, 37–38, 40–41, 49, 52–53, 56, 80, 85, 91, 103–104, 106, 112, 119–120, 125–127, 137–138, 140

San Ramón Mountain, 9, 47, 66, 106

San Ramón Pueblo, 23–24, 41, 52; and being generous, 92, 94–95, 102; census director of, 15; current state of, 125, 132; description of, 8–10, 106–107, 111; economic prosperity of, 20, 111; emphasizes collective work, 79, 88, 92–93, 95, 98–101; future of community, 40, 78, 83, 88, 91, 139–140; and health/wholeness of community, 105–106, 111, 114, 116; history of, 99–102, 106; and language loss, 37, 42–43; members leave, 37; members return to, 119; political climate at, 11–12; prevalence of English at, 18–20; progress in, 119–120; and respecting elders, 92, 96–97; sociopolitical climate of, 85, 94, 102, 132–134, 138; and tensions with neighboring Pueblos, 101; traditions of, 89–90

Santa Clara Pueblo, 13–14

Santa Clara Pueblo et al. v. Martinez et al., 13–14

Santa Fe, 8–11, 14, 17–20, 68, 89, 110

Santa Fe Indian Market, 11

Santa Fe New Mexican, 14

Saxon, Leslie, 62

Schoolcraft, Henry Rowe, 88

secrecy, 4–6, 11–12, 53, 102; and anthropology, 47, 141, 144n5; and avoidance, 33, 49; and concealment, 138–139; emphasis on, 35; and exchange, 45–46; and information control, 43; and literacy, 26, 49,

103–104; local beliefs of, 64; logic of, 7, 141; and perfectibility, 7, 103; poorly enforced, 42–46; produces excitement, 47–48; produces value, 45–46, 48; productive ability of, 42, 139; and revelation, 48, 141; and *As the Rez Turns*, 123; and San Ramón dictionary, 64; and scarcity, 45–46, 48; in social science literature, 41–49, 53; theorizing of, 41–52, 103–104; and writing, 26–27

secret societies, 41–42, 47, 144n5

Seminole gaming, 10, 126

sensitive information, 24, 41, 49, 57, 60, 64, 80

Silverstein, Michael, 27–28, 60, 75–76

Simmel, Georg, 41–42, 45–48, 53

Smithsonian Institution, 55, 57

soap opera. *See As the Rez Turns* soap opera

social: action, 49; categories, 72–73, 79; change, 28, 85, 110–113, 126; climate, 85, 87, 94, 102; contexts, 23, 76; critiques, 112, 131–135, 140; forces, 139; goals, 64; imaginary, 141; issues, 120; life, 9–10, 13–14, 24, 61, 139; movements, 26; norms, 88; order, 73, 116; phenomena, 7; positions, 79; power, 72; practices, 102; projects, 106, 113–114; solidarity, 34; values, 29, 39–40, 61–62, 65, 83, 85; work, 7, 26, 33, 41, 48, 73–74, 103–104, 117, 120–122

social science literature, 6, 41–49, 53, 104

sociality, 7, 90, 135, 138

solidarity, 29, 34, 40, 47, 77, 123

South Africans, 113

Soviet Union, 111

Spanish: language, 18–20, 22, 28–33, 39, 75, 79, 92, 145n8; loanwords, 31, 51, 82, 109; and Pueblo Revolt, 143n8; reconquest, 16–17, 28, 101, 144n8; repression, 29, 42, 105; and word lists, 62

speaking: Keiwa, 33, 37, 40, 46, 48, 55, 70, 79, 88, 105, 112, 114; "the past," 93–97, 102; ways of, 6, 79–88, 108, 120, 127, 132, 135

"Speaking and Writing" (Chafe), 38

speech: acts, 73; behavior, 33; ceremonial, 79–80, 90; communities, 36–37, 48, 73, 84–85, 87, 107; events, 60, 71–72; forms, 6, 61, 71, 95; genres, 26, 47, 64, 77, 84–88, 91–97, 100, 102, 120, 122, 127, 130–132, 134; ritual, 60, 66; styles, 79–89

status, 9, 46, 76

stereotypes, 75, 120, 123–124, 127

Stewart, Kathleen, 107–109, 111–112

storytelling, 47, 93–96, 106–108, 120, 127. *See also As the Rez Turns* soap opera; *Bowl Story, The*

Sturm, Circe, 15–16, 18

Summer Institute of Linguistics (SIL), 21–22, 31, 39, 55, 57–58, 62–63, 83, 96, 145n2

Suslak, Daniel, 135

Sutton, Logan, 24

TallBear, Kim, 16

Tekakwitha, Kateri, 12

temporality, 7, 26, 114–115

Tewa, 8, 28, 33, 35, 50, 80, 93–94, 102

Texas, 4, 8, 35, 145n1

"The Things We Do with Words" (Rosaldo), 73

Time and Other (Fabian), 141

Tiwa, 8

Towa, 8

traditional: clothing, 17, 90, 101; contexts, 89–90, 138; cultural attitudes, 32; cultural forms, 90; definition of, 33; faith, 12, 19–20; foods, 78, 89, 94; technologies, 93, 95–97; way of life, 36, 79; ways of speaking, 83

Trager, George, 20

tribal council, 9–12, 15–16, 42–43, 90, 99–100, 111, 137

tribal leaders, 11–12, 20, 42–43, 59, 99–102, 107–108, 137–138, 145n2

tribal membership, 24, 139, 143n1; disenrollment; and changes in policy, 15–16, 132–134; at Cochiti, 36; controversy about, 12–14, 95, 100–102, 119; critiques on, 49, 132–134; destructive decisions about, 70; determination of, 13–16, 143n5; economic benefits of, 13–15; and Indian/English names, 130, 145n9; and Indian identity, 14–18, 110; and language programs, 45; at Santa Clara, 13–14; and tribal affiliation, 129–130; and women, 11–12, 100–101, 134. *See also* children: and tribal membership

Tzotzil Maya, 98

United States: Dept. of Housing and Urban Development, 9, 14; education system, 60, 130; educational contexts, 104; foreign language classes, 91–92, 122, 130; government, 16; Supreme Court, 13. *See also* federal Indian schools

University of New Mexico, 11, 21, 23–24, 30, 92, 138

Uto-Aztecan, 24

veiling, 48, 52, 74, 76, 81, 84, 90, 103, 116, 121, 126, 132, 135, 139

Wallace, Anthony, 112

Warner, Michael, 7, 49

wealth, 14, 21, 102, 125–126

Webster, Noah, 61

Weigel, William, 63

Western Apache, 100, 102, 120, 144n9

Whiteley, Peter, 36

Whorf, Benjamin, 90, 113

writing, 7–8, 91, 104, 138, 140; of indigenous languages, 20, 35–38, 108, 114; of Keiwa, 5–6, 37–41, 44–46, 49, 55, 61, 64, 119; and language programs, 21, 35, 44–46, 120; negative consequences of, 36, 38, 40–41, 120; at San Ramón Pueblo, 28, 33–34, 36–37, 40, 55–56; and secrecy, 7, 26–27; as technology, 29, 36–38, 40–41, 52

Ysleta del Sur Pueblo, 8, 145n1

Yucatec Maya, 62–63

Zuni Pueblo, 8, 18, 24, 102

Made in the USA
San Bernardino, CA
12 March 2016